W8-BXR-130

Ar'n't I a Woman?

Ar'n't I a Woman?

Female Slaves in the Plantation South

DEBORAH GRAY WHITE

Revised Edition

W · W · NORTON & COMPANY

New York   London

The text of this book is composed in Baskerville.
Book design by Jacques Chazaud

Library of Congress Cataloging in Publication Data

White, Deborah Gray.
  Ar'n't I a woman?

  Bibliography: p.
  Includes index.
  1. Women slaves—Southern States.   2. Plantation
life—Southern States—History.   3. Slavery—Southern
States—Condition of slaves.   I. Title.
E443.W58   1985   975'.00496073   85.4842

ISBN 0-393-31481-2

W. W. Norton & Company, Inc.
500 Fifth Avenue, New York, N.Y. 10110
W. W. Norton & Company Ltd.
10 Coptic Street, London WC1A 1PU
 1   2   3   4   5   6   7   8   9   0

For my mother,
Eddie Florence Gray

Contents

Acknowledgments

Throughout the course of this project I have been fortunate to have met and been helped by many people who thought a book on slave women was needed and could be done. Among the first were my fellow graduate students at the University of Illinois at Chicago, especially Stephen Hansen, Arnold Hirsch, and Jacqueline Petersen. My dissertation advisor, Robert Remini, was always encouraging and helpful, as were the other members of my dissertation committee, particularly Daniel Scott Smith and Marilyn Miller. Several of my colleagues in the History Department at the University of Wisconsin–Milwaukee read and commented on the dissertation and first drafts of the book manuscript. I thank Margo Conk, Reginald Horseman, and Carole Shammas for the time and the effort they put into it. Special thanks are extended to Margo Conk, who for six years never stopped pushing me to finish this work and who was always so confident that things would work out. I also benefited from the seminars held in the

Department of Afro-American Studies at the University of Wisconsin—Milwaukee. My colleagues Osei-Mensah Aborampah, Lloyd Barbee, Nana Korsah, Richard Lewis, Frank Martin, and Winston Van Horne made useful and insightful comments on several chapters of the manuscript. Milton Cantor and Catherine Clinton read earlier drafts and I am indebted to them for their comments. A special note of thanks is extended to Anne Firor Scott, who read the dissertation and the manuscript. Her comments were invaluable and her encouragement even more so. I would also like to thank Jacqueline Hall and Elizabeth Fox-Genovese for comments made on articles that I have written. Many of their thoughtful suggestions are incorporated here, as are those of my editor, Robert Kehoe. I have benefited just as much from the kind word as from kind criticism. For the former I thank Darlene Hine, Blanche Hersh, James Oakes, Harold Rose, and Walter Weare. I am indebted to The American Association of University Women and The Southern Fellowship Foundation for providing funds for the research and writing of this book, and to Marie Mayer, Jessica Myers, and Ilga Strazdins for typing it over and over again.

To my friends outside of the university world and to my family I extend deep feelings of gratitude. Many thanks to Melanie James for her patient assistance with the final editing and galleys. Heather Crooks, Charlene Griffin-Jordon, and Clara Rogers-Green probably do not know how much I was bouyed by their enthusiastic words of support. Had it not been for the child-care and homemaker help of my mother, Eddie Florence Gray, my mother-in-law, Lodilleen Iona White, and Jean Parker and her family, this book would have taken even longer to produce. My daughters, Maya and Asha, were an inspiration for the book and I hope that when they get older they will be inspired by it. I thank my mother and father for the support they have given me through the years and also Patrick White for being my own private resource center and a wellspring of compassion and wisdom.

Ar'n't I a Woman?

Revisiting *Ar'n't I a Woman?*

History is supposed to give people a sense of identity, a feeling for who they were, who they are, and how far they have come. It should act as a springboard for the future. One hopes that it will do this for black women, who have been given more myth than history. The myths have put black women in a position where they must, as Sojourner Truth did in 1858, *prove* their womanhood. Despite all that she has come through and accomplished, the American black woman is still waiting for an affirmative answer to the plaintive question asked over a century ago: "Ar'n't I a woman?"

THIRTEEN YEARS AGO I ended *Ar'n't I a Woman? Female Slaves in the Plantation South* with the above statement. At that time the Civil Rights and Black Power movements had spawned a renaissance in African-American Studies. Books on every aspect of black life were in demand, and, as outlined in the *Ar'n't I a Woman?* introduction, an abundance of books on slavery attempted to restore to black men the masculinity Americans had denied them. Yet, African-American women were close to invisible in historical writing.

Not because there was no need or audience for black women's history. Rather, black women were invisible because few historians saw them as important contributors to America's social, economic, or political development, and few publishers identified an audience for books that connected black women's thoughts and experiences to the history of other Americans. Two decades ago African-American women's records were often deemed suspect or otherwise nonauthentic often because they *were* black women's records.[1] Manuscripts that drew heavily on them were dismissed as nonobjective, as were the historians, especially black women historians, who wrote them.[2] Today we take the publication of black women's history for granted, but in the early 1980s publisher after publisher rejected manuscripts on black women, including *Ar'n't I a Woman?* for these very reasons. To legitimize black women's history, black women historians, in particular, were put in the ironic and untenable position of having to be especially careful to corroborate black women's sources with those of whites and black men—the very source material that made black women invisible in the first place.[3] Had my Ph.D. dissertation not been rescued by one of the pioneers of American women's history, Anne Firor Scott, who took it to W. W. Norton and Company, *Ar'n't I a Woman?* might never have seen the light of day.[4]

I gladly report that on this, the eve of the twenty-first century, things have changed. New source material on black women has been unearthed and historians are using it in inventive ways. History books on African-American women have multiplied and a new language now expresses the difference between black men and women, and black women and white people. We now understand that race, class, gender, sexuality, and other identity variables do not exist independently. Nor do they compete for supremacy, but reinforce, overlap, and intersect each other. The history of black women's enslavement has filled out. We know far more today than in 1985 about women's resistance, religion, medical care, and sexual and labor exploitation. We know that colonial white America's perceptions of racial difference were founded on the different way they constructed black and white women. A body of writing now allows us to determine the legacy of the black woman's enslavement; we understand how slavery impacted on her postbellum employment history, migration, self-image, and on her involvement in the family and the nineteenth- and twentieth-century movements for political and civil rights. In fact, unlike in 1985, there is now more history than myth. This history indeed gives black women a greater sense of themselves, but it is not clear that it has liberated them from the task of *proving* their womanhood. Aspects of the mythology's dismantling have been disquieting. Most unsettling perhaps is the documented revelation that Sojourner Truth did not stand before the 1851 Akron, Ohio, Woman's Right's convention and ask the penetrating question "Ar'n't I a Woman?"

If I were writing *Ar'n't I a Woman?* today I would still use that discredited speech as theoretical grounding, but I would also use the significant body of new work on difference and black female consciousness.[5] In 1985, the empirical record made it relatively easy to discern the difference between male and female slavery and black and white women. Conceptualizing the difference was considerably more difficult. What did it mean for black women to share some identity and disability of both black men and white women and yet be very different from both? Today, a stronger light shines on my subject. I would never write that the "slave woman's condition was just an extreme case of what women as a group experienced in America." I would not say that "the powerlessness and exploitation of black women was an extreme form of what all women experienced because racism, although just as pervasive as sexism, was more virulent." Nor would I argue that "the contour, if not the content" of the lives of all American women was "paradoxically similar."[6]

These statements presume that racism and sexism can be added to produce a prejudice more severe than either racism or sexism alone. In fact, black women did not experience sexism the same way white women did. Owing to their color white men saw black women differently and exploited them differently. Race changed the experience of black womanhood. The rape of black women, their endless toil, the denial of their beauty, the inattention to their pregnancy, the sale of their children were simultaneous manifestations of racism and sexism, not an extreme form of one or the other. For black women, race and sex cannot be separated. We cannot consider who black women are as black people without considering their sex, nor can we consider who they are as women without considering their race.

Similarly, white women endured their own race-determined sexism. The silence and submissiveness demanded of them, their exile to the home and from schools, their inability to own property rested on a notion of femininity that made piety, delicacy, morality, weakness, and dependency the reserve of white women alone.

Black and white womanhood were interdependent. They played off one another. The white woman's sense of herself as a woman—her self-esteem and perceived superiority—depended on the racism that debased black women. White women were mistresses *because* black women were slaves. White women had real power over enslaved women because black women were really powerless. Black and white women had so little in common because the sexism they both experienced kept them apart.

New studies on the origins of slavery and the relationship between black and white Southern women make these differences clearer than did *Ar'n't I a Woman?* For example, Kathleen Brown's insightful analysis of seventeenth-century Virginia laws that taxed African women's labor on the same basis as laboring men demonstrates that African women were at the center of attempts to create concepts of racial difference.[7] English women might work in the tobacco fields and not be taxed because white womanhood was construed to be domestic, physically weak, and economically dependent on men. In contrast, laws that taxed African women construed them to be physically strong and quite able to make a living from the tobacco they grew. So powerful were these distinctions in seventeenth-century Virginia that *class* differences between free and servant English women virtually disappeared. The very definition of "English" came to represent a privileged womanhood; on the other hand, the term "negro," which in the 1660s had lacked precise definition, soon after became associated with the debased labor of African women. The pervasive connection of black women's bodies with the uncivilized is underscored by Jennifer Morgan's work on Barbados and South Carolina. Here, too, Englishmen constructed the black woman's body as monstrous and grotesque, bestial enough to deem all Africans inferior in contrast to the civility and superiority of the English.[8]

By the nineteenth century this difference was fixed in the American mind. Elizabeth Fox-Genovese reminds us that while slave masters controlled both black and white women, the latter wielded power over the former. As mistress of the house she was the master's delegate, his implementer. Today, we might view slaveholding women as victims of male dominance; few of them, however, would have seen themselves so. They might deplore their men's excessive drinking, sexual philandering, and abuse of power, but they rarely rejected the system "that established their sense of personal identity within a solid community."[9]

Of course, enslaved women rejected slavery's system and the raw power it granted to white men and women alike. Recent studies of female enslavement have described more graphically than *Ar'n't I a Woman?* the cruelty and excesses of white power. In so doing they have made resistance a defining aspect of female slavery, one that shaped relationships and identity. For example, Brenda Stevenson convincingly argues that enslaved women saw even the most compassionate white women as "unholy" and "unchristian" because the power they wielded forced enslaved women to hide their real selves—forced them to steal food, feign illness, and participate in all kinds of covert activities.[10] On the other hand, they viewed their own resistance to rape, to the sale of their children, to the white woman's never-ending and often petty demands, as proof of their moral superiority to white women. In fact, the pride and esteem they had for women who resisted openly—who fought off rapists, who refused to be whipped, who verbally assaulted masters and mistresses—revealed their reverence for heroism and their celebration of it as a feminine trait. They did not see aggression and independent behavior as unfeminine, but a means to "protect their most fundamental claims to womanhood; . . . their female sexuality and physicality, and their roles as mothers and wives."[11]

The increased focus on brutality and resistance has shifted the historiography and language of slavery. African and African-American women were not born degraded but rendered so by enslavement. Were I to write *Ar'n't I a Woman?* today, I would use the verb "enslaved" rather than the noun "slave" to implicate the inhumane actions of white people. The noun "slave" suggests a state of mind and being that is absolute and unmediated by an enslaver. "Enslaved" says more about what *happened* to black people without unwittingly describing the sum total of who they were. "Enslaved" forces us to remember that black men and women were Africans and African-Americans before they were forced into slavery and had a new—and denigrating—identity assigned to them.

"Enslaved" also nudges us to rethink our ideas about black resistance under slavery. In 1959 Stanley Elkins argued that the master's absolute power translated into the slave's absolute dependency. Black people, therefore, became perpetual children. This view of Elkins's spawned a historiographic movement bent on proving him wrong. As part of this revisionist history *Ar'n't I a Woman?* argued that "despite the brutality and inhumanity, or perhaps because of it, a distinct African-American culture based on close-knit kinship relationships grew and thrived, and that it was this culture that sustained black people."[12] Like others I focused on the community of the quarters and the slave family, but I also highlighted the network of enslaved women, their will to quietly resist and avoid total domination. I held then and still believe that "in the assimilation of culture, in the interaction of blacks and whites, there were gray areas and relationships more aptly described in terms of black over white."[13]

I would make the same argument today but with strong qualifications. Over the course of writing *Ar'n't I a Woman?* I had two children—two girls. I could not escape the vulnerability and dependency that these female experiences gave rise to. When I was pregnant I thought about how it would feel to pick cotton or dig ditches, or be beaten or raped. Some critics allege that I muted slavery's brutality—and the consequent dogged resistance. If so, it was because the historiographic moment and the historical record supported the emphasis on agency and survival, and my findings fit with what I needed to believe about the sheer will and courage of African-American women—that they could overcome their many tribulations. Subsequent works like Stevenson's *Life in Black and White: Family and Community in the Slave South*, Melton A. McLaurin's *Celia, A Slave*, Dorothy Roberts's *Killing the Black Body*, and Nell Painter's "Soul Murder: Toward a Fully Loaded Cost Accounting of Slavery" have nudged me to reconsider the agency I ascribed to African-American women, and the entire body of literature written after, and in response to, Stanley Elkin's "Sambo theory."[14]

Without diminishing the role of religion, the family and kinship networks, and the female community in the survival and emotional health of enslaved African-Americans, more attention needs to be paid to the psychological costs of enslavement. As Nell Painter has argued, we need to "investigate the consequences of child abuse and sexual abuse on an entire society in which beating and raping of enslaved people was neither secret nor metaphorical."[15] Given what we know today about the effects of abuse, the way it spawns feelings of anger, low self-esteem, depression, and even self-hatred, can we discuss black female survival without tackling the rage that dwelled within? Enslaved women endured repeated rapes, were surrounded by and were victims of violence. As mothers they were beaten in front of their children, watched their children be beaten, and very often beat them themselves, if only to spare them later violence at the hands of masters and mistresses. Enslaved women were treated inde-

cently during sale and some had experimental gynecological operations and cesarean sections performed on them—without
benefit of anesthesia.[16] Rose Williams, whose story of coerced
sex at age sixteen is related on pages 102–103, survived long
enough to be interviewed in the 1930s. Her testimony that "after
what I does for the massa, I's never wants no truck with any man,"
suggests that the price she paid was life without male sex, love, or
companionship. Maybe women who managed to resist personal
violence avoided the debilitating psychological anguish that
Williams endured. Maybe. Still, today, I would pay more attention
to the psychological impact of violence and abuse as a way to emphasize the resistance waged against it. In the context of violence
and its psychological impact, enslaved women never look as
strong, nor as heroic, as when viewed as agents in their family, religious, female, or kinship networks. They look vulnerable and
even frail, traits not generally associated with African-American
women.

Pairing the psychological with the enslaved woman's means
of survival has helped us analyze many patterns that emerged
after slavery. Recent work has traced black female migration, dissemblance, institution and community building back to abuse
of the black female body.[17] America's constant concern with
black women's morality, chastity, and respectability flow from
slavery's legacy, as well as the rape, medical experimentation,
and reproductive control that black women continued to endure
through the twentieth century. As work continues on the psychological dimensions of abuse, on the enslaved woman's body
as the site of interracial masculine conflict, on African-American
ways of healing, we will know more than we ever knew about
black women's ways of resisting, surviving, and living.[18] If pursued
with the rigor that the subject demands, the violence done to
black women might well de-center lynching as the primary site
and preeminent expression of white (sexual) anxiety on the
black body.

I believe, however, that new scholarship should not and will not alter the identification of enslaved women with the words "Ar'n't I a woman?" Both Carleton Mabee and Nell Painter have demonstrated that twelve years after the 1851 Akron, Ohio, Woman's Rights meeting, Frances Dana Gage, and not Sojourner Truth, wrote the famous "Ar'n't I a Woman?" speech.[19] According to Painter, Gage, the white presiding officer at the meeting, deliberately set her sights on writing a more engaging account of Truth than Harriet Beecher Stowe, who in 1863 captured the nation's attention by romantically characterizing Truth as the "Libyan Sibyl." Gage, thinking herself a more talented writer than Stowe, sought to shape popular perceptions of Truth. She thus fictionalized the Akron convention, a convention electrified as much by Truth's presence as by her speech. Placing Truth at the center, Gage substantially embellished and dramatized her remarks. We know enough about Truth to celebrate her on her triumph over physical and sexual abuse, her religious commitment, and her fight for her children. Even so, it is Gage's invention that black and white Americans cling to. We have the history but much prefer the myth—the idea that a strong powerful black woman, in defiance of vehement opposition, and by sheer force of character, overcame illiteracy and mesmerized many a hostile audience with a wisdom that defied the logic of America's racists and sexists. According to Painter, in embracing Gage's account, we have shown how much more we need the symbolic Sojourner Truth—the strong black woman triumphing against the odds— than the real one, whose struggles were heroic but hardly mythic.[20]

Painter and Mabee have given us the facts. Let us add, however, that when we understand the ideas expressed in the "Ar'n't I a Woman?" speech, and Truth's struggle to prove herself a woman (such as in 1858 when she showed her breast to her audience), we also understand more deeply the essence and dilemmas of American black womanhood. Contrary to Painter's contention, I did not make Truth stand for enslaved Southern women;[21] I made her stand for black women across the nation whose lives, as I noted in 1985, stood "in stark contrast to that of most nineteenth-century white American women." Like Truth, black women were unprotected by men or by law, and they had their womanhood totally denied.[22] Inasmuch as Truth overcame the tribulations of enslavement and invented herself, she perfectly represents women who found a way and a will to survive and reconstruct their womanhood. Even to the extent that Truth was invented by others, she still represents black women, whose victimization has been minimalized and whose personae have been buried under layers of mythology. It is indeed ironic—and disappointing too—that a white woman penned the rhetorical question which, as Painter notes, "inserts blackness into feminism and gender into racial identity";[23] but black women can take pride in the fact that Truth's real remarks and life history obviously inspired the question "Ar'n't I a woman?" Regardless of authorship that phrase still captures the difference between white and black antebellum women, and still locates black women at the intersection of racial and sexual ideologies and politics.

D. G. W.

May 1998

Introduction

WHEN SOJOURNER TRUTH took the podium at the Akron, Ohio, Women's Rights convention she was greeted with boos and hisses. It was 1851, just nine years before the Civil War debacle, and in the minds of many the infant feminist movement was linked to the threatening abolitionist crusade. For Truth, both racism and sexism mediated against the democracy with which Americans had become comfortable, yet as a former slave, a black, and a woman, Sojourner Truth made many Americans uncomfortable. Issues concerning slavery and black or female status seemed to be tearing apart the nation's fabric, and some Americans could not look at, much less listen to, Truth, without being reminded of the nation's woes.[1]

Truth's supporters secured her a place on the program and her very first sentences served notice that she would talk about women's rights without ignoring the equally controversial topic of the abolition of slavery:

Well, chilern, whar dar is so much racket der must be
something out of kilter. I tink dat 'twixt de niggers of de
Souf and de women at de Norf all a talking' 'bout rights,
de white men will be in a fix pretty soon.[2]

Having launched her indictment of the status quo, Truth
proceeded to draw on her own slave experience to demonstrate how slavery and racism made a mockery of the logic
upon which sex discrimination was based:

Dat man ober dar say dat woman needs to be lifted ober
ditches, and to have de best place every whar. Nobody eber
helped me into carriages, or ober mud puddles, or gives
me any best place and ar'n't I a woman? Look at me! Look
at my arm! I have plowed, and planted, and gathered into
barns, and no man could head me—and ar'n't I a woman?
I could work as much and eat as much as a man (when I
could get it), and bear de lash as well—and ar'n't I a woman?
I have borne thirteen chilern and seen em mos' all sold off
into slavery, and when I cried out with a mother's grief,
none but Jesus heard—and ar'n't I a woman?[3]

Sojourner Truth went on to reprove the males in her audience for withholding rights from their mothers, sisters, and
wives, but she had already made her point. Her life stood in
stark contrast to that of most nineteenth-century white American women. The safety of a pedestal, questionable as it was,
had not been extended to her. She, like most black women of
the time, plowed, planted, and hoed, did as much work as a
man, endured the brutal punishment meted out by slaveholders and their overseers, and also fulfilled her ordained role of
motherhood. Judged by her life experience, all theories of
inequality based on the assumption that women were weaker
than men and that their physical and mental constitution suited
them only for domestic duties were false. In fact, perhaps more
than any group of American women, black women, particularly slaves, proved daily that sexual discrimination based on
such assumptions was not justified.

The slave woman's condition was just an extreme case of what women as a group experienced in America. Many activities were circumscribed and hopes blunted by the conventional wisdom that a woman's place was in the home. Women were overworked and underpaid in factories and other work places because they were denied the legal and social sanctions necessary to fight unjust and intolerable working conditions. "In education, in marriage, in religion, in everything," lamented feminist Lucy Stone, "disappointment is the lot of women."[4] So inhibitive were society's norms that many women's rights advocates likened the husband-wife relationship to that of master and slave. The English philosopher John Stuart Mill wrote in his famous essay "The Subjection of Women" that the wife "is the actual bond servant of her husband, no less so as far as legal obligation goes, than slaves commonly so called."[5] Mary Boykin Chesnut, the wife of a prominent Southern politician, concurred: "All married women, all children and girls who live in their father's house are slaves."[6]

For antebellum black women, however, sexism was but one of three constraints. Most were slaves, and as such were denied the "privilege," enjoyed by white feminists, of theorizing about bondage, for they were literally owned by someone else. They were slaves because they were black, and even more than sex, color was the absolute determinant of class in antebellum America. To be of color was a mark of degradation, so much so that in most Southern states one's dark complexion was *prima facie* evidence that one was a slave. Black in a white society, slave in a free society, woman in a society ruled by men, female slaves had the least formal power and were perhaps the most vulnerable group of antebellum Americans. Certainly Sarah and Angelina Grimké thought so. For these two abolitionist and feminist leaders no other group of people were so degraded and brutalized. The whip on the slave woman's shrinking flesh became for them a symbol of male inhumanity and more than enough reason for American women to unite.

Few, they thought, could fail to believe that the slave woman's lot was the most intolerable, the most sorrowful, and the most pitiable of all.[7]

Indeed it was, but let us, for the moment, take our cues from Sojourner Truth. Inasmuch as she was a very articulate former slave who traveled the country speaking to audiences about women's rights and black rights, she was unique among antebellum African-American women, most of whom spent their lives anonymously tilling the soil. Yet Truth's question, "Ar'n't I a woman?" should make us pause to consider exactly what kind of status slave women considered ideal. Like Truth, they stood beyond the boundaries of Victorian womanhood, but did they want the empty deference given to those within its bounds? The feeling in antebellum America was that women needed male guidance because women were fickle and weak-willed. Slave women demonstrated that sex was not an absolute determinant of skill, will power, aptitude, or even strength. Undoubtedly they wanted the whip off their backs and an end to all the other iniquities that came with slavery, but did they want America's ideas about a woman's place to envelop them?

There are other questions that need attention. We now know enough about antebellum bondage to appreciate that most female slaves had to rely on themselves for protection against the sexual attacks of masters and overseers, that for them marriage did not translate into protection or security. We know that the plantation was akin to a psychological battleground where slaves vied with the whites in a neverending clash of wits, and that slaves did not—could not—regard the development of crafty and subtle survival strategies as solely a male affair. We know too that slave women, just as their male counterparts, performed taxing field labor from dawn to dusk, that motherhood did not exempt them from that work, and that a good many had husbands on distant plantations whom they did not see from one end of the week to the next.[8]

What did all this add up to? American white women were expected to be passive because they were female. But black women had to be submissive because they were black and slaves. This made a difference in the sex roles of black and white women, as well as in the expectations that their respective societies had of them, but how? Surely biological and social motherhood had different implications for slave women than it did for white women. Did being a wife and mother anchor slave women to the position of inferiority in slave society as it did white women in American society at large? How did slave women maintain a sense of worth and what standards did they use to judge their own conduct?

These are very important questions. The answers would provide clues to a host of other questions about the history of black family and community life. How curious, therefore, that despite the wealth of information that we now have about African-American slavery, so few scholars have dealt realistically with these questions.[9] Two reasons come to mind for this gap in our knowledge about female slaves. The first has to do with the way the issues of the recent debate over slavery were defined; the second, with the difficulty in finding source material that throws light on the experience of slave women. Let us examine the recent debate first.

The 1960s and 1970s witnessed a debate among historians concerning the nature of the slave personality. Stanley Elkins began by alleging that the American slave master had such absolute power and authority over the bondsman that the slave was reduced to childlike dependency. "Sambo," Elkins argued in his book *Slavery, A Problem in American Institutional and Intellectual Life,* was more than a product of Southern fantasy. He could not be dismissed as just a "stereotype." "Sambo," the docile, infantile, lazy, irresponsible personality was real, the product of a system of slavery that required absolute conformity and limited the slave's choice of "significant others." The distinct quality of American slavery, explained Elkins, was its "closedness." All lines of authority descended from the master and all alternative social bases that might have supported alternative standards were systematically suppressed. Absolute power for the master meant absolute dependency for the slave—"the dependency not of the developing child," insisted Elkins, "but of the perpetual child."[10]

Elkins' thesis had a profound effect upon the research and writing of the history of slavery. Indeed, it spawned research that otherwise might not have been undertaken. The direction that the research took, however, was in large part predetermined because Elkins' *Slavery* defined the parameters of the debate. In a very subtle way these parameters had more to do with the nature of male slavery than with female slavery.

Elkins *seemed* to be dealing with the entire black race when he wrote *Slavery*. "American slavery operated as a 'closed system,' " he wrote, "one in which, for the generality of slaves in their nature as men and women . . contacts with free society could occur only on the most narrowly circumscribed of terms." As he searched in vain for evidence of Sambo in Africa, Elkins again implied that infantilization was something that happened in America to the race as a whole. In Africa, he observed, the docile personality was absent, men's and women's work was clearly delineated: "Women did the cultivating, the heavy labor was performed by men."[11]

What Elkins said and what he implied, however, were two different things. In recounting Southern lore about Sambo, Elkins quipped that "the merest hint of Sambo's 'manhood' might fill the Southern breast with scorn." Later, quoting a noted antebellum Southern pro-slaveryite, he recounted: "The Negro . . . in his true nature is always a boy, let him be ever so old."[12] Perhaps Elkins' use of the terms "manhood" and "boy" as examples of Southern thinking about Sambo represents the very common practice of grammatical neutralization of the sexes. On the other hand, Elkins' description of other aspects of slavery reveals a subliminal exclusion of black females from the Sambo theory. For instance, while elaborating on the preslavery life-style of the West African, Elkins claims that "the typical West African tribesman was a distinctly warlike individual. . . . If he belonged to the upper classes of tribal society . . . he might have had a considerable experience as a political or military leader."[13] Elkins' portrait of traditional West Africa was rather distorted and rested heavily on the role of African males. There were many sedentary tribes, and many nonwarlike nomadic tribes, and while West African women contributed much to their societies, they were not generally warriors or soldiers.

There was also a problem with Elkins' discussion of the Middle Passage. Blacks, he insisted, traveled the Atlantic in the holds of slave ships. Elkins was right in his assertion that holds were "packed with suffocating humanity." However, both sexes did not travel the passage the same way. Women made the journey on the quarter and half decks.[14]

Elkins also emphasized men, to the exclusion of women, in his discussion of Latin American slavery. He claimed the Sambo personality was absent in Latin America because a variety of significant others mediated on the slaves' behalf. According to Elkins, slaves in this region could also play different roles, roles that allowed them to internalize behavior different from that of a Sambo. Not surprisingly, the list of significant others, which included the friar, the priest, the Jesuit, the local magistrate, and the king's informer, included no female models. Similarly, Elkins' list of roles fulfilled by Latin American slaves, that of artisan, peddler, merchant, truck gardener, priest, independent farmer, and military officer, also included no female roles.[15]

That Elkins seemed to omit women altogether was accentuated by his description of slaves whom he identified as part of an American "underground," those who never succumbed to Samboism. Among those mentioned were Gabriel, who led the revolt of 1800, Denmark Vessey, leading spirit of the 1822 plot at Charleston, and Nat Turner, the Virginia slave who fomented the rebellion of 1831.[16] An omission, conspicious by its absence, was Harriet Tubman, a woman who in her own way waged a successful little private war against Southern slaveholders. If Elkins had really been thinking of slaves of both sexes he would hardly have forgotten this woman, who became known widely as the Moses of her people.

Where were the women, then, in Elkins' theory? They clearly stood beyond Samboism in his thinking. Following the lead of E. Franklin Frazier and Kenneth Stampp, Elkins maintained that women were allowed the alternative role of mother: "The mother's own role loomed far larger for the slave child than did that of the father. She controlled those few activities—household care, preparation of food, and rearing of children—that were left to the slave family." The etiquette of plantation life, explained Elkins, even deprived the black male of the honorific attributes of fatherhood.[17] Since Elkins' Sambo theory rested, in part, on the absence of significant alternative roles for the slave, to recognize the role of mother was tantamount, on Elkins' part, to arguing that black women escaped Samboism.

Elkins' implications aside, it is clearly insulting to a race to be called Sambos, but while the insult is to the race, the onus is on black men. No one expects women to be assertive and aggressive. For centuries white women have been characterized, indeed, rewarded, for being childlike and silly. Humility has been seen as a mark of class in a woman, and weakness an indication of grace. Women have sometimes been offended by these characterizations but inasmuch as Samboism involves "feminine" traits, it is the men of the race characterized as such who bear the burden of the insult.

At times in the black man's past, such a characterization was not an automatic disparagement. Comparing it to the crass materialism that seemed to pervade white America, some African-Americans, the twentieth-century political activist

W. E. B. DuBois, for example, took pride in the black man's natural meekness and spirituality.[18] But the byword for blacks at the time Elkins' *Slavery* was circulating was "militancy," the ideology was black power. If the stage Elkins set for the debate over slavery was one that reemphasized the femininity of the race, those who did most of the debating were bent on defeminizing black men, sometimes by emphasizing the masculine roles played by slave men, and sometimes by imposing the Victorian model of domesticity and maternity on the pattern of black female slave life.

A quick historiographic survey bears out this observation. One of the first full-length works to appear after *Slavery* was John Blassingame's *The Slave Community, Plantation Life in the Antebellum South*. The work is a classic but much of it deals with male status. For instance, Blassingame stressed the fact that many masters recognized the male as the head of the family. He observed that during courtship men flattered women and exaggerated their prowess. There was, however, little discussion of the reciprocal activities of slave women. Blassingame also described how slave men gained status in the family and slave community, but he did not do the same for women.[19] Robert Fogel and Stanley Engerman in their book *Time on the Cross, The Economics of American Negro Slavery* claimed that "for better or worse, men played the dominant role in slave society." As proof they noted that slave men occupied all managerial and artisan slots, that masters recognized the male as head of the family group, and that only men performed the heavy labor of plowing, while women predominated in the kitchen and at the washtub.[20] Eugene Genovese argued in *Roll, Jordan, Roll, The World the Slaves Made*, that female slaves did not assert themselves, protect their children, or assume other normally masculine activities.[21] In his epic work, *The Black Family in Slavery and Freedom, 1715–1925*, Herbert Gutman made so much of the role of slave men—in protecting slave women and children, in naming offspring, in

the stabilizing effect of their presence in slave households—
that women's roles were reduced to insignificance and largely
ignored.[22] Thus, the emphasis of recent literature on slavery
has been on negating Samboism. The male slave's "masculinity" was restored by putting black women in their proper
"feminine" place.

Fortunately, however, the content of Truth's 1851 remarks
as well as the reality of slave life gives us reason to suspect that
we do black women a disservice when we rob them of a history that placed them at the side of their men in their race's
struggle for freedom. This present study takes a look at slave
women in America and argues that they were not submissive,
subordinate, or prudish and that they were not expected to
be so. While the focus is primarily on Southern antebellum
plantation life it does not ignore bonded women in the colonial and early American South. Women, it will be seen, had
different roles from those of men and they also had a great
deal in common with their African foremothers, who, in many
precolonial West African societies, held positions not inferior
but complementary to those of men.[23] This study also argues
that mutual respect characterized relationships between the
sexes. If the male supremacy of the Big House did not infil-
trate the quarters it was in part because the jobs and services
performed by slave women for the community were not
peripheral but central to slave survival. Evidence presented
here also suggests that slave women had a high degree of sex
consciousness and that it was encouraged by the plantation
work regimen, which required women and girls to work
together in groups and which made black women highly
dependent on each other.

At this point a note on sources is in order. Elkins set the
stage for the distortion of female slave sex roles but the dearth
of source material makes documenting their real role difficult. Anyone familiar with the traditional historical sources of
slavery, including plantation records, travelers' accounts,

newspapers, slave narratives and ex-slave interviews, slave-owner letters and diaries, and pro and antislavery pamphlets, understands the problems associated with reconciling the different and often contradictory sources with such variables as time, region, plantation size, crop, and slave owner idiosyncracies. In short, it is very difficult, if not impossible, to be precise about the effect of any single variable on female slaves. Source material on the general nature of slavery exists in abundance, but it is very difficult to find source material about slave women in particular.[24] Slave women were everywhere, yet nowhere. They were in Southern households and in Southern fields but the sources are silent about female status in the slave community and the bondwoman's self-perception. In fact, the material sheds little light upon the way sex and race shaped her self-concept.

The source problem is directly related to what was and still is the black women's condition. Few scholars who study black women fail to note that black women suffer a double oppression: that shared by all African-Americans and that shared by most women. Every economic and political index demonstrates the black woman's virtual powerlessness in American society at large.[25] A consequence of the double jeopardy and powerlessness is the black woman's invisibility. Much of what is important to black Americans is not visible to whites, and much of what is important to women is not visible to men. Whites wrote most of antebellum America's records and African-American males wrote just about all of the antebellum records left by blacks. To both groups the female slave's world was peripheral. The bondwoman was important to them only when her activities somehow involved them. Few sources illuminate the interaction of slave women in their private world.

A related problem has to do with the matter of subversive activity. Source material on slavery does not bear out the popular notion that black women were allowed to express their aggression because they were less "threatening" than black men.[26] Rather, it seems that slave women understood the value of silence and secrecy. Being both black and female they knew to be true what Simone de Beauvoir would elaborate nearly a century after formal bondage ended. Women, like slaves and servants, deliberately dissemble their objective reality. Like all who are dependent upon the caprices of a master, they hide their real sentiments and turn toward him a changeless smile or an enigmatic impassivity.[27] Paul Lawrence Dunbar, speaking specifically of black Americans, had made a similar reference over half a century earlier:

> We wear the mask that grins and lies,
> It hides our cheeks and shades our eyes,
> This debt we pay to human guile;
> With torn and bleeding hearts we smile,
> And mouth with myriad subtleties.[28]

It is unfortunate, but so much of what we would like to know about slave women can never be known because they masked their thoughts and personalities in order to protect valued parts of their lives from white and male invasion.

For this reason it is often necessary to make inferences. I relied heavily on the Works Projects Administration's interviews with female ex-slaves. I found them the richest, indeed almost the only black female source dealing with female slavery. I have studied them in light of what anthropologists know about women who do similar things in analogous settings. Thus, while the emphasis is primarily on female slaves, the approach taken here is at times cross-cultural in that slave women are compared to other women who are not slaves but who are or were members of preindustrial black agricultural societies. This approach obviously presents problems since the bonded woman's circumstances were unique. However, it may be the best way available to handle this rather difficult topic.

The history of slavery has come a long way since Ulrich B. Phillips described the plantation as a school, and the slave the blissful, yet eternal, student.[29] Through the diligent and meticulous study of antebellum sources subsequent scholars taught us what unyielding demands the institution made on the slave, and still others enlightened us as to the demands the slave made on the institution. We have learned that race relations were never so clear-cut as to be solely a matter of white over black, but that in the assimilation of culture, in the interaction of blacks and whites, there were gray areas and relationships more aptly described in terms of black over white. We have also begun to understand that despite the brutality and inhumanity, or perhaps because of it, a distinct African-American culture based on close-knit kinship relationships grew and thrived, and that it was this culture that sustained black people through many trials before and after emancipation. This study aims to enrich our knowledge of antebellum black culture and to serve as a chapter in the yet unwritten history of the American black woman.

CHAPTER ONE

Jezebel and Mammy: The Mythology of Female Slavery

From the intricate web of mythology which surrounds the black woman, a fundamental image emerges. It is of a woman of inordinate strength, with an ability for tolerating an unusual amount of misery and heavy, distasteful work. This woman does not have the same fears, weaknesses, and insecurities as other women, but believes herself to be and is, in fact, stronger emotionally than most men. Less of a woman in that she is less "feminine" and helpless, she really *more* of a woman in that she is the embodiment of Mother Earth, the quintessential mother with infinite sexual, life-giving, and nurturing reserves. In other words, she is a superwoman.[1]

THE UNIQUENESS OF the African-American female's situation is that she stands at the crossroads of two of the most well-developed ideologies in America, that regarding women and that regarding the Negro. Although much of the race and sex ideology that abounds in America has its roots in history that is older than the nation, it was during the slavery era that the ideas were molded into a peculiarly American mythology. As if by design, white males have been the primary beneficiaries of both sets of myths which, not surprisingly, contain common elements in that both blacks and women are characterized as infantile, irresponsible, submissive, and promiscuous. Both blacks and women have generally been dependent politically and economically upon white men. Both groups are consigned to roles that are subservient, both groups have shared a relationship of powerlessness *vis-à-vis* white males, and both groups, as a matter of automatic response, have been treated as outsiders and inferiors.[2]

The black woman's position at the nexus of America's sex and race mythology has made it most difficult for her to escape the mythology. Black men can be rescued from the myth of the Negro, indeed, as has been noted, this seems to have been one of the aims of the historical scholarship on slavery in the 1970s. They can be identified with things masculine, with things aggressive, with things dominant. White women, as part of the dominant racial group, have to defy the myth of woman, a difficult, though not impossible task. The impossible task confronts the black woman. If she is rescued from the myth of the Negro, the myth of woman traps her. If she escapes the myth of woman, the myth of the Negro still ensnares her. Since the myth of woman and the myth of the Negro are so similar, to extract her from one gives the appearance of freeing her from both. She thus gains none of the deference and approbation that accrue from being perceived as weak and submissive, and she gains none of the advantages that come with being a white male. To be so "free," in fact, has at times made her appear to be a superwoman, and she has attracted the envy of black males and white females. Being thus exposed to their envy she has often become their victim.

When antebellum Southerners thought about black women they did not conjure up images of an indolent Sambo, a rabid rapist, or an affable helpmeet. The first two explained black men, the latter, Southern white women. Black women had something in common with both black men and white women and the characterization of them, while unique, was an odd blend of the ideas formed about these two groups. In antebellum America, the female slave's chattel status, sex, and race combined to create a complicated set of myths about black womanhood.

One of the most prevalent images of black women in antebellum America was of a person governed almost entirely by her libido, a Jezebel character. In every way Jezebel was the counterimage of the mid-nineteenth-century ideal of the Victorian lady. She did not lead men and children to God; piety was foreign to her. She saw no advantage in prudery, indeed domesticity paled in importance before matters of the flesh. How white Americans, and Southerners in particular, came to think of black women as sensual beings has to do with the impressions formed during their initial contact with Africans, with the way black women were forced to live under chattel slavery, and with the ideas that Southern white men had about women in general.

The idea that black women were exceptionally sensual first gained credence when Englishmen went to Africa to buy slaves. Unaccustomed to the requirements of a tropical climate, Europeans mistook seminudity for lewdness. Similarly, they misinterpreted African cultural traditions, so that polygamy was attributed to the Africans' uncontrolled lust, tribal dances were reduced to the level of orgy, and African religions lost the sacredness that had sustained generations of ancestral worshippers.[3]

The travel accounts of Europeans contained superficial analyses of African life and spurious conclusions about the character of black women. Perhaps it was the warm climate of Africa that prompted William Bosman to describe the women he saw on the coast of Guinea as "fiery" and "warm" and "so much hotter than the men."[4] William Smith must have fallen under the same influence, since he wrote of "hot constitution'd Ladies" who "are continually contriving stratagems how to gain a lover."[5] Smith also reported that orangutan like creatures "often attack and use Violence to the Black Women whenever they meet them alone in the Woods."[6]

Similar descriptions are found in the writings of North American and Caribbean travelers and planters. From Jamaica came a poem dedicated to "The Sable Venus," in which "sooty dames well vers'd in Venus' school, Make love an art and boast they kiss by rule."[7] These ideas found their way to the continent, and in 1736 one could read in the *South Carolina Gazette* about "African Ladies" of "strong robust constitution" who were "not easily jaded out," but able to serve their lovers "by Night as well as Day."[8] Even in the Chesapeake, ideas about promiscuous black women held firm. Suggesting that black women mated with orangutans, Thomas Jefferson was certain that this animal preferred "the black woman over those of his own species."[9]

By the nineteenth century, coarse jokes about "negro wenches" were commonplace, and both Northerners and Europeans accepted the premise upon which they rested. Alexander Wilson, a European poet, wrote from Savannah that "the negro wenches are all sprightliness and gaiety." Citing circulating rumors, he continued, "if report be not a defamor," the sexual habits of black women "render the men callous to all the finer sensations of love and female excellence."[10] Another visitor, Johann Schoepf, wrote that "in almost every house there are negresses, slaves, who count it an honor to bring a mulatto into the world."[11] Even the abolitionist James Redpath wrote that mulatto women were "gratified by the criminal advances of Saxons."[12]

Many antebellum Southerners found little in the black female's character to compliment. Some were convinced that slave women were lewd and lascivious, that they invited sexual overtures from white men, and that any resistance they displayed was mere feigning. While Samuel Cartwright, a Louisiana proslavery theorist, spoke of "lewd and lascivious" black females, easily thrown into "paroxysms of unconsciousness" and "vulgar hysterics" when dancing with members of the opposite sex, a Louisiana planter expressed his belief that there was not "a likely-looking black girl in this state that is not the paramour of a white man."[13]

The view that black women were exceptionally libidinous was nourished by the conditions under which slave women lived and worked. The matter of reproduction provides an excellent example. American slavery was dependent on natural increase of the slave population, and through the use of innumerable incentives, planters made sure that slave women were prolific. Since causal correlations have always been drawn between sensuality and fecundity, the increase of the slave population seemed to be evidence of the slave woman's lust. A Mississippi planter associated the two when he attributed the rapid increase on his plantation to the early onset of sexual activity among female slaves. An Alabama slave owner also associated reproduction and promiscuity when he linked the high birthrate of slaves on his plantation to the fact that he "did not know more than one negro woman that he could suppose to be chaste. . . ."[14]

The actual rate of increase did not lend nearly as much credence to the reality of Jezebel as did the public attention that was given to the procreative capacity of slave women. Major periodicals carried articles detailing optimal conditons under which bonded women were known to reproduce, and the merits of a particular "breeder" were often the topic of parlor or dinner table conversations.[15] The fact that something so personal and private became a matter of public discussion prompted one ex-slave to declare that "women wasn't nothing but cattle."[16] Once reproduction became a topic of public conversation, so did the slave woman's sexual activities. People accustomed to speaking and writing about the bondwoman's reproductive abilities could hardly help associating her with licentious behavior.

The conditions under which women worked, were sold, and were punished also fostered an atmosphere conducive to such thoughts. Southerners were extremely squeamish about the "place" of women in antebellum society. Layers of clothing adorned the "respectable" white woman, and she never exposed even her legs or arms to public view without arousing the ire of her husband and the contempt of her community. The slave woman's body, however, commanded no such respect. Just as with reproduction, that which was private and personal became public and familiar.

Very often on the auction block women's bodies were exposed and handled to determine their capacity for child-bearing. Slave buyers sometimes kneaded women's stomachs in an attempt to determine how many children a woman could have.[17] Thomas Hamilton, an English visitor, attended the auction of a woman who was obviously ill, and noted how several men felt the poor woman's ribs.[18] Sometimes examinations approached a level of indecency. A historian of the slave trade cited an auction where the auctioneer introduced a woman with the following remarks: "Show your neck, Betsey. There's a breast for you; good for a round dozen before she's done child-bearing."[19] Occasionally, when there was doubt about a woman's reproductive ability, she was taken by the buyer and a physician to a private room where she was inspected more thoroughly.[20] Since Southern society associated public nudity with lascivity, this exposure of the slave woman's body led to an unconscious equating of black women with promiscuity.

The majority of Southerners never attended a slave auction, but conditions on the plantation had the same, if not a more profound, effect. More than likely, planters did not purposefully expose their female slaves; a few even took pains to clothe them properly and to prohibit indecent punishment practices. But such precautions were often insufficient, especially on large plantations of absentee owners where the dress of slaves was particularly ragged. Some women had such tattered clothes that they were almost naked. Sometimes bond-women were exposed because of the nature of their work. Female slaves on rice plantations worked in water with their dresses "reefed up" around their hips, exposing their legs and thighs. Similarly, many female field hands worked with their skirts pinned up to keep them out of dirt and mud, and house servants pulled up their skirts to wash and polish floors.[21]

The very sight of semiclad black women nurtured white male notions of their promiscuity. Even the usually objective Frederick Law Olmsted, the famous Northern architect, had trouble avoiding the association. He stood for a long time watching slave women repair a road on a South Carolina plantation. The women had their coarse gray skirts "reefed up" around their waist and did no more than complete their assigned tasks. Nevertheless, Olmsted's impressions of them were distinctly negative. He described them as "clumsy," "gross," and "elephantine," yet added that in their demeanor the women were "sly," "sensual," and "shameless."[22] In the South, where it was not unusual for female slaves to work bent over with their skirts up, it was easy to come to such conclusions.

The exposure of women's bodies during whippings had similar consequences. Christopher Nichols, an escaped slave living in Canada, remembered how his master laid a woman on a bench, threw her clothes over her head, and whipped her. Another refugee remembered that when his mother was whipped, she was stripped completely naked: "Dey didn't care nothing 'bout it. Let everybody look on at it."[23] Similarly, Henry Bibb reported a whipping where a woman's "naked quivering flesh" was "tied up and exposed to the public gaze of all."[24]

Without doubt, some whippings of female slaves were sexually suggestive. The man who whipped Henry Bibb's wife was often heard by Bibb to exclaim that "he had rather paddle a female than eat when he was hungry."[25] The whipping of a thirteen-year-old Georgia slave girl also had sexual overtones. The girl was put on all fours "sometimes her head down, and sometimes up" and beaten until froth ran from her mouth.[26] Solomon Northup's master was not above whipping his slave Patsey in such a manner, either. According to Northup, Master Epps was a man possessed with "brute passion." Nothing satisfied him more than having a few drinks and whipping Patsey.[27]

The conditions under which bonded women lived and

worked helped imprint the Jezebel image on the white mind, but traders and owners also consciously and unconsciously created an environment which ensured female slave behavior that would fulfill their expectations. The choice put before many slave women was between miscegenation and the worst experiences that slavery had to offer. Not surprisingly, many chose the former, though they were hardly naive. Many expected and often got something in return for their sexual favors. There was no reason for them to believe that even freedom could not be bought for the price of their bodies. Some women, therefore, took the risk involved and offered themselves. When they did so, they breathed life into the image of Jezebel.

Although not all white male–black female relationships were exploitive, most began that way, and most continued that way. For instance, Cynthia, an acquaintance of William Wells Brown, was given a choice by the slave trader who bought her: If she would accept his proposals he would take her back with him to St. Louis and establish her as his housekeeper at his farm. But, if she persisted in rejecting him, he would sell her as a field hand on the worst plantation on the Mississippi River. Cynthia accepted the offer and became the trader's mistress and housekeeper.[28] A similarly desperate choice was made by Malinda Bibb. Malinda tried to escape with her husband, Henry, but both were caught. While they were imprisoned, Malinda managed to fight off a lecherous slave trader by herself. She and Henry were sold apart, but while he eventually escaped North she became the concubine of her new owner. Henry was bitter when, years later, he was told of her situation. He reasoned that she undoubtedly "became reconciled to it . . . she was much better treated than she had ever been before."[29]

Other women proved more eager than either Cynthia or Malinda. Mary Boykin Chesnut wrote that she saw a slave woman on an auction block who seemed delighted with her plight. The woman sometimes ogled the bidders, and "her mouth never relaxed from its expanded grin of excitement."[30] Solomon Northup, a kidnapped slave had a similar experience. He was imprisoned in a slave pen with a woman who "entertained an extravagantly high opinion of her own attractions." Northup was shocked when she haughtily declared that she expected, upon arrival in New Orleans, to be bought by a "wealthy gentleman of good taste."[31] Undoubtedly the thought of silks and satins and jewelry lured such women. In cities like Charleston and New Orleans travelers did indeed see the mulatto and quadroon slave mistresses of wealthy merchants strolling down boulevards.[32]

Sadly enough, though, what was one woman's boon proved another's bane. While some women remained the concubines of their white lovers and eventually obtained freedom for themselves and their children, just as many, if not more, were sold off to plantations where they shared the misery of all slaves. Sometimes their lovers married and settled into a stable family life with a white woman. Sometimes a jealous wife put an end to her husband's carousing by insisting that the slave woman be sold away. Occasionally, the black woman who had been treated like a family member since childhood became the rival of a jealous wife. Whatever the reason, there were enough "fallen women" to demonstrate how risky it was to expect liberation from one's enslavers.

In the Southern slave pens, such women were distinguished by their dress and manners. Fredericka Bremer, a Swedish visitor, was amazed to find such a well-dressed woman in a slave pen in Washington, D.C. The slave keeper related the tragic story of the woman who was "brought up in all respects 'like a lady' " who "could embroider and play piano, and dress like a lady, and read, and write, and dance." The slave keeper went on to explain that the woman was sold by the whites who had raised her because "her mind had grown too high for her; she had become proud, and now, to humble her, they had brought her here . . . to be sold."[33]

Abolitionist Levi Coffin related the story of Rose, another "fallen woman." Although Rose was a slave, "she had never experienced any of the hardships and cruelties of slavery." She had been treated kindly by her master and mistress, had a comfortable home, did the lightest household tasks, and had been taught to sew. However, when she gave birth to the master's child her mistress turned vengeful and hired Rose out to another family. When the term of service ended, and Rose was faced with the reality of having to return to her original master *and* the possibility of sale, she decided to take her chances as a fugitive. Unlike so many other women, Rose was a successful runaway. Not only had she acquired the manners and language skills necessary to escape, but because she was so exceptionally light skinned she was also able to pass as a white female.[34]

Other slave women of similar attainments were often less fortunate than Rose. When Solomon Northup first met Eliza he knew she was no common slave. She was arrayed in silk, with rings upon her fingers, and golden ornaments suspended from her ears. "Her air and manner, the correctness and propriety of her language, all indicated that she had enjoyed opportunities denied to most slaves." Eliza had been the concubine of a planter who had separated from his wife and built a new house that he shared with Eliza and the two children born to them. He promised to free Eliza and her children but domestic problems prohibited it. Instead of receiving her manumission papers, a bill of sale was issued to a slave trader who at once separated Eliza from her two children and sold all of them into slavery. Only a few months passed before her face became ghastly and haggard and her once elegant form became bowed under the weight of her physical and mental oppression. The tragedy was captured by Northup: "Freedom—freedom for herself and her offspring, for many years had been her cloud by day, her pillar of fire by night. . . . She had ascended to the top of Pisgah, and beheld the land of promise. In an unexpected moment she was utterly overwhelmed with disappointment and despair. . . . Now she weepeth sore in the night and tears are on her cheeks."[35]

Frederick Olmsted also met a very sad slave woman just days after she had been cast aside. The woman was with several men who had recently been sold and were now on their way to a plantation in South Carolina. While her slave companions bundled their blankets and slept close to the fire, the woman stood apart. The scene, as narrated by Olmsted, was full of melancholy: "The woman, bareheaded, and very inadequately clothed . . . stood for a long time alone, erect and statuelike, her head bowed, gazing in the fire. She had taken no part in the light chat of the others, and had given them no assistance in making the fire." Olmsted noted that the woman's dress "was not the usual plantation apparel." Without knowing the story connected with the woman Olmsted concluded: "It was all sadly suggestive."[36]

The scene Olmsted witnessed suggested the existence of the "Fancy Trade," the sale of light-skinned black women for the exclusive purpose of prostitution and concubinage. New Orleans seems to have been the center of the trade, but "fancy girls" could be found in other cities, especially Charleston, St. Louis, and Lexington.[37] Bremer saw "fancy girls" on two occasions, once in Columbia, South Carolina, and again in Richmond, Virginia. While touring a slave market in Richmond, she noticed that the dealer kept a few mulatto women in a separate jail. The slave keeper told her that the women were "fancy girls for fancy purchasers." In Columbia, she found a similar arrangement. There, the slave keeper informed her that on the day before her visit a handsome woman had been sold for fifteen hundred dollars.[38]

Some women sold for more. The aforementioned Eliza had a daughter named Emily who was sold away from her. Eliza's purchaser was loath to separate mother and daughter and wanted them both, but the slave trader would not hear of it. He had other plans for Emily. Indeed, "there were heaps and piles of money to be made of her . . . when she was a few years older. There were men enough in New Orleans who would give five thousand dollars for such an extra handsome, fancy piece as Emily would be. . . . No, no he would not sell her then. She was a beauty—a picture—a doll—one of the regular bloods—none of your thick-lipped bullet-headed, cotton-picking niggers—if she was might he be d—d."[39]

Whether or not slave women desired relationships with white men was immaterial, the conventional wisdom was that black women were naturally promiscuous, and thus desired such connections. If, in order to ease the burdens of slavery, they made themselves available, they only fulfilled the prophecy of their lustfulness, which in turn made it more difficult for other black women to reject the overtures made by white men. While slave women became the easy prey of profligates, justification for their exploitation came from the lips of some of the South's leading statesmen. This was particularly true after Northern abolitionists questioned the moral health of Southern society, a society that degraded and exploited a class of its women and ignored the involvement of its male youth with women alleged by Southerners themselves to be immoral. Rather than fault themselves, some Southern spokesmen blamed black women.

Those who used this rationalization found morality wanting in black society as a whole. Black men and women were thought to have such insatiable sexual appetites that they had to go beyond the boundaries of their race to get satisfaction. It was black women who, many claimed, tempted men of the superior caste. White men, it was argued, never had to use authority or violence to obtain compliance from bonded women because the latter's morals were so relaxed. Proponents of this line of reasoning actually celebrated the societal stratification that made black women available but put white women out of reach. Northerners, they argued, debased the civilized; they defamed the white prostitute, cut her off from the hope of useful and profitable employment, immured her in a state of depravity. By contrast, Southern white women were kept free and pure from the taint of immorality because black women acted as a buffer against their degradation.[40]

The most succinct statement of this argument was made by William Harper, chancellor of the University of South Carolina. After citing the imperfect morality of the black female, he asked his audience to compare the female slave with white prostitutes of the North:

> She is not a less useful member of society than before. If shame be attached to her conduct, it is such shame as would be elsewhere felt for a venial impropriety. She has not impaired her means of support or materially impaired her character, or lowered her station in society; she has done no great injury to herself, or any other human being. Her offspring is not a burden but an acquisition to her owner; his support is provided for, and he is brought up to usefulness.

Harper continued by noting that under such advantageous conditions, it was hardly surprising that the slave woman should "yield to temptation."[41]

Although Harper seemed comfortable with his rationalization of the white male's exploitation of black women, many Southerners approached the subject with much more caution and a good deal of uneasiness. Obviously, Southern white women remained unimpressed by the supposed superiority of Southern sexual arrangements. Many shared the belief that black women were naturally promiscuous, but they saw no advantage in having a spouse who spent his spare time in the slave cabins. Moreover, many felt stifled by the sexual straitjacket they were forced to wear. From the white women of the South, Harper demanded "purity of conduct" and "purity of manners."[42] To many white women this was proof enough of their subordination to white males. Others became convinced that black women had unlimited sexual freedom.

Mary Chesnut was of both opinions. According to her, white men held all the cards, and black women did not do too badly, either. The magnate who ran a black harem under the same roof with his white daughters, she fumed, lost no social prestige. He still held his head high, still posed as a model of all human virtues, still thundered and stormed at his family as if he had never done wrong in his life. Chesnut, however, had no pity for slave women, nor did she show any understanding of their problems. Instead, she echoed Harper's views: "Who thinks any worse of a Negro or mulatto woman for being a thing we can't name." If white women behaved like either white men or black women, she wrote, they would be "ridiculed," "abandoned," and sent out of any decent house.[43] Chesnut was not the only Southern mistress to voice such complaints. A Virginia mistress also wrote with distress about the conduct of many Southern "gentlemen." White mothers and daughters of all classes, she complained, had "seen their dearest affections trampled upon, their hopes of domestic happiness destroyed, and their future lives embittered" by their husbands, sons, and brothers.[44]

An event certain to destroy domestic happiness was the birth of a half-white child to a slave woman. Unlike Chancellor Harper, white women did not just add another digit to the profit side of the ledger. Half-white children told a story of a white man's infidelity, a slave woman's helplessness (though this concerned few whites), and a white woman's inability to defy the social and legal constraints that kept her bound to her husband regardless of his transgressions. Unable to do anything about it, many a Southern white woman feigned ignorance of illicit, interracial relationships, at least those that occurred under her own roof. According to Chesnut, "any lady is ready to tell who is the father of all the mulatto children in everybody's household but their own. Those she seems to think drop from the clouds."[45] Of course, the slaves on a given plantation could have advised their mistress of the paternity of a mulatto child, for they usually knew with which slave women the master was sleeping. Out of fear they dared not, and these secrets of slavery remained, as Linda Brent reported, "concealed like those of the Inquisition."[46]

That was in public; in the privacy of her household the mistress let her true feelings show. Savilla Burrell explained what happened on her plantation: "Old Marse was de daddy of some mulatto chillun. De 'lations wid de mothers of dese chillun is what give so much grief to Mistress. De neighbors would talk 'bout it. . . . My mistress would cry 'bout dat."[47] Mary Reynolds told how her mistress heard two mulatto children tell her own white children: "We ain't no niggers, 'cause we got the same daddy you has, and he comes to see us near everyday and fotches us clothes and things from town." The mistress threatened to go away but "she didn't never leave, and Massa bought her a fine, new span of surrey hosses. But she don't never have no more children, and she ain't so cordial with the Massa."[48]

As court records indicate, on some plantations unpleasant three-sided relationships led to bitter confrontations and disruptions of white family life. One Alabama mistress returned to live with her parents because her husband abandoned her bed to "embrace a Negro woman belonging to him." A North Carolina planter insulted his wife by allegedly putting his slave concubine in charge of all domestic duties and by sleeping with her in their bedroom. Similarly, a South Carolina mistress brought a suit against her husband and claimed that he daily insulted her and encouraged his slave mistress to do the same.[49]

Southern white women were powerless to right the wrongs done them, but some did strike back, not always at Southern patriarchs, but usually at their unwitting and powerless rivals, slave women. Light-skinned children were sometimes sold by

irate slave mistresses who suspected or knew that their husbands were the fathers.[50] When a child was not involved, some
women took their revenge directly on the female slave. Patsey, the slave woman mentioned previously in connection with
whippings, was truly a pitiable woman. Edwin Epps' sexual
appetite was masochistic, and Mistress Epps' jealous behavior
bordered on sadism. She had Patsey whipped whenever the
opportunity presented itself.[51]

Many of the ex-slaves who had unfavorable memories of
the mistress were light-skinned black women who unwittingly
incurred the mistress's emnity. One such ex-slave remembered her mistress as a mean woman: "She was jealous of me
because I was light, said she didn't know what her husband
wanted to bring that half-white nigger there for." Ellen Craft's
mistress was so disturbed by Ellen's presence that she gave
Ellen to her daughter as a wedding present. Ellen's husband
figured that the "tyrannical old lady" objected to Ellen's complexion, which was as fair as any white child's.[52] The reaction
of some mistresses to slave women with long straight hair was
to have the hair cut short. When Rebecca was a slave her hair
was purposely kept short to offset her likeness to her white
father's young sister. Louisa Piquet's hair was cut when her
mistress feared it put her own daughter's to shame.[53] If such
episodes illustrate the abject condition of slave women, they
also demonstrate the white mistress's complicity with a system
that made victims of all women.

Linda Brent understood the predicament of Southern white
women, yet she faulted them for having so little compassion
for slave women. She thought white mistresses should have
felt for her as she felt for them. Brent was caught in a three-
sided affair involving her master and mistress. Mr. Flint would
make sexual overtures to her, and Mrs. Flint would then stalk
her to determine the extent of the relationship and assail her
whenever the opportunity presented itself. Brent yearned for
some show of sympathy from Mrs. Flint, as she put it "one

word of kindness from her would have brought me to her feet." Indeed, Brent felt sorry for Mrs. Flint because Flint's marriage vows had been desecrated and her dignity insulted. She reasoned that Flint pitied herself as a martyr but could not feel pity for another's shame and misery. Surmising further, Brent thought that "slaveholders' wives feel as other women would under similar circumstances." Describing Mr. Flint as a "hoary-headed miscreant" who would try the patience of any woman, she empathized with Mrs. Flint, who simply did not know what to do.[54]

There was little white women could do when problems of this sort arose, but they were not alone in their opposition to miscegenation. They were joined by white men who feared what they called "mongrelization," or race mixing, that would inevitably result in the disappearance of the "pure" Caucasian. These men heeded the teachings of Southern scientist Josiah Nott and Northerner J. H. Van Evrie, both of whom cautioned the South against becoming too much like its racially mixed Spanish neighbors to the south. According to them, mulattoes were treacherous and ultimately sterile beings. Implicit in this characterization was a plea to white men to put an end to the sexual connections that increased the mulatto population.[55] Others objected to illicit sex with black women out of fear for their white adolescent boys, who, some thought, could never learn discipline or respect for Christian continence as long as they felt they could compel black women to sleep with them. This anxiety motivated a Louisiana planter to send his boys North to be educated. As he saw it "there was no possibility of their being brought up in decency at home."[56]

Finally, white women were joined by those who were uncomfortable with the negative characterization of black women, those who could not reconcile the image of Jezebel with the close contact white children had with black house servants. This concern was given voice by a writer in the *Southern Cultivator* who warned that "if, in this association, the

child becomes familiar with the indelicate, vulgar, and lascivious manners and conversation, an impression is made upon
the mind and heart, which lasts for years—perhaps for life."[57]

These objections reveal how ill at ease many Southerners
were with interracial sex. Proslavery arguments like that put
forth by Harper served to increase their sensitivity. In fact, it
touched a raw nerve because implicit in the argument was an
admission of impropriety, namely that black women were
indeed kept in a state of prostitution by white men who had
little incentive to exercise self-control. Furthermore, the Jezebel characterization of black women left the South vulnerable
to Northern charges that Southern white women could hardly
respect chastity when they were surrounded by black women
who had learned from childhood that virtue was something
that could be traded for food.

To successfully rebut abolitionist charges of Southern
degeneracy, Southerners had to come up with alternative jus-
tifications of slavery and a more postive image of black women.
Their society and their labor system had to be exalted on the
basis that everyone benefited, both black and white. Slavery
had to be explained in a context that was in keeping with the
idea of white moral supremacy. Since in her role as mother
and wife it was woman's responsibility to be the guardian of
morality, much of the South's defense hinged on how virtuous it could show its women, both black and white, to be.

To this end, Southern men claimed that slavery uplifted
white women. It was argued that only those women at the
very lowest rung of society debased themselves by having illicit
sex. For those in the middle and upper strata of society slavery had an ameliorative effect. William Drayton argued that
one of the first fruits of slavery was to rescue women from
"their undeserved and wretched fate" and afford them leisure time to improve themselves. The Southern white woman
gained from slavery in several ways: "Her faculties are developed; her gentle and softening influence is seen and felt; she

assumes the high station for which nature designed her; and happy in the hallowed affections of her own bosom, unwearily exerts those powers so well adapted to the task of humanizing and blessing others."[58] George Fitzhugh argued that women in the slave South had not been robbed of the softness of their own sex, as was the case in the North where women had been thrown into the arena of industrial war. Women in the North, he argued, were in a false position. In contrast, "be she white, or be she black, she is treated with kindness and humanity in the slaveholding South."[59]

As suggested by Fitzhugh black women also benefitted from slavery. While Chancellor Harper was resigned to the debasement of black women, and actually found some advantage in it, others argued that slavery was at the root of the black woman's reformation. Fitzhugh maintained that "the intercourse of the house-servants with the white family assimilated . . . their moral conduct to that of the whites."[60] George S. Sawyer, an antebellum Louisiana lawyer, thought that slavery afforded the female slave "encouragement to lead a virtuous life." If she chose to avail herself of the opportunity, the institution of slavery would throw a "shield of protection" around her.[61] In some proslavery rhetoric, therefore, Jezebel was made chaste, and the idea of chaste slave women was soothing to many Southern whites.

To those who rebutted the abolitionist charge that the South was a land of immorality, the regenerative power of slavery was an extremely convenient concept. Once they embraced it they argued that slaveholders never came in contact with the most debased slave women because none but the most righteous were allowed to serve in Southern households. Thus, a Southern clergyman insisted that whenever a house servant was found to be immoral, he or she was immediately sent to the fields. For abolitionists who assumed that white children were being "ruined in the nursery by being committed to negro kitchens," this minister had only rebuke. Just as white nurses in the North could be dismissed when found to be unworthy, slave nurses could also be discharged. If a suitable replacement could not be found on the plantation, then the slave market had an abundant supply of black women who had been "trained . . . in the point of honesty, morality and intelligence."[62]

Those so trained became trusted servants who, according to this proslavery argument, were well cared for, even through old age. Thomas Cobb thought this one of the most beneficent aspects of slavery. Once a slave became part of the "white family," that slave was cared for through the aged and infirm years. While abolitionists criticized those conditions that made sexual liaisons between adolescent white boys and female slaves a probability, Southerners like Cobb were more apt to emphasize the innocent quality of the relationship between white children and slave women. So strong were the ties, said Cobb, that "even the young spendthrift experiences a pang in sundering a relation he has recognized from his infancy."[63]

Southerners, therefore, were hardly of one mind concerning African-American women. Jezebel was an image as troubling as it was convenient and utilitarian. When forced to defend it many Southerners quickly retreated and revised their thinking. They did not necessarily abandon Jezebel nor their rationalizations of her. Rather many Southerners were able to embrace both images of black women simultaneously and to switch from one to the other depending on the context of their thought. On the one hand there was the woman obsessed with matters of the flesh, on the other was the asexual woman. One was carnal, the other maternal. One was at heart a slut, the other was deeply religious. One was a Jezebel, the other a Mammy.

* * *

Who was the black Mammy? What did she do and how did she do it? Most of what we know about Mammy comes from memoirs written after the Civil War. The descriptions are written with a certainty and definitiveness that seem to defy question. According to these accounts, Mammy was the woman who could do anything, and do it better than anyone else. Because of her expertise in all domestic matters, she was the premier house servant and all others were her subordinates. Thus, Susan Bradford Eppes grew up on a Florida plantation where Mammy was selected for "her worth and reliability." Her authority extended to all the "subnurses" and she ruled them with a "rod of iron."[64] Louisa Campbell Sheppard described Mary, the Mammy on her father's Missouri plantation, as a cook who not only ruled supreme in the kitchen, but who was the general superintendent of the younger servants as well.[65] Susan Dabney Smedes, the daughter of a wealthy Virginia planter, characterized Mammy Maria as a "field marshall who gave out work and taught the plantation women to sew."[66] Similarly, in her description of social life in New Orleans, Eliza Ripley recalled that Mammy was a "supernumerary" who, after the children grew up, "managed the whole big and mixed household." In her father's house, everyone was made to understand that "all applications" were to go through Mammy Charlotte. "Nobody thought to go to the judge or his wife for anything . . . if they required anything from a riding horse to a fresh stick on the fire, from a mint julep to a bedroom candle, they had only to call Charlotte. She was never beyond the reach of a summons day or night."[67]

In these and similar sources, Mammy is especially remembered for her love of her young white charges. Mrs. Smedes did not think Mammy "could be angry more than a minute with her white children."[68] On the White Hill plantation in Virginia Mammy seemed to be always around to humor and protect. "No cry from the school room escaped her ears," for Mammy was always there to defend "her children."[69] For Susan Eppes it was Mammy who stood between her "honey chile' and the cold, cold world."[70]

Considering Mammy's supposed intimate involvement in all aspects of domestic life in the Big House, it is not surprising that she was thought of as someone special, not just another house slave. Thus, in accounts of Mammy, her occupation is infused with great emotion. "Hers was a case both of greatness thrust upon one and of greatness achieved," said Susan Smedes of Mammy Maria.[71] "Mammy was an out and out aristocrat," reported Mrs. Eppes. Anyone "who to her mind did not come strictly up to the mark" was discouraged from associating with her "nurslings." Herself a model of politeness, she tolerated "not the least touch of vulgarity." Her favorite admonition, recorded Eppes, was "you ain't got no call ter say dat—you ain't no pore white trash—nor no nigger nuther—take yer finger out yore mouth—held up your hed an' don't forgit yore manners."[72] The Mammy on the White Hill estate also drew comparisons between "niggers" and "whitefolks." According to one of her charges, Mammy was "exclusive and had never encouraged our playing with the young negroes." In fact, she concluded, "her nature was passionate."[73] So respected was Mammy that she often served as friend and advisor to master and mistress. Susan Smedes recalled that her father never returned from the field without stopping to talk to Grannie Harriet. "He consulted her about his plantation affairs as did no one else and her judgment was so sound that he relied on it."[74]

Ex-slaves also remembered Mammy. Drucilla Martin recalled that her mother was in full charge of the house and all "Marse" children. Her mother, herself "clean as a new pin," insisted on their cleanliness and made each white child pass a daily inspection. When white boys came to court, her mother would inspect them with the same attentiveness: "Do you think my daught is gwin' to marry any Por' white trash'," she would say. "Be-gone, don' come back."[75] An Alabama woman named Katherine Eppes remembered that her mother worked in the Big House, "aspinnin an' anussin de white chillun." Eppes proudly reported that the mistress was quite solicitious of her mother, so much so that when she learned that the overseer had whipped the woman whom everyone called "Mammy," she dismissed him and gave him until sundown to remove himself and his family from the plantation.[76] A Louisiana black woman's recollections, like those of Susan Smedes, made Mammy seem almost majestic: "All the niggers have to stoop to Aunt Rachel just like they curtsy to Missy."[77]

This, therefore, is the broad outline of Mammy. She was a woman completely dedicated to the white family, especially to the children of that family. She was the house servant who was given complete charge of domestic management. She served also as friend and advisor. She was, in short, surrogate mistress and mother.

The Mammy image is fully as misleading as that of Jezebel. Both images have just enough grounding in reality to lend credibility to stereotypes that would profoundly affect black women. For instance, most house servants were, indeed, female. Black women served in all capacities, from cook to waiting maid, from wet nurse to mantua maker, or seamstress. In very wealthy Southern households there were many female servants. While the Mammy tradition is usually associated with upper-class whites, black women also served in less wealthy households, though they were not as numerous, and they sometimes doubled as field workers. Children in these homes could become just as attached to female servants as children of wealthier families, and in their adult years when they laid claim to the status that went along with having had a black Mammy they could do so with some credibility.

If the Mammy myth is grounded in the reality of black female house service, the idyllic aspect of the myth also gains support from the fact that house service was less physically demanding than field work, and very often translated into better care for the housemaids involved. Hard as cleaning, cooking, sewing, dairy work, and child care were, they were

not as physically taxing as a sun up to sun down day in the
crop—be it sugar, rice, or cotton. On the whole, house women
could expect to eat better, dress better, and get better medical
care than field women, if only because they were more familiar to the master and mistress, not to mention nearer to the
kitchen and potential hand-me-downs. Some women were
given relatively exceptional wedding services, others were
allowed an opportunity, rare for slave women, to leave the
plantation as waiting maid for their traveling mistresses. Still
others were taught to read and write by members of the white
family. Furthermore, genuine affection sometimes developed
between the white children and house servants on Southern
plantations and farms. There was, therefore, much in the reality
of house service on which to base a romantic view of female
household help.

Such a view required that some of the uglier and perverse
aspects be overlooked. If, as Eliza Riply claimed, Mammy
Charlotte was never beyond a summons day or night, then
Mammy Charlotte was a very tired woman. Indeed, house
servants were on call at all hours. They probably had less private time than field workers. They were always under the
scrutiny of the white family and far more subject to their mood
swings, particularly to those of the mistress, than other slaves.
House servants had to be on guard constantly lest a master or
mistress, angry at who knows what, swung an open palm or
closed fist in their direction. Obsequious behavior was, therefore, more of a must for them, and the pretty, even the comely,
could never rest easy once the master's sons reached puberty,
or the master himself developed a roving eye. That roving
eye, of course, presented a problem that is ignored in romantic views of female house service. As noted earlier, there was
conflict between black and white women in many ante'bellum
households. Conflict precipitated by the indiscretions of white
men did little to contribute to smooth household management.

In fact, the complaints of many white women give rise to questions about how smoothly Southern households functioned. One would think that with efficient and tireless Mammies around, wealthy Southern women would lead lives of leisure. However, during her visit to America, Harriet Martineau found the opposite to be the case. All too often it was the Southern mistress, not a female slave, who carried the keys of the household. The wives of slaveholders, said Martineau, "are as they and their husbands declare, as much slaves as their negroes." When domestic problems arose, it was the mistress who ran to the rescue. According to Martineau, if the white lady of the house "will not have everything go to rack and ruin around them, they must superintend every household operation, from the cellar to the garrets; for there is nothing that slaves can do well." Martineau apparently did not find many black women in charge of Southern white households, for she further noted that it was the white mistress who "is forever superintending, and trying to keep things straight, without the slightest hope of attaining anything like leisure and comfort."[78]

The diaries of white mistresses confirm Martineau's observations. For instance, Meta Morris Grimball, a South Carolinian, complained continuously about the work she had to do, even when ill or pregnant. In her Civil War diary she recorded how she used to drag herself "with weak and wretched feelings" about the house doing her duties. She complained that for eight out of her twelve pregnancies she had no nurse, and when she had them their stay was too short. Grimball's complaints are curious in light of the presence of at least two slave women in her household who could have eased her burdens. There was a black woman, referred to as Old Mauma, who apparently was charged with the care of the white children and who had been with Grimball for some time. There was also another woman named Patty who had lived with Grimball for thirty-six years "being a skillful seamstress, tailoress,

Mantuamaker, washer and ironer." One can only assume that even working in tandem, Old Mauma and Patty could not do all that needed to be done in Grimball's Big House, and therefore did not fulfill the role traditionally associated with Mammy.[79]

Probably there was too much work in Southern households for any *one* woman, black or white. Everyday chores like cooking, cleaning, washing, ironing, and milking were not aided by many time- or labor-saving devices.[80] Childcare duties were performed in addition to everything else and, contrary to legend, not all Southern wealthy white women handed over the care of children to a black Mammy. Mrs. Isaac Hilliard, for instance, had several house slaves, but would not allow her son Henry to be cared for by anyone but herself. "I cannot conceive," she wrote, "how a mother can rest satisfied, to put her tender and helpless babes out to nurse. Who but a mother, would patiently undergo the fatigue and sleepless nights."[81]

The portrait slaves paint of Southern mistresses is very similar to the one painted by Southern women themselves, if not more revealing. Southern white mistresses were anything but idle. Along with house slaves they often spun thread, wove cloth, and sewed garments. Polly Colbert observed that while slave women did the spinning and weaving "Miss Betsey cut out all de clothes and helped wid de sewing. . . . She learnt all her women to sew. . . . She done all the sewing for de children."[82] On W. J. Snow's plantation the mistress made dye to color the thread before she wove the cloth. Miss Maugurite, a Mississippi mistress, had eight slaves, including Mollie Williams, who helped around the house as a child. Miss Maugurite not only made dresses for the slave women but cooked for the slaves and her own white family after the cook died.[83] Anna Parkes' recollections of her "Ole Miss" confirm Martineau's observation that the white mistress, not a black mammy, had charge of the keys to the cupboards. As a child, Parkes was overjoyed when the mistress allowed Parkes to tag behind her as she went from one room to the next opening closets. Sometimes Parkes even got to carry the keys.[84]

White women also played a role in slave child care, and while a legend has been built around the black nurses who helped raise Southern white children, the role that white women played in raising slave children has largely been ignored. If there was no elderly or disabled slave woman to supervise slave children during the day when their parents worked in the field, the responsibility fell to white mistresses. White women also played an important role in the health care of slave children. Adele Frost made a typical comment: "We ain't had no doctor, our Missus an' one of de slave' would tend to the sick."[85] The care white mistresses gave to sick slave children was probably no better or worse than that administered by slave nurses. In fact, white women, like slave nurses, often used herbal medicines and folk cures. Hester Hunter's testimony that her mistress took good care of her when she was sick was not unusual. On Master Jones' plantation in Fayette County, Texas, an old slave woman gathered herbs for medicines in the woods and the "old Miss would line up all de chillen and give dem a dose of garlic and rum." Alice Houston's mistress made the slave children wear a piece of lead around their necks to ward off malaria and nose bleeds.[86]

Tradition holds that the black Mammy socialized her white charges, but a much overlooked aspect of the Southern mistress's activities was the role she played in the socialization of black children. Some mistresses, motivated by a desire to protect their possessions, made lessons about theft and honesty standard when they read the Bible to slave children on Sunday mornings, frequently intoning "Thou shalt not steal."[87] Yet, sometimes genuine affection flowed between white mistresses and slave children. Dora Franks, for instance, grew up in the Big House with a mistress whose children were all grown by the time she arrived, and Franks believed that the mistress was so kind to her because she had no little ones of her own to care for.[88] Ester King Casey was taught to be "respectable and truthful" by Miss Susan, the "white lady," who once whipped her for playing with neighboring white children. Like the Mammy who supposedly made sure her white children were socialized properly, Miss Susan was concerned that these white children, being the offspring of the town jailer, were not good company: "She said that she wanted to raise me to be good and truthful, and that the jailer's little white children told lies and talked bad."[89] Frankie Goole's mistress was similarly maternal toward Frankie, and gave her advice any mother might give to a daughter: "She tole me ter alluz be a good girl, en don't let a man er boy trip me."[90]

If those who assume that every white family had a capable Mammy overlook the complaints of the Southern mistress and the role she played in raising black children, they pay just as little attention to the number of antebellum Southerners who shunned black nurses and employed white women instead. Mrs. Chesnut, the mother of the distinguished politician, James Chesnut, would have no black Mammy. According to her daughter-in-law, "after all her outspoken praises of Negroes, she would never trust her children except to a white head nurse."[91] The son of the Reverend Charles Colcock Jones would not trust his child to a black nurse, either. Although this Georgia family praised the exemplary conduct of their house slaves, when Charles, Jr., needed a nurse for his newborn son he secured a white nurse.[92] If Catherine Edmundson, a wealthy Southern mistress, can be believed, even Jefferson Davis, the president of the Confederacy, employed a white nurse.[93]

The mythology of Mammy has her well cared for in old age, but in reality many old female house servants were mistreated and many were abandoned. Frederick Douglass' grandmother suffered such a fate. She had been a faithful nurse and housekeeper all of her life, yet she lived to see her children, her grandchildren, and her great-grandchildren divided like so many sheep and sold away. In her final years she was of little value to her owners, and despite her frail condition they took her to the woods, built her a little hut with a mud chimney, and left her there to support and care for herself. As Douglass put it, they turned her out to die.[94] Other forms of abuse were not unknown to Mammies. Former slave Jacob Stroyer told a particularly harrowing story of a women named Aunt Betty. She had nursed her master through infancy, lived to see him become a drunk, and then became his victim when, during one of his drunken rampages, he took his shotgun and killed her.[95]

In reality there were no certainties for Mammy, but she could hope that the odds would come up in her favor. One may well assume that self-preservation motivated Mammy as much, if not more, than any particular loyalty she had to her owners. This is Genovese's view. He noted that Mammy was probably not nearly as "white-washed" as the legend has it. Genovese cautioned against simplistic analyses of Mammy and reminded us of Mammy's many positive traits. He noted, for instance, that Mammy carried herself with "courage, compassion, dignity and self-respect." She served her white folks well, but she was ever-mindful of the well-being of her own family. Mammy knew that by becoming a friend, confidante, and indispensable servant to the whites, she and her family might gain some immunity against sale and abuse. According to Genovese, Mammy did not always denigrate black people. She knew what was fair and proper, and often even defended black dignity, or championed the cause of an abused slave. "Her tragedy lay, not in her abandonment of her own people," said Genovese, "but in her inability to offer her individual power and beauty to black people on terms they could accept without themselves sliding further into a system of paternalistic dependency."[96]

Genovese did much to reshape the image of Mammy but there is still something about Mammy that is enigmatic. If the reality of Mammy and female household service does not square with the Mammy legend, why was the image of this domestic necessary at all and why did the image take the form it did? In order to answer the latter question one has to consider the period in American history when the first comprehensive descriptions of Mammy appear, namely during the thirty or so years prior to the Civil War. As advisor and confidante, surrogate mistress and mother, as one who was tough, diplomatic, efficient, and resourceful, Mammy was not merely a female slave housekeeper who identified more with her master than her fellow slaves. The image of Mammy taking care of the children, performing and supervising household chores, lending an ear and offering advice to master, mistress, and white children, was in keeping with the maternal or Victorian ideal of womanhood prevalent in nineteenth-century America.

The maternal ideal achieved its quintessential expression in the writings of the mid-nineteenth century. Women, according to the prevailing Victorian image, were supremely virtuous, pious, tender, and understanding. Although women were also idealized as virgins, wives, and Christians, it was above all as mothers that women were credited with social influence as the chief transmitters of religious and moral values. Other female roles—wife, charity worker, teacher, sentimental writer—were in large part culturally defined as extensions of motherhood, all similarly regarded as nurturing, empathetic, and morally directive.[97]

In the antebellum South this ideal found expression in writings that delineated the virtues of the farm wife. This genre cautioned women against too much fashion and too many leisure pastimes and ornamental attainments. The proper woman was one who made the home her primary sphere, who was a helpmeet to her husband, who raised her children according to Christian principles, who knew how to cook, sew, and garden.[98] Thus, in a typical contribution on this subject to the *Southern Cultivator,* "Advice to the Girls" admonished:

Girls do you want to get married—and do you want good husbands? If so, cease to act like fools. Don't take a pride in saying you never did housework—never cooked a pair of chickens—never made a bed, and so on. Don't turn up your pretty nose at honest industry—never tell your friends that you are not obliged to work. When you go shopping, never take your mother with you to carry the bundle. Don't be afraid to be seen in the kitchen cooking steak.[99]

Not surprisingly, much of the Southern literature which espoused the "cultural uplift" theory of slavery also preached the gospel of domesticity. John Pendleton Kennedy's *Swallow Barn* was the first in a long string of novels that did both. Of the blacks on the Swallow Barn plantation he wrote that "no tribe of people have ever passed from barbarism to civilization whose middle stage of progress has been more secure from harm, more genial to their character, or better supplied with mild and beneficient guardianship." The mistress of Swallow Barn, Lucretia, is typical of all his white female characters. She takes care of the household affairs "as one who had a reputation to stake upon her administration." Lucretia raises housekeeping to a science. Mornings were the best time to watch her operate as she "rather tyranically enforced her regimen against the youngsters of her numerous family, both white and black." Reminiscent of Mammy's supposed magic in the kitchen, Kennedy's Lucretia made such fantastic breakfasts that "a small regiment might march in upon her without disappointment."[100]

Beverly Tucker similarly described blacks and women. In *George Balcombe* the blacks are servile, loyal, and affectionate, the women are all models of domesticity. In one of his many soliloquies Balcombe reasons that only effeminate men marry educated women. Most men, he claims, "prefer the plain housewifely girl, who reads her Bible . . . darns her stockings, and boils her bacon and greens together."[101] Caroline Gilman's fictionalized account of her life repeated the same theme.

In *Recollections of a Southern Matron,* the blacks are perfect, and the women are model housewives. Of her mother she wrote:

> Home was her true sphere; there everything was managed with promptitude and decision. No one ever managed an establishment better; but there was no appeal from her opinions and I have known her ever eloquent in defending a recipe. . . . Her sausages were pronounced to be the best flavoured in the neighborhood; her hog's cheese . . . was delicacy itself; her curds made in a heartmould, covered with nutmeg and cream, won the hearts of many a guest.[102]

In the antebellum South, therefore, ideas about women went hand in hand with ideas about race. Women and blacks were the foundation on which Southern white males built their patriarchal regime. If, as seemed to be happening in the North during the 1830s, blacks and women conspired to be other than what white males wanted them to be, the regime would topple. Thus, George Balcombe advises his friend William to rest easy and accept the benefits of white manhood: "Let women and negroes alone," he cautions. "Leave them in their humility, their grateful affection, their self-renouncing loyalty, their subordination of the heart, and let it be your study to become worthy to be the object of their sentiments."[103]

Mammy was, thus, the perfect image for antebellum Southerners. As the personification of the ideal slave, and the ideal woman, Mammy was an ideal symbol of the patriarchal tradition. She was not just a product of the "cultural uplift" thoery, she was *also* a product of the forces that in the South raised motherhood to sainthood. As part of the benign slave tradition, and as part of the cult of domesticity, Mammy was the centerpiece in the antebellum Southerner's perception of the perfectly organized society.

Mammy's roots in the cult of domesticity run deep. Her very title was steeped in maternal sentiment. Everything she supposedly did was in harmony with the tradition of woman as guardian of the hearth. Lucretia of Swallow Barn and Caroline Gilman's mother were no more or less accomplished in culinary skills than Mammy. Margaret Isabella Weber, a Southern mistress, asserted that Mammy was "her Majesty" in the kitchen.[104] Louisa Sheppard claimed that even the most fastidious had small complaint with Mammy's cooking.[105] Like images of Southern women, Mammy indefatigably raised the children while she managed other household responsibilities. Thus, polemicist E. A. Pollard described a black woman named Aunt Debby as one who "managed" his parents' Georgia plantation. She was fond of "usurping the authority of her mistress below the stairs," and "if at times her mistress disputed her authority," Aunt Debby was sure to resume the reins once peace was restored.[106]

Central to the maternal ideal was the characterization of women as religious.[107] The best wives and mothers were steeped in virtue and piety. Mammy did not come up short on this count. In Pollard's *Black Diamonds,* for instance, all of the black women are sanctified. Of Aunt Debby, Pollard wrote, "the religious element is very strong" in her character. Of Aunt Belinda, a woman who Pollard claimed "nussed" him, he wrote, "the religious element is quite as marked in her character as in that of Aunt Debby." Pollard described other women similarly. About Aunt Judy he noted, "especially do I remember the intensity of her religious sentiment." Aunt Marie was like all of Pollard's other black women. Her very last gesture as she lay gasping for breath on her deathbed, struggling to live on, was to join her hands in prayer.[108] When Hannah, the "good and faithful servant" of Thomas Butler King died in August 1854, King wrote that her honesty and moral character were beyond reproach. Hannah, a woman who seemed to fit the Mammy mold, was eulogized as being utterly devoted to her owners. King was sure that she died "resigned with firm trust in her redeemer."[109]

A popular fictionalized account of Mammy was not very different from Pollard's supposedly real life sketches. In Mary Eastman's novel, *Aunt Phyllis's Cabin, or Southern Life As It Is,* Aunt Phyllis is industrious, honest, and humble. Typical of many portraits of nineteenth-century women, Aunt Phyllis is virtuous; her whole life, as the narrator puts it, had "been a recommendation of the religion of the Bible." Her conduct was so exemplary that the narrator concludes: "I wish my chance in Heaven were half as good as hers."[110]

If Mammy stands apart from the moral mother tradition she does so on at least two points. The children and household upon which she lavished her attentions were, of course, not her own. There was room for black women in the Victorian tradition only to the extent that Mammy's energies were expended on whites. The other distinct feature about Mammy was her advanced age. This is probably explained by the fact that age is understood in both absolute and relative terms. A sixty-year-old woman may be considered old by some standards, yet to a child a twenty-year-old woman is also old. Mammies were always older than their charges and when white children reached adulthood and recorded their remembrances they were likely to remember Mammy as elderly. However, Mammy's age might also be a metaphor for the asexuality attributed to her. Among Anglo-American Protestant middle and upper classes, the Victorian maternal ideal was understood in terms of asexuality.[111] Very likely the Jezebel image of black females got in the way of a perception of young or middle-aged black women as maternal domestics. Old age, thus, put Mammy beyond the pale of the carnal, above the taint of Jezebel.

In sum, the forces that made the Mammy image were many. It cannot be fully understood independent of the Jezebel conceptualization because they are inverse images that existed simultaneously in the Southern mind. They are black images but, being almost as old as the images of Eve and the Virgin

Mary, they are also universal female archetypes. When, beginning in the 1830s, Southerners were forced to justify slavery and race relations, they adjusted their thinking to make slavery a positive good. At the same time that the "positive good" proslavery argument was presented, the maternal-domestic ideal was being perfected. It was a small matter, but a major necessity, to incorporate this ideal into the "cultural uplift" theory that was being applied to female slaves. The image of Jezebel excused miscegenation, the sexual exploitation of black women, and the mulatto population. It could not, however, calm Southern fears of moral slippage and "mongrelization," or man's fear of woman's emasculating sexual powers. But the Mammy image could. Mammy helped endorse the service of black women in Southern households, as well as the close contact between whites and blacks that such service demanded. Together Jezebel and Mammy did a lot of explaining and soothed many a troubled conscience.

In the long run Mammy was of special importance to Southern perceptions, for she reflected two traditions perceived as positive by Southerners—that of the idealized slave and that of the idealized woman. For proslavery advocates, Southern apologists, antifeminist propagandists, and for those who genuinely loved their black nurses, Mammy was a Godsend. The last group took particular comfort in the belief that their black guardians were regarded by some as highly as Southern white women. For the others, Mammy symbolized race and sex relations at their best. She was at once black and female. In reality, as well as in mythology, both blacks and women were ultimately subservient to white males. Thus in 1897, Thomas Nelson Page, a Virginia romanticist, could describe both groups as slaves.[112]

CHAPTER TWO

The Nature
of Female Slavery

Slavery is terrible for men: but it is far more terrible for women. Superadded to the burden common to all, *they* have wrongs, and sufferings, and mortifications peculiarly their own.[1]

THE IMAGES OF African-American women that grew out of the slavery era reflect the fact that black males and females did not experience slavery the same way. For both sexes the broad outline of racial oppression was similar, as was the general way in which the race resisted and survived. However, within the institution of racial slavery there were two systems, one for women, the other for men. This was due, in part, to the different expectations that slave owners had of male and female slaves. Different expectations gave rise to different responsibilities, and these responsibilites often defined the life chances of the male or female slave. The discussion that follows is not meant to be a comprehensive study of the institution of slavery as it functioned in antebellum America for blacks and whites. Such a task goes beyond the purposes of this study, and would require several chapters. However, a review of the system is necessary in order to show how black women fit into it. What follows, therefore, is a general discussion of American slavery with emphasis on the divergent experience of black men and women.

Male and female slavery was different from the very beginning. As noted previously, women did not generally travel the middle passage in the holds of slave ships but took the dreaded journey on the quarter deck. According to the 1789 Report of the Committee of the Privy Council, the female passage was further distinguished from that of males in that women and girls were not shackled. The slave trader William Snelgrave mentioned the same policy: "We couple the sturdy Men together with Irons; but we suffer the Women and children to go freely about."[2]

This policy had at least two significant consequences for black women. First, they were more easily accessible to the criminal whims and sexual desires of seamen, and few attempts were made to keep the crew members of slave ships from molesting African women.[3] As one slaver reported, officers were permitted to indulge their passions at pleasure and were "sometimes guilty of such brutal excesses as disgrace human nature."[4]

Conversely, African women were occasionally able to incite and/or assist slave insurrections that occurred at sea. For instance, in 1721 the crew on board the *Robert* was stunned when they were attacked by a woman and two men intent on gaining their freedom. Before they were subdued by the captain and other crew members, the slaves, including the woman, had killed several sailors and wounded many others. In his investigation into the mutiny, Captain Harding reflected on the near success of the slaves and found that they had been assisted by the woman "who being more at large, was to watch the proper Opportunity." The woman had served as a lookout and alerted the leader as to the number of sailors on deck. She had also stolen all the weapons used in the mutiny. For her exceptional participation she paid dearly: "The Woman

he hoisted up by the Thumbs, whipp'd, and slashed her with
Knives before the other Slaves till she died."[5]

In another incident, in 1785, the captain of a Bristol slaver
was attacked by a group of women who tried to throw him
overboard. When he was rescued by his crew the women threw
themselves down the hatchway. Some died from the injuries
incurred in their desperate plunge. Others starved themselves to death.[6] Nine years earlier a similar incident had
occurred aboard the Rhode Island vessel, *Thames.* As reported
by Dr. Bell, the physician on board, two women aided thirty-
two men and two boys in their attempt at mutiny. In a letter
to his employer, John Fletcher of London, Bell indicated that
the women played a limited role only because the revolt had
been so spontaneous that the men did not have time to consult and plan with the women. "Had the women assisted them,
in all probability your property here at this time would have
been small."[7]

It would seem that a primary reason for allowing women
to go without irons was the natural assumption that women
could be overpowered. However, since seventeenth- and
eighteenth-century merchants and captains were convinced
that "prime male slaves generally sell best in any market,"
slavers crammed the holds full of men and brought women
almost as an afterthought. The most common instruction given
to slavers was to bring one woman for every two men, yet,
Captain William Ellery's 1859 instructions to "buy no girls,
and few women" were hardly unusual."[8]

Therefore, for most of the seventeenth century and for at
least the first third of the eighteenth, the system of slavery
relied mostly upon black males. This was the case in both the
Chesapeake and Carolina regions. For the period from 1658
to 1730 black men in colonial Maryland outnumbered women
by roughly one and one half to one.[9] Indeed, the entire Chesapeake area had many more slave men than women. In Surry
County, Virginia, the ratio was about 145 men to 100 women

in the 1670s and 1680s, and rose to over two to one in the 1690s and 1700s.[10] In South Carolina, too, men outnumbered women. In 1720 in St. George's Parish the sex ratio was 129 to 100. A sample of slaves taken from inventories in 1730 and 1731 revealed that on sizable plantations throughout the colony slave men outnumbered slave women 180 to 100.[11]

The uneven sex ratio clearly made colonial slavery different for black men and women; it was much harder for a man to find a wife than for a woman to find a husband. Until about 1730 a significant number of men could expect to die without ever having had a spouse, and because plantations were small it was likely that many of those with wives had had to seek them on other plantations and therefore did not live with them. On colonial plantations both married and unmarried men lived together in small groups. In short, the emphasis that white colonialists put on muscle and brawn in the development of their plantation systems made early colonial slavery very lonely and desolate for men.[12]

The situation was different for the bonded woman. Few went without husbands and even though plantations were small the preponderance of men made it likely that a woman would be able to live with her spouse. Nevertheless, many women had husbands on plantations other than their own, and these women lived with their children and raised them without the daily company of their husbands.[13]

These sex-segregated living arrangements did have some imperfect analogs in the African experience. Like their American counterparts, seventeenth- and eighteenth-century West African women usually did not raise small children with the help of their husbands, but raised them alone or with the assistance of other women. While West African men lived with their spouses in the same compound, and couples were free to come together at will, they did not share the same hut or area of the compound. But in Africa segregated living arrangements flowed from the corporate nature of the family and from a belief in the inherent differences of the sexes. The Africans' definition of family extended far beyond parents and children, or the nuclear family, to aunts, uncles, and grandparents. Since a husband and wife did not alone compose a family there was no reason for them to reside alone together. A woman's duty was to bear and raise small children, a duty that was hers alone. In colonial North America the African woman was separated from the cultural foundations and environment that had lent meaning to sex-segregated living and independent child rearing in Africa, but the demographics of slave settlement caused such living and rearing patterns to persist in a not too dissimilar form.[14]

Slavers separated the black woman from most of what had lent meaning to her life. In Africa, her primary role had been motherhood, yet in the early years of plantation settlement she figured in some plantation building as a means of keeping male slaves content. Between 1763 and 1783 Britain attempted to establish a plantation colony in East Florida modeled after that of South Carolina. The slaves involved in this endeavor were mostly men. Correspondence among the governor, his overseer, and those assisting in the undertaking reveals a concern that women be purchased and transported forthwith lest the men become dissatisfied and run away. Thus, the Earl of Egmont wrote that the slaves could not be happy and content without each having a wife. This, he wrote, "will greatly tend to keep them at home and to make them Regular."[15]

The use of black female labor in the fields tended to make farming profitable for seventeenth-century Virginia planters. Although some Virginia white women did field work, this was generally assumed to be a temporary state of affairs and therefore no taxes were levied on their labor. No such assumption was made about the field labor of black women. In fact, in 1629, in colonial Virginia, a tax was levied on any person who worked in the ground, and subsequent laws defined those subject to taxation as black and white male servants and "negro women at age of sixteen years." Because the cost of a female slave was less than that of a male slave, female slave labor was cheaper than male slave labor, particularly when planters applied to black women the same tax-exempt status that applied to white female servants. Naturally, Virginia planters did just that, necessitating another series of laws, passed between 1662 and 1672, reiterating that tithes were to be paid on all field workers including black women.[16]

Surprisingly, slaveholders were slow to appreciate the economic value of the slave woman's procreative ability, but by the middle of the eighteenth century most slave owners, especially those with twenty or more slaves, had come to realize the potential benefits. Thomas Nairne, an eighteenth-century South Carolina planter, expected bondwomen to do the same work as his male slaves. They would, he thought, clear, plant and hoe three acres of land in six months. Besides doing field work he expected them to have children, and thus, by natural means increase the slave population. In 1732, Nairne estimated that the yearly advantage from this increase would be 540 British pounds.[17]

Athough many planters made similar calculations, they did not move to increase the number of female slaves through importation.[18] In the years prior to the American Revolution, the female slave population grew more as a result of natural increase than by importation. It was not until sometime between 1730 and 1750 that the sex ratio evened out. The first African-American women began childbearing earlier than their African mothers, and thus had more children, including more females, than their mothers. The second generation also had more children than the first, and on, and on until the ratio was even.[19]

Although a one to one sex ratio was achieved slowly the consequences were astounding. First, the presence of an even slave sex ratio made American slavery unique in the Western Hemisphere. Everywhere else that slavery reared its ugly head, black men composed the overwhelming majority of the labor force. A related consequence was the creation by North American slaves of monogamous families. In Latin America and the Caribbean black men lived in barracklike environments and had far fewer opportunities to establish long-lasting emotional relationships with black women.[20] Taken together, these two facts suggest that North American male slaves had a more balanced life than their Caribbean or South American counterparts. However, the Earl of Egmont's request for wives to make men more "regular" suggests that powerless North American male slaves were more easily manipulated, because their spouses and children could be held hostage and compelled to answer for their transgressions. Black women, unfortunately, proved to be mirrors for black men. Each time the former was abused, the latter's own helplessness was reflected.[21]

For black women the consequences of the even sex ratio were also severe. Once slaveholders realized that the reproductive function of the female slave could yield a profit, the manipulation of procreative sexual relations became an integral part of the sexual exploitation of female slaves. Few of the calculations made by masters and overseers failed to take a slave woman's childbearing capacity into account. This was particularly true after Congress outlawed the overseas slave trade in 1807. The slave woman's "marital" status, her work load, her diet all became investment concerns of slaveholders, who could maximize their profits if their slave women had many children.[22]

It was little consolation for slave women—in fact, they may not have even realized it—that when slaveholders put a premium on female slave childbearing, slaveholders unwittingly supplied another thread of continuity between Africa and North America. As noted, in the seventeenth and eighteenth century many first-generation African slave women raised their children without a lot of male assistance, much as they had done in Africa. In all likelihood this helped preserve that part of African culture that put emphasis on motherhood, and the African mother probably passed it on to her daughters. When mid-eighteenth-century slaveholders made female slave childbearing their desired goal and acted on that goal, they reinforced a cultural attitude which for African-American women now had roots in both Africa and North America. The nature and conditions of black motherhood in Africa and the North American South obviously differed because the motivations of Africans, African-Americans, and slaveholders were different. But for the purpose of our current discussion it is important to note the continuity. We will return to the differences in subsequent chapters.

In the one hundred years after 1750 the American black population, 90 percent of which was enslaved, was notable for, among other things, its fertility. In the pre–Civil War period black women were very prolific. According to demographers the crude birthrate exceeded fifty per one thousand, meaning that each year more than one fifth of the black women in the 15- to -44 age cohort bore a child.[23] This statistic indicates a major functional difference between male and female bondage. Male slavery centered mostly around the work that black men did for whites. Female slavery had much to do with work, but much of it was concerned with bearing, nourishing, and rearing children whom slaveholders needed for the continual replenishment of their labor force. This does not mean that work and childbearing were always kept in perfect balance. The extent to which the slaveowner consciously emphasized one or the other ultimately depended on his needs. In antebellum America, these were often determined by the region of the country in which he was settled. The lower black fertility rates in the lower and newer regions of the south (Alabama, Mississippi, Louisiana, and Texas) may be an indication that female labor in the fields superseded childbearing in importance. In both the upper and lower South however, slave owners attended to the proverbial bottom line by striving to maximize profits. Few ignored the important role that natural increase played in the realization of that goal.[24]

Meanwhile, the responsibilities of childbearing and child care seriously circumscribed the female slave's life. The limits were reflected in patterns of female resistance. Studies of fugitive slaves reveal that their ranks were not swelled with women. Seventy-seven percent of the runaways advertised in colonial South Carolina during the 1730s were men. This pattern persisted throughout the century.[25] South Carolina was by no means unique. The 1,500 newspaper advertisements published in Williamsburg, Richmond, and Fredricksburg, Virginia, from 1736 to 1801 evince much the same pattern. Of the runaways whose sex could be discerned 1,138 were men, while only 142 were women.[26] The same pattern existed in antebellum Huntsville, Alabama, where, between 1820 and 1860, of the 562 fugitives advertised, 473 were listed as male and only 87 as female.[27] In North Carolina from 1850 to 1860, only 19 percent of the runaway ads described women.[28] In 1850, 31.7 percent of the runaways advertised for in New Orleans newspapers were women.[29]

Some of the reasons why women were underrepresented in the fugitive population had to do with childbearing. Most runaways were between sixteen and thirty-five years old.[30] A woman of this age was either pregnant, nursing an infant, or had at least one small child to care for. While all that men between sixteen and thirty-five could count on was hard work and severe punishment if they angered the master or overseer, it was during these years that many slave women got their best care. Slave owners were less likely to insist on a full day's heavy workload when the laborer involved was a pregnant woman.

Also important in understanding why females ran away less frequently than men is the fact that women tended to be more concerned with the welfare of their children, and this limited their mobility. Fugitive men loved their offspring, but unlike the runaway male, the slave woman who left her children behind could not be certain that they would be given the best possible care. A father could not provide for a suckling infant because "in dem days no bottle was given to no baby under a year old."[31] Moreover, since women and small children were often sold as a group, a father was more likely to be sold away from his children.[32] Sometimes the children of runaway mothers were lucky enough to have an aunt or grandmother on the same or nearby plantation, and sometimes a father or uncle cared for the child. But, for those fugitive women who left children in slavery, the physical relief which freedom brought was limited compensation for the anguish they suffered. Of the same one hundred fifty-one fugitive women advertised for in the 1850 New Orleans newspapers, none was listed as having run away without her children.[33]

This, of course, was no secret to slaveholders and probably accounts for the casual attitude many masters and overseers had about female runaways. For years the Flint family's hold upon Linda Brent's children kept her from fleeing. In her narrative Brent explained: "I was certain my children were to be put in their power, in order to give them a stronger hold on me."[34] Similarly, in 1838 a slave named Clarissa was sent to Philadelphia even though there was some concern about her running away once she reached free territory. Mrs. Trigg, her mistress, had few qualms because Clarissa's husband and children remained in Kentucky.[35]

Women would probably have escaped more often if they could have done so with their husbands and offspring but children, in particular, made the journey more difficult than it already was and increased the chances of capture. For instance, although Josiah Henson successfully reached Cincinnati with his wife and children he had to carry his two stout toddlers most of the way and listen to their cries of hunger and exhaustion at night.[36] Henry Bibb also tried to escape with his family but was unsuccessful. With his wife, Malinda, and small child, he started on his journey north, but a pack of blood-thirsty canines and patrollers put a stop to his quest for freedom. For Bibb, the difficulties of escaping with a wife and child proved insurmountable, and although he regretted his capture he was actually relieved. Some time later he escaped, but without Malinda or his child.[37] Another couple that fled with an infant from Alexandria, Virginia, was also unlucky. Although the parents successfully reached Philadelphia, cold weather caused the death of the infant.[38]

If women in the company of men encountered insurmountable difficulties, imagine the problems encountered by women and children escaping alone. For conductors and directors of the Underground Railroad, fugitive women with children were a tremendous source of anxiety. William Still, the chairman of the Vigilance Committee of the Philadelphia Underground Railroad, was always nervous about transporting women with children since they stood a greater chance of being caught. "Females," he wrote, "undertook three times the risk of failure that males are liable to."[39] William Penn, who worked with the Underground Railroad, also expressed apprehension. Speaking of two women, both of whom had two children, he noted: "none of these can walk so far or so fast as scores of *men* that are constantly leaving."[40] The director of one of the many "depots" described a woman and her children who took refuge in her house as a "very helpless set." Hours were spent trying to arrange the escape of this mother and her five children. Finally, they were split up and some of them left with the mother's aunt and uncle who had no children.[41]

The few women who ran away did so for a variety of reasons. Some escaped with men and many left for the same reasons as men—cruel treatment or the fear of it, fear of sale or sale of a loved one, or just the desire to be free. Not surprisingly, for many women it was the children, or more properly, the fear of losing them, that provided the incentive to flee. The desperation of some slave mothers was captured in Harriet Beecher Stowe's fictionalized account of the escape to freedom by Eliza Harris and her son across the ice floes of the Ohio River. Many took the heart-rending tale of Eliza's flight as evidence of Stowe's vivid imagination, but actually Stowe described in fiction what was a real life episode for a few women.[42] One such woman was a Kentucky slave who feared that her two little girls were to be sold away from her. Surviving only on fruits and green corn she managed to cross the river.[43] The odds were formidable even when there was no river to cross. For instance, there was the Maryland slave named Maria who with the help of the Underground Railroad escaped in 1859 with all *seven* of her children.[44]

Many female fugitives were much less fortunate than Maria and had to leave some of their children behind. On the night she escaped, Louisa Bell of Norfolk, Virginia, was saddened by the thought of leaving her children enslaved:

> . . . she felt more keenly than ever for her little children, and she readily imagined how sadly she would mourn while thinking of them hundreds of miles distant, growing up only to be slaves. And, particularly would her thoughts dwell upon her boy, six years of age; full old enough to feel deeply the loss of his mother, but without hope of ever seeing her again.[45]

Similar thoughts must have been entertained by Emeline Chaman as she fled from Washington, D.C., leaving two children and a husband behind.[46] A Maryland slave woman named Vina was forced to choose which of her children would be free and which would remain enslaved. She fled to New Jersey to meet her husband with her two daughters after having consigned her two small sons "into the hands of God." The journey still proved to be too much for her; she left one of them on a lonely road to be retrieved by her husband.[47] The story of Mary Montgomery is especially hearbreaking. Although sickly, Mary had a nursing infant at her breast. According to Christopher Nichols, a successful fugitive, Mary had been given conflicting work orders by the overseer and master. Unable to satisfy both she "took to the woods" and disappeared. "It was said that she got to the North, but nobody knew." Mary Montgomery did what few other bondwomen did; she left her suckling infant behind to die for lack of nourishment.[48]

Such desperate decisions inevitably induced emotional trauma and psychological torment. At age twenty-seven, when she fled to Pennsylvania to escape the sexual overtures of her master, Linda Brent made a decision similar to Mary Montgomery's. She knew her grandmother would keep a watchful eye on her son and daughter. However, she feared her mistress's vengeance would put them in danger of severe punishment, even sale. The advice she sought and was given served only to confuse her and increase her anxiety. From her friend and accomplice, Betty, she received encouragement to escape: "Lors, chile! What's you crying 'bout? Dem young uns vil kill you dead. Don't be so chick'n hearted! If you does, you vil nebber git thro' dis world." But, her grandmother, who, unlike childless Betty, had helped raise three generations of black children, admonished: "Stand by your own children, and suffer with them till death. Nobody respects a mother who forsakes her children; and if you leave them, you will never have a happy moment."[49]

Truancy seems to have been the way many slave women reconciled their desire to flee and their need to stay. Studies of female runaways demonstrate that females made the most likely truants because they were more concerned about breaking family ties.[50] Benjamin Johnson of Georgia remembered that "sometimes de women wouldn't take it an' would run away an' hide in de woods. Sometimes dey would come back after a short stay an' den again dey would have to put de hounds on dere trail to bring dem back home."[51] Short-term absences of this sort were not mere flights of fancy. Truants were often no less angry, resentful, and frightened than their fugitive bretheren who chose to flee to the North. If anything they were more frightened of the unknown to the North than of the certainties they left behind. However, this frightful ambivalence did not keep them from shouldering substantial risk. Thus we find cases such as that of a St. Simon's woman who, after being severely beaten by her master, found the rattlesnakes of the South Carolina rice swamps more comforting than her own cabin. Sickness induced by hunger finally forced her back to her plantation.[52]

For many women truancy became a way of life. While Nellie, a slave of Mr. Elderet of Louisiana, hid in a corn crib for three days, others spent a much longer time away from the plantation. Such a woman was Celeste, another Louisiana slave who, determined not to be beaten by the overseer, built her own rude hut from dead branches and camouflaged it with leaves of palmetto on the edge of a swamp not far from the master's residence. Every evening she returned to the plantation for food and lived like this for the better part of a summer.[53]

Such behavior was not unique to the nineteenth century. As early as 1710 Virginian William Byrd recorded a case of truancy that had a tragic ending. One of his slave women ran away on June 25, 1710, and was found on June 28, only to disappear again two days later. She was recovered again on July 8, but ran away again on the fifteenth. Three weeks later she turned up again, but in November she disappeared and was soon found dead.[54]

Motherhood structured the slave woman's behavior but so too did the female slave work experience. The division of labor on most plantations conferred greater mobility on male than on female slaves. Few of the chores performed by bondwomen took them off the plantation. Usually masters chose their male slaves to assist in the transportation of crops to market, and the transport of supplies and other materials to the plantation. More male than female slaves were artisans and craftsmen, and this made it more difficult to hire out a female slave than a male slave. Fewer bondwomen therefore had a chance to vary their work experience. As a consequence, more men than women were able to test their survival skills under different circumstances.[55]

Another factor affecting slave mobility was the "abroad marriage," a marriage between slaves who resided at different locations. When "abroad" spouses visited each other, usually once a week, it was most often the husband who traveled to the wife. All in all, it was female bondage, more than male bondage, that meant being tied to the immediate environment of the plantation or farm. This was a liability when it came to running away. The would-be female fugitive, including the domestic who conceivably had more polished verbal and language skills than the field slave, had to consider her unfamiliarity with the surrounding countryside before fleeing. She also had to consider how conspicuous a lone black woman or group of black women would be in a countryside infrequently traveled by such humanity. Some female fugitives overcame this last impediment by disguising themselves as males.[56] However, the small number of female runaways indicates that more bondwomen than bondmen just "stayed put."

This does not mean that they did not resist enslavement or sexual exploitation. As historians have been quick to point out, the dearth of large-scale slave revolts suggests that in the United States slave resistance often manifested itself in intransigent behavior. If resistance in the United States was seldom politically oriented, consciously collective, or violently revolutionary, it was generally individualistic and aimed at maintaining what the slaves, master, and overseer had, in the course of their relationships, perceived as an acceptable level of work, shelter, food, punishment, and free time. Slaves may have thought about overthrowing the system of slavery but the odds against them were so overwhelming that the best most could hope for was survival with a modicum of dignity. Slave resistance was aimed at maintaining what seemed to all concerned to be the status quo.[57]

Bondwomen, like bondmen, were adept in inventing schemes and excuses to get their own way. After her mistress died, Alcey, the cook on the Burleigh plantation in Virginia, decided she no longer wanted to work in the kitchen. When her request to be transferred to the field was ignored, she found another way to make her desire known. "She systematically disobeyed orders and stole or destroyed the greater part of the provisions given to her for the table." When that failed "she resolved to show more plainly that she was tired of the kitchen": "Instead of getting chickens for dinner from the coop, as usual, she unearthed from some corner an old hen that had been sitting for six weeks and served her up as a fricassee!" Alcey achieved her objective and was sent to the field the following day without even so much as a reprimand.[58]

While some Southern whites called such behavior "rascality," slaves understood it to be an effective form of resistance.[59] For instance, Josiah Henson knew Dinah, a fellow slave, to be as "clear witted, as sharp and cunning as a fox." Yet, she purposely acted like a fool or idiot in order "to take advantage of her mistress." According to Henson, "When the latter said, 'Dinah, go and do your work,' she would reply with a laugh, 'Yes, yes; when I get ready, or 'Go do it yourself.' Sometimes she would scream out, 'I won't; that's a lie—catch me if you can'; and then she would take to her heels and run away." Henson revealed that Dinah was always doing odd things, but she escaped the whipping that other slaves received because her mistress thought she was an idiot.[60]

Some bondwomen were more direct in their resistance. Some murdered their masters, some were arsonists, and still

others refused to be whipped.[61] Overseers and masters learned
which black women and men they could whip, and which would
not be whipped. Sometimes they found out the hard way.
Equipped with a whip and two healthy dogs, an Alabama
overseer tied a woman named Crecie to a stump with inten-
tions of beating her. To his pain and embarrassment she jerked
the stump out of the ground, grabbed the whip, and sent the
overseer running.[62] Women fought back despite severe consequences. An Arkansas overseer decided to make an example of a slave woman named Lucy "to show the slaves that he
was impartial." Lucy, however, was not to be made an example of. According to her son, "she jumped on him and like to
tore him up." Word got around that Lucy would not be beaten.
She was sold, but she was never again whipped.[63]

Slave women also sometimes violently resisted sexual
exploitation. Since Southern laws did not recognize the rape
of a black woman as a crime, often the only recourse slave
women had was to fight off their assailants. When Jermain
Loguen's mother was attacked she picked up a stick and dealt
her would-be rapist a blow that sent him staggering. She stood
her ground even as he rebounded with a knife, and finally
she knocked him out cold.[64] Gus Feaster's mother had help
in doing what Cherry Loguen managed to do by herself. Along
with another woman Feaster's mother was approached by an
overseer who tried to abuse them both. Their protestations
that they were religious women did not halt his advances, which
were made under the threat of the lash. The women had the
choice of fighting or yielding. After the overseer had taken
off his clothes, the women pounced upon him, wrestled him
to the ground, and then ran away.[65]

Bondwomen used dissembling tactics and force much as
bondmen did. It is probably safe to assume that women chose
violent resistance, particularly that which involved fisticuffs,
less often than did men. However, it should also be remembered that such resistance was not really a viable option for

bondmen, either. A bullet through the head, a jail cell, a merciless whipping, and / or sale was the likely fate of any slave, male or female, who demonstrated aggressive behavior, even in self-defense.

A less overt form of resistance involved the use of poison and this suited women because they officiated as cooks and nurses on the plantation. As early as 1755 a Charleston slave woman was burned at the stake for poisoning her master, and in 1769 a special issue of the *South Carolina Gazette* carried the story of a slave woman who had poisoned her master's infant child.[66] No one will ever know how many slave owners and members of their families were poisoned. The slave's objective was not to get caught because punishment was sure and swift. A case in point was recorded by Mary Chesnut in her diary. A friend of hers told her the story of a man named Dr. Keitt who was chronically ill. Dr. Keitt's friend suggested to him that his slaves were perhaps trying to kill him: Dr. Keitt promised to be prudent and to come the next day. As soon as his friend left, a Negro woman brought him a cup of tea. In stirring it, a white powder became evident, settled in the bottom of the cup. In a moment he believed what his friend had suspected. He dashed the tea in her face. "You ungrateful beast, I believe you are trying to poison me." Next morning, he was found with his throat cut from ear to ear. It was found that the woman, in league with two male slaves, was putting a poison in Dr. Keitt's coffee every morning and when discovered they murdered him outright. Interestingly enough, and consistent with female runaway statistics, the men successfully escaped but the woman was caught and hanged.[67]

Perhaps the most important difference between male and female slave resistance was the greater propensity of women to feign illness in order to gain a respite from their work or to change the nature of their work altogether. This strategy was feasible precisely because childbearing was a primary expectation that slave owners had of slave women. The perpetuation of the institution of slavery, as nineteenth-century Southerners knew it, rested on the slave woman's reproductive capacity. In an age when women's diseases were still shrouded in mystery, getting the maximum amount of work from women of childbearing age while remaining confident that no damage was done to their reproductive organs was a guessing game that few white slave owners wanted to play or could afford to lose. A Virginia planter summed up the "problem" when he complained of the "liability of women, especially to disorders and irregularities which cannot be detected by exterior symptoms, but which may be easily aggravated into serious complaints." He further explained that women were rendered "nearly valueless" for work because of the ease with which they could impose upon their owners. His frustration was obvious as he told Frederick Olmsted that "they don't come to the field and you go to the quarters and ask the old nurse what's the matter and she says, 'Oh, she's not . . . fit to work sir'; and . . . you have to take her word for it that something or other is the matter with her, and you dare not set her to work; and so she will lay up till she feels like taking the air again, and plays the lady at your expense."[68] Although few slave women were given as much latitude as this planter suggested, they did sometimes "play the lady" and get away with it.

By the time Olmsted heard this complaint slave women had been engaging in such behavior for some time. On Landon Carter's eighteenth-century Virginia plantation, this form of resistance was raised to an art. Although Carter was certain that Mary faked her fits, her violent and uncontrollable howls always got the better of him, and she spent a good deal of time away from the fields. Another woman, named Sarah, laid up for *eleven* months before delivering her infant. She, no doubt, "played the lady" at Carter's expense, and even tried to do it again during her next pregnancy. To her chagrin she met a wiser Landon Carter who was determined not to let her get away with it. Sarah was determined, too, and proved to be as good at truancy as she was at feigning illness. Although "big with child" she took to the woods and stayed over a week. Sarah may have learned her tricks from fellow slavewomen on Carter's plantations, for he complained of two other women who had fooled him as Sarah had: "Wilmot, . . . whenever she was with Child always pretended to be too heavy to work and it cost me twelve months before I broke her," wrote Carter. "Criss of Mangorike fell into the same scheme and really carried it to a great length for at last she could not be dragged out."[69]

Female complaints proved a constant source of frustration to other slaveholders as well. George Washington spoke of slaves who "will lay up a month, at the end of which no visible change in their countenance, nor the loss of an ounce of flesh, is discernable; and their allowance of provision is going on as if nothing ailed them." He listed women as among the principal offenders.[70] On the nineteenth-century Newstead plantation, the situation was much the same. Although women usually got their way, the master was convinced that "there's not much the matter with any of them."[71] Richard J. Arnold's overseer had nine women report ill in one week. Although he whipped some of them, he was unsuccessful in getting them to work.[72] On the Bayside plantation in Louisiana a slave woman named Milly missed thirty-eight consecutive days because of sickness.[73]

The case of Maria, one of President James Polk's slaves, is particularly revealing. Since Polk spent a good deal of time away from his plantations, they were run by overseers with the aid of a few of his close friends. With the exception of Eophraim Beanland, all of Polk's overseers had trouble with Maria, who was always complaining of some malady. Maria began pleading illness in May 1839, significantly, after the strict Beanland was replaced by the more indulgent George Bratton. At that time, Bratton wrote to Polk that "she has bin in bad helth since the first of march and is likely not to be able to do any sirvice." Bratton died that year and was replaced by John Garner who also had difficulty making Maria work. In June 1840, Garner informed Polk that Maria "has spels onste a month very bad." A week later he explained in greater detail that "she is in a very bad condishon every thre or fore weks, so very bad onst this spring she was thone into fits of spasms." Maria's health continued to keep her from the fields and finally she was reassigned to the house where she was taught to weave. She was particularly good at weaving and Garner soon reported that "Marier aperes to enjoy as good helth at present as any person." In fact, Maria had such a miraculous recovery, and became so good at weaving that she informed Polk that she had increased her worth by at least thirty dollars.[74]

Maria was "fortunate" because many slave masters refused to accept even obvious illness as an excuse to lay off work. James Mercer, for instance, had a strict formula for judging illness: "No woman was allowed to 'lay up' unless her illness was accompanied by a fever."[75] Some masters insisted on giving the "patient" a thorough examination before excusing her from work. After sending his slave, Caroline, to the fields in spite of her protestations, a Mississippi Valley planter claimed: "We have to be sharp with them; if we were not, every negro on the estate would be abed."[76]

The subject of feigning illness is as difficult for the historian as it was for the planter. Was Maria actually ill or was she deceiving the overseers? The description of her complaint suggests a menstrual disorder but she could also have been quite an actress. Whatever we conclude we must not overlook the important point that Maria's behavior, feigned or otherwise, is what landed her the easier seamstress job. This case, and the many like it, suggest that while slaveowners had a vested interest in keeping pregnant women healthy, the relatively better care expectant mothers received was as much a result of the pressure slave women exerted as of self-serving benevolence extended by slave owners and overseers. If slave women frequently "played the lady," as the Virginia planter argued, it was only after they risked a lot to be treated humanely.

Data on slave illness on Southern plantations reveal that plantations were havens for disease, and that slaves were indeed plagued by sickness. Slaves suffered and often died from pneumonia, diarrhea, cholera, and smallpox. The slave diet was high in calories but suffered from dangerously low levels of protein and other nutrients. Lean meats, poultry, eggs, milk, and grain products other than corn—foods needed to help the human immune system produce antibodies to fight off infections—were only sporadically seen on most slave's plates. In addition, most slaves did not get nearly enough fruits and vegetables. Blindness, sore eyes, skin irritations, rickets, toothaches, pellagra, beriberi, and scurvy were among the many afflictions that resulted from vitamin dificiencies caused by the monotonous daily servings of rice, fat-back, corn meal, and salt pork.[77]

Slave women suffered from these illnesses as well as from those associated with the menstrual cycle and childbirth. According to Todd Savitt, Virginia bondwomen probably lost more time from work for menstrual pain, discomfort, and disorders than for any other cause. Among the menstrual maladies were amenorrhea (lack of menstrual flow), abnormal bleeding between cycles (sometimes caused by benign and malignant tumors), and abnormal discharges (resulting from such conditions as gonorrhea, tumors, and prolapsed uterus). Although the 1850 mortality statistics for Virginia indicate that slave women were slightly less likely than white women to die from complications of pregnancy, bondwomen suffered during childbirth. Convulsions, retention of placenta, ectopic pregnancy, breech presentation, premature labor, and uterine rigidity were among the difficulties they faced. Birthing was complicated further by the unsanitary practices of midwives and physicians who delivered a series of children in the course of a day without washing their hands, thereby triggering outbreaks of puerperal (child bed) fever. These infections of the reproductive organs were often fatal.[78]

Still it is difficult to ascertain whether bondwomen who claimed to be ill were actually sick or whether they were practicing a kind of passive resistance. They certainly had more leverage in the realm of feigning illness than men but they also perhaps had more reason than men to be ill. This does not mean that women were more disadvantaged than black men in this regard. It does suggest, however, that their health experiences were radically different. Although women may have had a less healthy day-to-day existence they could generally expect to outlive their male counterparts, probably because men were engaged usually in heavier and more dangerous work. On the average, antebellum black women outlived their men by two years.[79] This average varied depending on the state. In Louisiana in 1850, for instance, at birth a black male could expect to live about twenty-nine years, while a black female had a life expectancy of about thirty-four years. At age thirty the life expectancy of a Louisiana black male was approximately another twenty-seven years. The thirty-year-old black women could expect to live for another thirty-one years.[80]

If it is hard to differentiate real sickness from passive resistance it is almost impossible to determine whether slave women practiced birth control and abortion. These matters were virtually exclusive to the female world of the quarters, and when they arose they were attended to in secret and were intended to remain secret. Some Southern whites were certain that slave women knew how to avoid pregnancy as well as how to deliberately abort a pregnancy. When Daph, a woman on the Ferry Hill plantation in Virginia miscarried twins in 1838 the overseer reported that Daph took some sort of abortifact to bring about the miscarriage.[81] Suspicions about slave abortions ran high enough to spur public comment. In an essay entitled "On the susceptibility of the Caucasian and African races to the different classes of disease," Dr. E. M. Pendleton claimed that planters regularly complained of whole families of women who fail to have any children.[82] A Tennessee physician, Dr. John H. Morgan said of slave women that "often they will attempt to bring all the aids into requisition that they can ascertain that will increase the parturient effort, either by medicine, violent exercise, or by external and internal manipulations." Morgan was relatively certain that black females declined the use of mechanical implements to effect miscarriage but he was convinced they used abortifacts. Among those he listed were the herbs of tansy and rue, the roots and seed of the cotton plant, pennyroyal, cedar berries, and camphor, either in gum or spirits.[83]

The suspicions of planters on this account were not without foundation. For example, an 1869 South Carolina court case revealed that a slave woman sold as "unsound" and barren in 1857 had three children *after* emancipation.[84] In another instance, a bondwoman refused to have children because her master forced her to marry someone she did not like. After she was sold and found someone of her own choosing, she had ten children.[85] Sarah Shaw of Missouri remembered that when her father was sold away, her master compelled her mother to take a new husband. Her mother complied but she was determined not to have any more children. "Mama said she would never marry a man and have children so she married my step-father Trattle Barber, because she knew he had a disease and could not be a father."[86]

The record on self-imposed sterility and self-induced miscarriages is ambiguous. Strenuous work might have been the culprit in many cases involving barrenness or abortion. For example, on the Ball rice plantations in South Carolina, from 1760 to 1865, the months of greatest hoeing and weeding activity—May, June, and July—produced the smallest num-

ber of conceptions resulting in birth.[87] Several physicians,
including Doctors Morgan and Pendleton, made the connection between the bonded woman's work regimen and sterility
and miscarriages. Dr. Morgan thought that slave fertility would
be higher if, among other things, female field hands were not
so "exposed" during menstruation and pregnancy: "When by
proper care and attention during these periods, in the way of
moderate labor, good clothing etc., they are much more thrifty
and fruitful."[88] A Dr. Baskette believed, with Morgan, that
the want of attention and care was "more generally the cause
of barreness than any other thing." Black women, he noted,
"were seldom consulted in regard to their catamenia, and if
there was any disturbance in that function it was treated with
indifference."[89] While Dr. Pendleton remained convinced that
"blacks are possessed of a secret by which they destroy the
foetus at an early stage of gestation," he too regarded slave
labor as "inimical to the procreation of the species from exposure, violent exercise, etc."[90]

The jury will have to remain out on whether slave women
were guilty of practicing birth control and abortion, but some
reasons why they might have been guilty as accused should be
considered. Certainly, they had reason not to want to bear
and nurture children who could be sold from them at a slave
master's whim. They had ample cause to want to deny whites
the satisfaction of realizing a profit on the birth of their children. But they also had as much reason as any antebellum
woman, white or free black, to shun pregnancy and childbirth. As long as obstetrics had not yet evolved into a science,
childbirth was dangerous.[91] We would also be remiss if we did
not at least suppose that a few abortions were motivated by
attempts to hide teenage pregnancy or marital infidelity. Black
women were slaves but they were also human.[92]

The entire subject of feigned illness, sterility, deliberate and
nondeliberate miscarriages illustrates some of the ways that
female slavery was different from male slavery; at the same

time it raises interesting points of comparison between ante-bellum black and white women. Although black women did considerably more heavy labor than white women, on a diet with less nutritional value, their fertility rate was usually similar to or slightly higher than that of Southern white women.[93] One explanation offered for the symmetry revolves around the natural immunity blacks have to malaria, or more specifically, the greater susceptibility of whites to this disease, which destroys male sperm by elevating male scrotal temperature. It has been argued that had not malaria been so devastating to whites, black fertility would not have compared so favorably, given the deprivation under which slave women functioned.[94] Historians have also observed that some white women of this period, particularly of the middle and upper classes, feigned illness or pretended to be very delicate in order to avoid sexual intercourse that could result in an unwanted pregnancy.[95] There seems to be no evidence to confirm or deny that slave women did the same. It is truly ironic, though, that while slave women probably shared with white women a natural fear of childbirth, slave women had to feign illness to ease the burden of work in order to make bearing a child easier. As we will see, some female slaves even got pregnant in order to avoid backbreaking field labor. The plight of both groups of women was unenviable but on the average white women were much more successful in avoiding pregnancies than black women. The white birthrate declined throughout the nineteenth century and continued to do so well into the twentieth century.[96] The black birthrate did not begin to show a significant decline until the very end of the nineteenth century.[97] Throughout the antebellum period especially, the incentives to have children were greater for black than for white women. Although they showed much concern, planters had little to worry about when it came to the rate of slave reproduction.

Did slave infanticide pose a serious threat? Probably not. There were some cases where mothers were accused of murdering their children, and a few women may have done so. In 1830 a North Carolina slave woman was convicted of murdering her own child.[98] A year later a Missouri slave was accused of poisoning and smothering her infant, and in 1834, Elizabeth, one of James Polk's slaves, was said to have smothered her newborn.[99] No one will ever know what drove these women to kill their infants, if they did. Some whites thought slave women lacked maternal feelings, yet a few women who killed their children claimed to have done so because of their intense concern for their offspring. Thus, an Alabama woman killed her child because her mistress continually abused it. In confessing her guilt, she claimed that her master was the father of the child, and that her mistress knew it and treated it so cruelly that she had to kill it to save it from further suffering.[100] Another woman killed her newborn because she knew that the master had plans to sell the baby, the same way he had sold her three older children. Years later Lou Smith recalled the incident: "When her fourth baby was born and was about two months old, she just studied all the time about how she would have to give it up, and one day she said, 'I just decided I'm not going to let Old Master sell this baby; he just ain't going to do it.' She got up and give it something out of a bottle, and pretty soon it was dead."[101]

These cases represent atypical behavior on the part of slave mothers. Runaway and truancy data suggest mothers cared dearly for their children, and recent historical and medical research suggest that many children who supposedly were suffocated by a mother were actually victims of what today is known as Sudden Infant Death Syndrome (SIDS) or "crib death." According to Michael P. Johnson the 1850 census showed that of the victims of suffocation 82 percent were slaves. The 1860 census showed a similar high percentage of slave deaths due to suffocation. Johnson estimates that between 1790 and 1860 smothering was reported to be responsible for the deaths of over sixty thousand slave infants.[102] Most white

Southerners attributed these deaths to the carelessness of slave mothers who rolled onto them while sleeping, deliberately murdered them, or otherwise provided insufficient care. Johnson and Savitt, however, argue that recent medical discoveries suggest that "crib death"—the sudden death of any infant or young child who does not have a history of illness and whose postmortem examination fails to demonstrate an identifiable cause of death—was probably responsible for the majority of such slave infant deaths.[103] Statistics compiled by Johnson show that most "smothered" slave infants died in the winter months, and a significant number were between two and four months old. Modern day physicians have pinpointed the peak age period for "crib death" victims to be between two and four months, and have found that more infants succumb between October and March than in any other time period.[104] In addition, a disproportionately high number of today's victims come from low socioeconomic groups, and are infants of women who are not likely to get good prenatal care.[105] Therefore, we can suppose that some of the infant deaths that planters attributed to infanticide and some that whites blamed on maternal carelessness were actually due to causes which even today baffle medical experts. We might also suppose that it was easier and cheaper for planters to malign slave women than to thoroughly investigate infant slave deaths and that, based on findings linking prenatal care and nutrition to SIDS, it was the planters who fed pregnant women too little and worked them too hard who were more responsible for "smothered infants" than the women who subsequently bore the guilt and blame.

Female slave bondage was not better or worse, or more or less severe, than male bondage, but it was different. From the very beginning of a woman's enslavement she had to cope with sexual abuse, abuse made legitimate by the conventional wisdom that black women were promiscuous Jezebels. Work assignments also structured female slave life so that women were more confined to the boundaries of the plantation than were men. The most important reason for the difference between male and female bondage, however, was the slave woman's childbearing and child care responsibilities. These affected the female slave's pattern of resistance and figured prominently in her general health.

CHAPTER THREE

The Life Cycle
of the Female Slave

"Us colored women had to go through a plenty."[1]

THE LIFE OF an individual in any society is a series of passages from one stage to another and from one occupation to another.[2] Yet, although each stage in a person's life may be very different from that which preceded it, an individual is not always aware that one period of his or her life has ended and a new one begun. For women, the beginning and cessation of the menses help define life's transitions, as does the beginning of motherhood. For the antebellum slave woman, biology combined with the demands made on her for plantation labor to delineate the series of passages that marked her life. The experiences of slave women from one plantation to the next, from one region of the South to the next, from the cotton, to the sugar, to the rice plantation were obviously different, but there was a pattern that defined the general contours of life for average bondwomen. This general pattern is the subject of this chapter.

For slave girls childhood was neither carefree nor burden-some. For the most part children lived in an age-segregated world so that with the exception of the elderly slaves whose responsibility it was to supervise the young, girls and boys had little contact with adult slaves who were away in the fields most of the day.[3]

But the children's world was by no means segregated by sex. Boys and girls were constant companions and it seems that neither work nor play was strictly differentiated on the basis of sex. There was almost no activity engaged in by girls that was not, at some time or another, also engaged in by boys. For instance, while girls were used as nurses, the term used by antebellum whites and blacks to describe someone who supervised infants and toddlers, so too were boys. Nelson Birdson of Alabama indicated that the first work he remem-bered doing was "nussing a baby boy."[4] Similarly, an Arkan-sas slave claimed that until he was old enough to chop cotton, all he did was "nurse babies."[5] That boys as well as girls were used as baby-sitters was also recorded by Frances Kemble, the English wife of a Georgia rice planter. She was incensed to find that girls and boys "from eight to twelve and older" did little more than "tend baby" while sickly women were forced to do field work.[6] Both sexes performed a variety of other kinds of work, such as "toting" water to thirsty field hands, collecting the mail, and tending livestock.

Similarly, play was not strictly differentiated or catego-rized as "masculine" or "feminine." Millie Evans explained that along with jump rope she busied herself "running, jumping, skipping and just everything."[7] Tag, or "You Can Catch Me," was another one of her favorite games. A Tennessee woman remembered that as a child she played a game called "Smut," which was just like cards except that it was played with grains of corn. Marbles was another game she played, but her big-gest amusement was "running through the woods, climbing trees, hunting grapes and berries."[8] Joseph Holmes's recollec-

tions of his sister's childhood in slavery also indicates that play
for little girls was not restricted to certain spheres: "If I jumped
in de ribber tuh swim, she did hit too; if I clum' a tree or went
th'ough a briar patch, she don hit right behin' me." His sister
was also his companion in hunting rabbits, coons, and tur-
tles.[9]

The memories of these former slaves suggest that girls were
not kept close to home in the exclusive company of women
and were not socialized at an early age to assume culturally
defined feminine roles. Black girls on the plantation spent
most of their time in a sexually integrated atmosphere. Even
the experience of the young female domestic offers little evidence of early differential socialization since boys were just as
likely as girls to be found doing kitchen and housekeeping
chores. This easy integration of boys and girls is perhaps
understandable in the context of their future plantation roles.
Since both girls and boys were expected to become field hands,
and they often found themselves doing similar work in later
life, it is not surprising that as children they did the same
chores and played the same games. This does not mean that
parents did not relate to girls and boys differently—there is
no way of knowing if they did or did not. It does seem, however, that parents were more concerned that children,
regardless of sex, learn to walk the tightrope between the
demands of the whites and expectations of the blacks without
falling too far in either direction. It was probably more
important for nine-year-old girls to learn that conversations
among blacks in the slave quarters were not for white con-
sumption, than it was for them to learn that cooking was a
"feminine" activity. Sometimes girls, as well as boys, found
that satisfying both masters and mistresses and fathers and
mothers could be difficult. Linda Brent, for instance, learned
at a young age just how hard it could be when she heard her
father chastise her brother for running to his mistress when
his father had summoned him at the same time. "You are *my*

child," said Brent's father, "and when I call you, you should come immediately, if you have to pass through fire and water."[10] If their activities of work and play are any indication of the degree of sex role differentiation which existed before age ten or twelve, then young girls probably grew up minimizing the difference between the sexes while learning far more about the differences between the races.

During the teen years, however, as girls were integrated into the work force, more strict role separation became the rule. In childhood, girls and boys had dressed much the same, in simple smocklike shirts or slips. But at some point in pre-adolescence, girls turned in their homespun shirts for dresses, and boys were supplied with pants.[11] While boys and girls, about twelve to sixteen, still performed the same kind of work, they were now more likely to be included in a work gang, which was sometimes called the "trash gang." The "trash gang" was assigned such tasks as raking stubble, pulling weeds, or doing light hoeing. At harvest time on cotton plantations they usually picked cotton.[12] Joining the "trash gang" had to be a more significant turning point for girls than for boys since this work gang, made up of pregnant women, women with nursing infants, young teenagers, and old slaves, was predominantly female. This was the first time that girls found themselves in an overwhelmingly female world. The importance of this step is underscored by recent evidence that pinpoints the peak growth spurt for slave girls, measured by height and weight, at around thirteen, and menarche approximately two years later.[13] Slave girls experienced these critical physiological changes at a time when their social milieu was shifting to include women who were about to become mothers, women who were nursing mothers, and elderly women, who, although past their childbearing years, had firsthand knowledge of the particulars of motherhood. Slave sources reveal little about the interaction of the members of this work gang, but its role in the socialization of adolescent girls was probably significant. At the very least it can reasonably be assumed that girls who worked and ate with childbearing and mature women daily developed some sense of what was expected of them in their future role of mother. It could very well be that the three-generational "trash gang" played a major role in teaching girls about life under slavery, as well as particulars regarding men, marriage, and sex.

Although the early teenage years brought hard work and a painful awareness of what it meant to be a slave, these years were also marked by puberty and a budding interest in boys. When girls traded their homespun shirts for calico dresses they usually dyed one dress a bright color for Sunday and special occasions.[14] If a young lady had attracted the eye of some young man, she was very likely to receive a hoop made out of a grape vine to wear under that dress. Gus Feaster of South Carolina observed that this was the age when young women stopped eating and claimed they had no appetite. Apparently, it was not "stylish" for "courtin' gals" to "eat much in public."[15] Instead of running and jumping and hunting 'coons, young adults "went to walk an' hunted chestnuts." The chestnuts were not for eating, however. According to Alabama born Lucindy Lawrence Jordon, "us would string dem an' put 'em 'round our necks an' smile at our fellers."[16]

If it was a transitional period for young ladies, it was also a period of apprehension for parents, especially mothers. The mother of slaves is very watchful, explained Linda Brent. "After they have entered their teens, she lives in daily expectation of trouble. This leads to many questions. If a girl is of a sensitive nature, timidity keeps her from answering truthfully and this well-meant course has a tendency to drive her from maternal counsels."[17] A slave mother's anxiety stemmed partly from her fear that her young daughters would fall prey to the licentious black and white men on the plantation. On Southern plantations mothers often schooled their daughters on avoiding the sexual overtures of these men. When one woman saw the overseer sneering at her daughter, she told her "not to let any of 'em go with her," and when Lucy McCullough's mother saw Lucy coming across the field with her dress rising too far, she promptly tore the hem out in the sight of everyone.[18]

In the long run, however, a mother could do little but hope that her daughter made it through adolescence and young womanhood unscathed by sexual abuse. In this respect homeliness could be a great asset, for antebellum sources seem to support Brent's statement regarding female slaves: "If God has bestowed beauty upon her it will prove her greatest curse," because "that which commands admiration in the white woman, only hastens the degradation of the female slave."[19]

A slave mother's uneasiness during her daughter's adolescence also grew out of her desire to protect her daughter from the responsibilities of adulthood. Mothers seemed to want girls to grow up slowly, and so they tried to limit their daughters' contact with members of the opposite sex. "Courtin' wasn't fast," noted one ex-slave.[20] W. M. Green complained that "girls acted like de old folks and dey did not carry on."[21] The vigilance of some mothers equalled that of a North Carolina woman who never let her daughter out of her sight when the latter was with her beau. It was one year before she allowed her daughter to walk with her future son-in-law and then she made sure that she was "setting dere on de porch lookin'."[22]

Some slave mothers apparently tried to shelter their daughters from the adult world by withholding knowledge of the mechanics of childbirth. For instance, Mississippian Frances Fluker claimed: "I come a woman 'for I knowed what it was. . . . They didn't tell me nothin'."[23] Another woman noted that at age twelve or thirteen, she and an older girl went around to parsley beds and hollow logs looking for newborn babies. "They didn't tell you a thing," she said. At age twenty she was still ignorant about reproduction: "I didn't know how long I had to carry my baby. We never saw nothing when we were children."[24] Minnie Fulkes, a Virginia woman, had a similar story. She married at the uncommon age of fourteen but knew nothing about sex: "I slept in bed, he on his side an' I on mine for three months."[25] Still others testified that their mothers told them that doctors brought babies, and that "people was very particular in them days. They wouldn't let children know anything."[26]

Try as they might, mothers could not forever shelter their daughters from the complex considerations that courtship involved. Despite the preferences of their mothers, teenage slave girls seem to have had a degree of sexual freedom unknown to Southern white girls. In a conscious comparison of the mores that bound white women to sexual prudery with those that afforded black women the opportunity to experiment with sex, Mary Boykin Chesnut, with a hint of envy, wrote: "These negro women have a chance here that women have nowhere else. They can redeem themselves—the impropers can. They can marry decently and nothing is remembered agains these colored ladies."[27] A plantation owner told Frederick Olmsted that slave men and women seldom married without "trying each other out . . . for two or three weeks, to see how they are going to like each other."[28] Black testimony also reveals premarital sexual contact between the sexes. Of his relationship with young single women, Oklahoma-born John White said: "I favor them with something extra from the kitchen. Then they favors me—at night."[29] Another male former slave recalled that boys sang a "vulgar" song to girls inviting them to "come out tonight."[30]

"Marriage" patterns and the way slave children were spaced also suggest that slave girls started sexual activities relatively early and were free to change their minds during the mate selection process. Usually female slaves had their first child in their nineteenth year (about two years earlier than Southern white women), waited a few years before having their second child, and then beginning with the second child had subse-

quent children at two and a half year intervals.[31] Most bonded
women married the father of their first child but many established a more enduring relationship with someone other than
their first child's father and went on to marry and have the
rest of their children with him.

If it is difficult for the historian to reconcile the contradic-
tions between the vigilance of slave mothers and the reality of
permissive sex, the problem only gets more complex when
planter demands are considered. Slave women in their late
teens and early twenties were not free to consider their future
without considering that their childbearing ability was of economic consequence to their owners. Since some masters figured that at least 5 to 6 percent of their profit would accrue
from natural increase, this period in the bondwoman's life
was beset with pressures that free women did not experience.[32] On one front there were norms and rites dictated by
the slave's culture, those designed to usher females out of the
asexual world of childhood, through puberty, and into the
sexual world of marriage and motherhood. The slow pace of
courtship dictated by anxious mothers is a good example of a
standard set not by the whites, but by black slaves. On another
front there was the white master whose sometimes subtle and
sometimes not so subtle manipulation of the slave woman and
her environment was aimed at maximizing the number of
children born to his slaves. Into these crosscurrents stepped a
very naive young woman who, along with the young men in
her life, had her own ideas about sex and courtship.

However she felt about the mores her mother tried to
inculcate, the young slave woman could not ignore her master's wishes which, in one way or another, were made quite
clear. Slave masters wanted adolescent girls to have children,
and to this end they practiced a passive, though insidious kind
of breeding. Thus, while it was not unheard of for a planter
to slap a male and female together and demand that they
"replenish the earth" it was more likely that he would use his

authority to encourage young slaves to make binding and permanent the relationships they themselves had initiated. Some did this by granting visitation privileges to a young man of a neighboring plantation who had taken an interest in a particular young woman. If the man and woman married, these visitations continued throughout the marriage. Occasionally, arrangements were made whereby a slave owner purchased a slave so that a man and woman could marry and live together.[33]

The typical plantation manual should arrest any thoughts that the attention masters paid to getting young slave women attached stemmed from unselfish benevolence. On the contrary, marriage was thought to add "to the comfort, happiness and health of those entering upon it, besides ensuring greater increase."[34] Indeed, on the morning after her wedding, Mammy Harriet of the Burleigh estate in Georgia was greeted by her mistress singing: "Good morning, Mrs. Bride. I wish you joy, and every year a son or daughter."[35] Malinda Bibb's master was a little less tactful. Henry Bibb recalled that when he asked Malinda's master for her hand in marriage, "his answer was in the affirmative with but one condition, which I consider to be too vulgar to be written."[36] Too often, when two people declared their intention to marry, as on a North Carolina plantation, all the master said was "don't forget to bring me a little one or two for next year."[37]

Beyond the verbal prodding used to encourage young women to reproduce were the more subtle practices that were built into the plantation system. For instance, pregnant women usually did less work and received more attention and rations than nonpregnant women.[38] This policy was meticulously outlined to overseers and managers. Richard Corbin of Virginia told his manager that "breeding wenches more particularly you must instruct the Overseers to be Kind and Indulgent to, and not force them when with child upon any service or hardship that will be injurious to him."[39] While this practice was designed to ensure the continued good health of mother and fetus alike, it also doubled as an incentive for overworked slave women to have children. As previously noted, the trash gang, to which women were assigned in the latter stages of pregnancy, did relatively lighter work than that done by other hands. On plantations where the work load was exhausting and back breaking, a lighter work assignment could easily have proved incentive to get pregnant as often as possible, and according to Francis Kemble it did just that. Writing about the women on her husband's Georgia and South Carolina rice plantations she noted: "On the birth of a child certain additions of clothing and an additional weekly ration are bestowed on the family, and these matters, as small as they may seem, act as powerful inducements." There can be little doubt that the women in the Georgia settlements were conscious of their owner's stress on natural increase. On one trip through the slave quarters, Kemble visited women who held their babies out for her inspection proclaiming: "Missus, tho' we no able to work, we make little niggars for massa."[40]

As part of their manipulation of reproduction some slave owners adopted the practice of rewarding prolific women. Every time a baby was born on one of Major Wallon's plantations, the mother was given a calico dress and a "bright, shiny silver dollar."[41] B. Talbert, a Virginia planter, took this policy to its extreme. In 1792 he bought a woman named Jenny and promised her that when she had a child for every one of his five children he would set her free. In the space of eleven years Jenny had six children, and in 1803, she and her youngest child were emancipated by Talbert.[42] Though only a few slaveholders were so "charitable," many adhered to the instructions in Plowden C. J. Weston's *Plantation Manual.* Weston advised that "women with six children alive at any one time are allowed all Saturday to themselves."[43]

If these inducements were not sufficient to secure the cooperation of the slave of childbearing age, the master always had recourse to punitive measures, such as the sale of women incapable of having children. Since much of a young woman's worth was in her unborn children, nonchildbearing women were less valuable to slaveholders than childbearing women. Both masters and slave traders were often unscrupulous in their methods of disposing of such women. In 1852 an Alabama master bought three women only to find that one of them had syphilis, another had gonorrhea, and the third suffered from the effects of an umbilical hernia, all of which rendered them, in the opinion of the buyer, "scarcely valuable as breeders." A Georgia farmer was likewise cheated out of the nine hundred dollars he had paid for a young woman. Less than a week after the sale, the woman was found to be suffering from a uterine infection. So common were such misrepresentations that judges and juries established a policy for dealing with such cases. If a buyer took possession of a woman who had been certified as fit to bear children by the seller, and it could be demonstrated that the seller knew the woman was incapable of having children, the sale was voided and the proceeds were refunded. These two planters got their money back, but some did not.[44]

Infertile women could, therefore, expect to be treated like barren sows and be passed from one unsuspecting buyer to the next. This was confirmed by a slaveholder who confessed to Northerner Frederick Olmsted that he had known a great many slave women to be sold off because they did not have children.[45] Berry Clay confirmed that "a barren woman was separated from her husband and usually sold."[46] Planter interest in a slave woman's offspring was long-range and often conflicted with that of a slave couple. For instance, Mary Reynold's husband wanted to buy her from her master, but her master refused because he was "never one to sell any but old niggers who was past working in the fields and past their breeding time."[47] John Tayloe of Virginia was similar in this respect, except he sold females both before and after their childbearing years. Of the twenty-nine females he sold off his Mount Airy plantation between 1809 and 1828, four were small children, sixteen were girls aged nine to seventeen, and the remaining nine were mature women. No childbearing women were sold. An ex-slave summed it up: If a woman was a good breeder, "they was proud of her;" if not, they got rid of her.[48]

If the subtle manipulations of slaveholders failed in their aim, and if a young bondwoman cared so little about her own security as to refuse to have children, then masters could and sometimes did resort to outright force. The story of Texan Rose Williams is a case in point. According to Williams she had been at Master Hawkins' place for about a year when Hawkins approached her and told her she was changing accommodations: "You gwine live with Rufus in that cabin over yonder. Go fix it for living." Rose attributed her naïveté to her youth (she was only about sixteen) for she assumed that she was only "to tend cabin for Rufus and some other niggers." She soon learned otherwise and promptly rebelled: "We-uns has supper, then I goes here and there talking till I's ready for sleep, and then I gits in the bunk. After I's in, that nigger come crawl in the bunk with me." Rose put her foot against him and shoved him on to the floor. An infuriated Rufus reported the incident to Hawkins who forthwith informed Rose of her duty to "bring forth portly children." Reinforcing his point, he told Rose that he had paid "big money" for her "cause I wants you to raise me childrens." She complied with his wishes only under his threats of a beating. But Rose Williams was influenced by more than fear of physical abuse. Her inclination to resist was tempered by the fact that Hawkins had bought her whole family off the auction block: "I thinks 'bout Massa buying me offen the block and saving me from being separated from my folks and 'bout being whipped at the stake. There it am. What am I's to do? . . . I yields." She gave in, but, as Williams herself revealed, the incident was shattering: "I never marries, 'cause one 'sperience am 'nough for this nigger. After what I does for the massa, I's never wants no truck with any man. The lord forgive this colored woman, but he have to 'scuse me and look for some other for to 'plenish the earth."[49]

The pressures on the female slave in young womanhood were not always laid to rest after marriage and childbirth. The birth of children bought some security for a married couple, but the vagaries of the market economy and a slave owner's death or peculiar whims were unpredictable factors that could result in the sale or permanent separation of a husband and wife. A young woman's search for another spouse with whom to have more children for her owner was expected to begin immediately. Not long after separation, both husband and wife would either find or be given a new spouse. When William Wells Brown asked Sally why she had married so soon after the sale of her husband, Ben, her earnest reply was that the master made her do it. So too, when Lavinia, another of Brown's acquaintances, was separated from her loved one, her master compelled her, on pain of the lash, to choose another. When she absolutely refused, she got a whipping.[50] Deacon Whitefield, one of Henry Bibb's masters, "graciously" provided one of his slave women with a slave named Steven, whom she quickly rejected. But the driver's lash made her think twice, and she reluctantly accepted him.[51]

If the evidence of the slaveholder's efforts to cajole and coerce slave women to have children in the cause of profit speaks for itself, the precise psychological and physiological effects of slave owner manipulation on young black women are more difficult to gauge. The ex-slaves' sensitivity on the subject suggests that bondwomen knew they were cogs in the plantation regime's reproductive machine. In all probability, slave owner manipulation was responsible for the two-year difference between the beginning of childbearing years in slave women and in Southern white women.[52] Although plantation owners succeeded in hastening the onset of the bonded woman's childbearing years, it appears that plantation blacks may have managed to deprive them of total victory. This conclusion is implicit in a study done by economists James Trussell and Richard Steckel, who have estimated the mean age of slave women at first birth to be 20.6 years. By using height and weight data obtained from the manifests of slave ships they also put the age of menarche at fifteen. Since a period of about 2.6 years of sterility usually follows menarche, the average female slave *delayed childbearing for at least two years* after attaining reproductive capacity.[53] Therefore, although slaveholders tried to get slave women to have as many children as physically possible, owners fell short of their aim.

Why? It could be that what owners perceived as better treatment and lighter work was not enough. Adolescent girls who did not get enough to eat, who suffered from any number of vitamin deficiencies, and who spent long days in the crop might have been unable to have children any earlier than they did. Moreoever, regardless of how good the treatment, how light the work, or how sufficient the diet, if planter policies made for a shortage of males, then bonded women would have to compete for mates. There was good chance that the woman who did not experience courtship during adolescence would begin childbearing later than her couterpart who had an adolescent courtship or might never have children at all. For instance, on some of the Ball plantations in antebellum South Carolina, Cheryll Cody found a direct correlation between the number of women who never bore children and an unbalanced sex ratio. On those plantations where women outnumbered men, there was also a significant number of women who never had children. The descendants of John Ball indirectly influenced female slave decisions on mate selection and childbearing through their sale, purchase, and dispersal policies.[54] Owners could also influence these decisions by prohibiting "abroad" relationships, those relationships between bonded men and women of different plantations.

All these are possible explanations for why the average young slave woman did not begin childbearing two years earlier than she did.

We must not, however, lose sight of the kind of pressure the blacks of the quarters exerted on young slave women. As Herbert Gutman has demonstrated, the slave family was remarkably stable, and served as a transmitter of culture. The care taken by slaves to obey the Seventh Commandment, the solemnity of the marriage ceremony, whether the bond was sealed in the Big House parlor or sand-covered yard, revealed that African-Americans understood their family to be a haven in a heartless Southland. It was within the slave family that a man, humiliated by the overseer's commands or lash, received respect. There, too, the overworked or brutally punished bondwoman received compassion.[55] We have noted how mothers agonized over their daughter's initial encounters with the opposite sex, how mothers tried to make courtship proceed at a slow pace, and how there seems to have been a virtual conspiracy against revealing the particulars of the mechanics of childbirth. If these slave mores were at odds with the slave owner's desire to turn every young black woman into a "brood mare," they were also at odds with the slave owner's stereotypical notion of slave women as Jezebels. Young adults in the slave community, eager to impress the opposite sex, and experiencing for the first time the excitement of courtship, might have resisted these mores. However, most older and more mature slaves knew that the unions that Southern whites could cavalierly dismiss as promiscuous and inconsequential were often buffers against slave owner callousness and insensitivity. Given the important place that the slave family occupied in the community of the quarters, slave parents had every reason in the world to caution young courting girls to proceed slowly.

Their attitude about motherhood supplied additional reason. For the bondwoman who adhered to the prevailing mores of the quarters, marriage sanctioned motherhood, not sexual intercourse. Prenuptial intercourse was not considered evil, nor was it, as too many Southern whites mistakenly assumed, evidence of promiscuity. Slaves rejected guilt-laden white sexual attitudes.[56] The African-American slave, like the Melanesian, the West African, the Bantu, the North American Indian, and the nineteenth-century Englishman living in Britain's agricultural districts, dissociated the two sides of procreation, and believed that marriage licensed parenthood rather than sexual intercourse.[57] If teenage girls were not bound to chastity by puritanical ideas that made it a sin to be anything but true to the traditional white worn on the wedding day, they were circumscribed by mothers who were intent on protecting their daughters against the premature assumption of maternal responsibility.

Many slave mothers adhered to mores that made motherhood almost sacred, mores rooted in the black woman's African past. In traditional West Africa, mothers, by virtue of their having and nurturing children, ensured the survival of the lineage, the consanguineal corporate group that controlled and dictated the use and inheritance of property, provided access to various political and/or religious offices, regulated marriages, and performed political and economic functions.[58] In matrilineal societies it was through the mother that affiliation to the lineage was established. Mothers were the genetically significant link between successive generations. Her line determined her children's succession, inheritance, rights, obligations, and citizenship. Though most political offices were held by men, political status was conferred by women.[59] In the more common patrilineal societies, fathers were the kinship link, yet mothers were still important. It was through a man's wife that his ancestral line was perpetuated. She gave him heirs through which he passed on his property and status. In all African societies having children meant having wealth, since their work translated into material gain.[60]

In traditional West Africa the most important responsibility of each individual was to have children. Thus women, as childbearers and nurturers, were absolutely central to African family and tribal life. In many societies a marriage was not considered consummated until after the birth of the first child. The birth of this child signaled a rite of passage for both partners, for they were no longer considered adolescents but adults. For some men it meant being able to set up an independent household away from their father's control. For women, having a child was the most important rite of passage in their life. It was after the birth of the first child that most African women left their family of origin to take up residence in their husband's compound, among the members of his lineage. African women were valued for their work, which contributed to the economic success of the family, but their greatest asset was their fecundity.[61]

West African women both respected and enjoyed their status as mothers. With their children, especially their daughters, they had their most enduring and cherished relationships.[62] Because mothers lived with and nurtured their children in a hut separate from their husbands, the mother-child relationship usually had more depth and emotional content than either the father-child or the husband-wife relationship.[63] At some point, often at puberty but sometimes earlier, sons left their mother's hut to join the men of the lineage segment, but they never severed the mother-son emotional bond. If they were members of a polygynous unit their attachment to their mothers was exceptionally strong since they shared her only with other blood siblings, while they shared their fathers both with blood siblings and the children of his other wives. In such a setting the African mother became the watchdog for her children, protecting their claim to inherit their father's property.[64]

For all the time and effort she invested in her children the traditional West African mother was generously repaid in her old age. Wives did not as a rule inherit their husband's property, and daughters usually did not inherit much, if anything, from their fathers. Thus, while they were important for lineage and wealth considerations, children, especially sons, were essential for women as a hedge against indigence in their elderly years. Then they were cared for and protected by children who themselves had superficial emotional relationships with their spouses and who found their mother the most important woman in their lives.[65]

While it would seem that the antebellum slave woman had little in common with her African foremother, motherhood was still the black girl's most important rite of passage, and mothers were still the most central figures in the black family.[66] They had been so during the colonial period before the European influence diluted the African culture, and when many recently arrived African mothers raised their children much as they had done in Africa, with only a little help from their husbands. In antebellum America the security that often accompanied motherhood served to reinforce its importance. Nonprolific women were sold; childbearing was a way to anchor oneself to a given plantation for an extended period of time, and thus maintain enduring relationships with family and friends. Childbirth also secured somewhat the nuclear family against breakup by sale. As in Africa, children brought wealth, though in the American South the financial gain accrued to the slaveowner, who was more likely to sell single men and nonchildbearing women than parents who were part of a nuclear unit that regularly increased itself. The slave woman's ability to bear many children and to nurture children through infancy was often the crucial element in the length and stability of a slave marriage. It is therefore not surprising to find, as Gutman does, slave women marrying the father of the first child after its birth.[67] In this the slave system encouraged the retention of the African custom that dictated a marriage consummated only after a woman had demonstrated her ability to have children.

Motherhood in slave communities was important for kinship reasons as well. Gutman found that slave children were more likely to be named after their fathers than their mothers. Since fathers were more likely to be separated from the family than mothers, slaves established this tradition to make the slave father important in the child's life even in his forced absence.[68] Gutman took this as partial evidence that fathers were the key figures in slave families. He failed to note, however, that when fathers were separated from their offspring, mothers were the crucial kinship link between the child and his or her unknown father. *She* supplied the information that made the father live in the child's mind.

Slaves seemed to have understood what slave mothers did for the individual slave and for the slave community, and therefore did not condemn motherhood out of wedlock. Frances Kemble was as shocked to find a woman with a child and no husband as she was by the woman's lack of guilt over her situation. A former slave who was asked if there was any illegitimacy in the slave community replied: "Yes, there was right smart of that." When asked if the mothers were slighted by slaves, he insisted, "No, they wouldn't do that." What they did do though was help these women. Elizabeth Botume found this out during her stay in the Sea Islands when she observed bondwomen helping pregnant slave women through labor and parturition regardless of the latter's marital status.[69]

Even if we take into account the expectations that both slave society and planters had of the adolescent female slave, we can only just begin to understand the pressures greeting her on the threshold of marriage and motherhood. On the one hand she had to deal with the fact that her master wanted her to have children for his profit's sake and that if she did not demonstrate her ability to give birth she might be sold away from family and friends. But then there were the values held by the slaves, especially by slave mothers, who, not wanting motherhood to be taken too lightly, cautioned the young woman to proceed with courtship slowly, to take her time before settling into womanhood. Marriage was hallowed in slave society for reasons held by the slave community and the individual slave girl, but at the same time masters and mistresses preferred and urged settled unions among their slaves for their own selfish reasons. Surely more than one slave girl found herself at eighteen or nineteen loving no particular male but having to find a husband in order to satisfy the whites and secure herself against abuse. If she was lucky, she fell in love, married, and had children with someone compatible. If she was unlucky she simply settled for something less. In any case, her standing in the quarters was probably more dependent on attaining motherhood than it was on marriage, because parenthood bought for slave families a measure of security against sale. Beyond that, living on the precipice of destruction as the individual slave did, giving birth was a life-affirming action. It was, ironically, an act of defiance, a signal to the slave owner that no matter how cruel and inhumane his actions, African-Americans would not be utterly subjugated or destroyed. Slave mothers gave African-Americans the right to say collectively what one slave woman once said of her offspring: "My child him is mine."[70]

Once a slave became pregnant she became much more dependent on other women than she was on slave men. Her interaction with elderly women and other pregnant women increased, especially on large plantations where the "trash gang" fostered intimacy. In some cases women, anywhere from five to nine months pregnant, were put to work sewing, weaving, or spinning in the company of elderly, pregnant, or nursing women. Once a young woman was cognizant of having conceived a child she was likely, on the advice of older women, to impose dietary restrictions upon herself, to wear some kind of charm, or to perform certain rituals. Such precautions were taken to "protect" the fetus or to ensure that a newborn was not "marked" in any way. For instance, some women thought it wise to stay away from strawberries lest a birthmark in the shape of the fruit be formed on the newborn's body. One midwife insisted that her patient put a spoonful of whiskey in her left shoe every morning to keep evil spirits from harming the unborn child.[71]

The dependence of pregnant women upon other women was particularly evident during and after childbirth. From the beginning to the end of their confinement slave women were attended by women, sometimes including the white mistress.[72] The midwife who attended the slave woman was often her everyday companion. Even when a midwife was sent to attend a woman on a neighboring plantation the odds were that the pregnant woman was an acquaintance of hers, since as a midwife hers was a familiar face to all slaves on farms and plantations adjacent to her own. Sometimes other women assisted the midwife at the birth, and for at least a week of postpartum, slave women, usually the assisting elderly females, were assigned to sit with the lying-in patient.[73]

Childbirth in the slave quarters was usually handled exclusively by women, but the gains derived from the companionship of familiar and sympathetic females could not compensate the birthing woman for the inadequate medical care she received. Of course, early nineteenth-century obstetric practice had not advanced much beyond traditional midwifery. Whether black or white, pregnant women had as much to fear from medical doctors and midwives as they had to gain.[74] Yet, ultimately, slave owners determined the nature and quality of the attention a pregnant slave woman received, and although many increased an expectant mother's food allotment and decreased her work load, the care received by slave women was nevertheless poor. This was partly due to neglect. It was widely believed by whites that slave women gave birth more easily and quickly than white women, and thus needed less attention during pregnancy and labor. A planter along the Mississippi River told Frederick Olmsted that because female slaves got so much exercise in their field work they "were not subject to the difficulty, danger and pain which attended women of the better classes in giving birth to their offspring." He, therefore, seldom employed a physician.[75] Some female slaves, like one Louisiana woman whose master was particularly insensitive, died painful deaths because their owners simply ignored their complaints of illness.[76] Other whites employed slave midwives rather than doctors as a means of cutting operating expenses. Midwives were often relatively competent but some of their techniques, such as their placement of an ax under the delivery mattress to "cut" the pain of childbirth, were based more on superstition than on proven medical science. Of course they could do little for women who suffered from illnesses resulting from the brutality and callousness of masters and overseers. Women who had been whipped or forced to perform heavy tasks during pregnancy had an especially hard time, as did those who were sent back to field work too soon after delivery. Slave women could have been spared backaches, uterine pains, and hernias if slaveowners had given more consideration to the condition of the women on whom they depended to reproduce the slave population.[77]

Motherhood bolstered the status of women in slave society but it also made a woman's day all the more exhausting. The first weeks after delivery were particularly difficult. Postpartum is usually accompanied by fatigue, especially for nursing mothers, and slave women almost always breast-fed their youngsters.[78] During the first two or three weeks after delivery women were usually put to work spinning, weaving, or sewing but even then they were sometimes hard pressed to finish the work assigned to them. When a slave child in Alabama, Cato attended "sucklers" or nursing women. Years later, he remembered how frustrating child care was for mothers of "fretin' babies." If they did not spin seven or eight cuts a day they got a whipping.[79] Once women returned to the field their day was still more tiring. As outlined by Clayborn Gantling, women on the Terrell County, Georgia, plantation of Judge Williams had it hard: "Women with little babies would have to go to work in de mornings with the rest, come back, nurse their children and go back to the field, stay two or three hours, then go back and eat dinner; after dinner dey would have to go to de field and stay two or three more hours and go and nurse the chillun again, go back to the field and stay till night."[80] Women were usually allowed half an hour to breast-feed, perhaps a little longer at noon. William Wells Brown reported that he was the cause of his mother's whippings. She would take William to the field on her back because the plantation did not have a nursery. She nursed him when he cried, but got whipped for taking time out from her work to feed him.[81] On most large plantations the cooking was done at a central place by cooks who did no field work, and slaves gathered and ate communally. But on plantations where there was no central kitchen, where women had to do field work and household cooking, child care was an additional bur-- den.[82]

Cooks and house servants could find it hard, too. Louis Hughes' wife had a neverending day. She nursed her infants before she hurried off to prepare breakfast and attend to the laundry. After cooking dinner she hurried back to nurse her babies again, but quickly returned to the Big House to cook supper. After all the dishes were washed and the kitchen was cleaned she returned to her little ones.[83]

Nursing and childcare did not relieve a slave woman of the burdens of field work. The combined responsibilities of nurturance and work were a source of constant anxiety as slave mothers tried to do their duty to both their children and their masters. Sometimes these conflicting demands required more acrobatics than an individual woman could perform. In the process, however, child care became a responsibility shared by many women, and the mother role, at least as it was defined by antebellum white America, was radically transformed.

The end of the childbearing years, around the age of thirty-nine or forty, was not marked by a diminution of work. Catherine Edmundson, a Southern mistress, once quipped: "I wish I could see a hearty negro woman—one who admitted herself to be over forty who was not 'Poorly.' " Of course, Edmondston knew why middle-aged slave women were full of complaints: "To be 'poorly' is their aim & object as it ends in the house & spinning."[84] And no wonder, since it was during the years after childbearing but before old age, the middle-aged years, that slave women did their hardest work. It was during this period, which was uninterrupted by pregnancy and the accompanying periods of "light" work, that women could probably be found "working like a man."[85] Indeed, this is perhaps the source of much of the confusion over whether or not field labor was differentiated by gender.[86] Travelers and ex-slaves who reported that women and men did the same work seldom reported the age of the women. Although some women of childbearing age plowed and ditched when they were pregnant, in view of the slave owners' concerns about natural increase it is more likely that women who did the same work as men were past their childbearing years. If this was the case, the middle-aged years were the most labor-intensive years of a woman's life. Slave owners who had already reaped the profit of a female slave's increase probably had no qualms about putting her in gangs that did exceptionally heavy work in a sexually integrated setting.

The slave woman's status in the slave community seems to have increased with old age as a consequence of her service as caretaker of children, nurse, and midwife. For many men this period was marked by decreased status because they no longer had the stamina and strength to perform physically demanding tasks and were sometimes reduced to doing such traditional female chores as spinning and child care.[87] Many older craftsmen found themselves replaced by younger, more energetic, and nimble slave artisans. Yet, as a woman aged she grew more knowledgeable in nurturing and "doctoring" and more experienced.

Although many senior women were put to work spinning, weaving, or sewing, their most common occupation, caring for the children of parents who worked in the field or the house, reinforced the importance of the mother role. Every morning young mothers could be seen taking or sending their children to the old "grannies" who looked after the children during the day. Frederick Olmsted visited a few of these plantation nurseries and was impressed at how well the elderly women handled their responsibilities. On a rice plantation in Georgia's tidewater region he found a "kind looking old negro woman" with "philoprogenitiveness well developed." Although the woman seemed to pay little attention to the children, except to chide some of the older ones for laughing or singing too loud, for the half hour he watched "not a baby of them began to cry." The same was true at two or three other plantation nurseries he visited.[88]

Mature women also served as nurses and midwives, and often the "granny" who ran the nursery was the same person who had brought most of her charges into the world. This is suggested by the instructions received by the overseer of Alexander Telfair's Georgia plantation. Telfair told his overseer that while the female slave Elsey was serving as midwife to both "black and white," one of her daughters was to "stay with the children and take charge of her business until she returns."[89]

In addition to serving as nursery superintendents, some old women served as folk doctors. A Georgia slave recalled that the same "old 'omans" who looked after sick slave women "knowed a heap about yarbs (herbs)."[90] The connection

between elderly female folk doctors and nursery supervisors
was drawn by a former South Carolina slave whose testimony
reveals the critical role played by old women in the raising of
children. "Fer de lil' chilluns and babies," she said, old women
"would take and chew up pine needles and den spit it de lil'
chilluns mouths and make dem swallow." Later "when dey
was a teachin' de babies to eat dey done de food de very same
way."[91] The same old women treated adults. They "made pine
rosin pills from de pine rosin that drapped from de pine trees
and give de pills to de folks to take fer de back ache." They
treated colds with horehound tea, pinetop, and lightwood
drippings in sugar. Pomegranate seeds and crushed mints were
brewed to cure fevers.[92]

Old bondwomen served a crucial role in the slave community on a plantation. They were likely to attend all slave
births and all slave deaths. Their accumulated knowledge
delivered one into life, helped one survive it, and sometimes,
as can be said of many physicians of the period, hastened one
to an early grave. As midwife and doctor they embodied the
link between the generations. And, it was partly through them
that a central aspect of black culture—the secret of the herbs—
was transmitted.

The world of the elderly female slave was highly circumscribed on the basis of sex. Few men were midwives, and
although some men looked after children in their old age, this
was also primarily a female occupation. Since black women
outlived men by at least an average of two years, undoubtedly
a large number of old women were widows, and their support
and care of pregnant women and women with small children
reinforced their ties to the female world.[93] When they engaged
in work other than nursing, baby-sitting, and sewing, they were
likely to be members of the "trash gang" along with the pre-
pubescent adolescents, pregnant women, and "suckers."

Although the prestige and status accruing to old women

who served as midwives and nurses may have reflected well on all elderly slave women, not all such women were so employed and not all fared well. Although slaveholders liked to boast that slavery was superior to the free wage system because of "cradle to grave" security, such was not usually the case. Old slaves probably received more care and attention from their friends and relatives than from their masters. Linda Brent, a fugitive slave, noted that "slaveholders have a method . . . of getting rid of *old* slaves whose lives have been worn out in their service." She personally knew a seventy-year-old woman who was sold for twenty dollars because she was of no further use to her owners.[94] Frances Kemble particularly lamented the condition of old women on her husband's Georgia plantations. A slave woman named Hannah was typical of the elderly slaves. Hannah's face and figure were "seamed with wrinkles and twisted with age and infirmity." Pitying the poor woman, Kemble noted that "as she crawled to me almost half her naked body was exposed through the miserable tatters that she held on with one hand."[95]

The unscrupulousness of some slaveholders can be inferred from statistics showing a disproportionately large number of elderly persons in Southern cities, especially those of the upper South. This suggests that some slaveholders disobeyed laws prohibiting the manumission of elderly slaves and simply freed them rather than assume the duty of feeding and clothing them.[96] It would not be an exaggeration to state that many slave owners shared the sentiments of a South Carolina overseer and welcomed the death of elderly women. Writing in 1864 to his employer, Adele Petigru Allston, he reported that an old slave woman named Grace, "the old woman that has bin sick fur 2 years," had died. He then added: "she was a Dead Expense to the Place."[97] Thus many old women found themselves either in a position similar to that of Hannah or Grace or destitute and lonely in a Southern city, dependent on their children and other relatives, slaves who valued the aged enough to share their meager rations and provisions with respected old folks.

At no stage in her life cycle was the plantation slave woman immune to the brutality of the system. And yet, most women enjoyed the love and companionship of other slaves throughout their lifetime, most knew the excitement of courtship and the joys of motherhood. In addition, most slave girls grew up believing that boys and girls were equal. Had they been white and free, they would have learned the contemporary wisdom of nineteenth-century America, that women were the maidservants of men, that women were feeble and delicate, intellectually unfit for all but the most rudimentary education. As it was, *because* they were black and slave they learned that black women had to be the maidservants of whites, but not necessarily of men. They learned, too, from both the whites of the Big House and the blacks of the quarters that becoming a mother was the most important of life's transitions for slave women and that caring for young children would always be an important female responsibility.

CHAPTER FOUR

The Female Slave Network

... the very symbolic and social conceptions that appear to set women apart and to circumscribe their activities may be used by women as a basis for female solidarity and worth.[1]

SLAVE WOMEN HAVE often been characterized as self-reliant and self-sufficient because, lacking black male protection, they had to develop their own means of resistance and survival. Yet, not every black woman was a Sojourner Truth or a Harriet Tubman. Strength had to be cultivated. It came no more naturally to them than to anyone, slave or free, male or female, black or white. If they seemed exceptionally strong it was partly because they often functioned in groups and derived strength from numbers.

Much of the work slaves did and the regimen they followed served to stratify slave society along sex lines. Consequently, slave women had ample opportunity to develop a consciousness grounded in their identity as females. While close contact sometimes gave rise to strife, adult female cooperation and interdependence was a fact of female slave life. The self-reliance and self-sufficiency of slave women, therefore, must not only be viewed in the context of what the individual slave woman did for herself, but what slave women as a group were able to do for one another.

It is easy to overlook the separate world of female slaves because from colonial times through the Civil War black women often worked with black men at tasks considered by most white Americans to be either too difficult or inappropriate for females. All women worked hard but when white women consistently did field labor it was considered temporary, irregular, or extraordinary, putting them on a par with slaves. Swedish actress Frederika Bremer, visiting the antebellum South, noted that usually only men and black women do field work. Commenting on what another foreign woman sarcastically claimed to be a noble admission of female equality, Bremer observed pointedly that "black [women] are not considered to belong to the weaker sex."[2]

Bremer's comment reflects what former slaves and fugitive male slaves regarded as the defeminization of black women. Bonded women cut down trees to clear lands for cultivation. They hauled logs by leather straps attached to their shoulders. They plowed using mule and ox teams and hoed, sometimes with the heaviest implements available. They dug ditches, spread manure fertilizer, and piled coarse fodder with their bare hands. They built and cleaned Southern roads, helped construct Southern railroads, and of course, they picked cotton. In short, what fugitive slave Williamson Pease said regretfully of slave women was borne out in fact: "Women who do outdoor work are used as bad as men."[3] Almost a century later Green Wilbanks was less remorseful than Pease but in his remembrances of his Grandma Rose, he implied that the work had a kind of neutering effect. Grandma Rose was a woman who could do any kind of job a man could do, a woman who "was some worker, a regular man-woman."[4]

However, it is hardly likely that slave women, especially those on large plantations with sizable female populations, lost their female identity. Harvesting season on staple crop plantations may have found men and women gathering the crop in sex-integrated gangs, but at other times women often worked in exclusively or predominantly female gangs.[5] Thus women were put in one another's company for most of the day. This meant that those with whom they ate meals, sang work songs, and commiserated during the work day were people with the same kind of responsibilities and problems. If anything, slave women developed their own female culture, that is, a way of doing things and a way of assigning value that flowed from the perspective that they had on Southern plantation life. Rather than being diminished, their sense of womanhood was probably enhanced, and their bonds to one another made stronger.

Since slave owners and managers seemingly made little of the slave woman's lesser strength, one wonders why they separated men and women at all. Gender must have provided a natural and easy way to divide the labor force. Despite their limited sensitivity regarding female slave labor, and the double standard they used when evaluating the uses of white and black female labor, slave owners did reluctantly acquiesce to female physiology. For instance, depending on their stage of pregnancy, pregnant women were considered half or quarter hands. Healthy, nonpregnant women were considered three-quarter hands. Three-quarter hands were not necessarily exempt from some of the herculean tasks performed by men who were full hands, but usually, when work assignments were being parceled out men were given the more physically demanding work unless there was a shortgage of male hands to do the very heavy work or a rush to get that work completed. A case in point was the most common differentiation: men plowed and women hoed.[6]

Like a lot of field labor, nonfield labor was structured so that women could identify with one another. In the Sea Islands slave women sorted cotton lint according to color and fineness and removed the cotton seeds the gin had crushed into the cotton and lint. Fence building often found men splitting rails in one area and women doing the actual construction in another. Men usually shelled corn, threshed peas, and cut potatoes for planting and platted shucks. Grinding corn into meal or hominy was woman's work; as were spinning, weaving, sewing, and washing.[7]

Female slave domestic work sealed the bonds of womanhood that were forged in the fields and other work places. Usually women spun thread, wove cloth, sewed, and quilted apart from men. Sylvia King grew up on a Texas plantation where women sewed together in the "spinnin' and weavin' cabins."[8] On Captain Kinsler's South Carolina plantation, as on countless others, "old women and women bearin' chillun not yet born did cardin' wid hand-cards." Some would spin, others would weave, but all would eventually learn from some skilled woman "how to make clothes for the family . . . knit coarse socks and stockins." Saturday afternoon was usually reserved for doing laundry, although sometimes women did it at night after coming from the fields.[9]

It is not at all clear what role slave women had in shaping their domestic work, or how they felt about it; what is clear is that they sometimes worked long after their return from the fields, and long after the men had retired. Frances Willingham of Georgia remembered that when slaves came in at night "woman's cleant up deir houses atter dey et, and den washed and got up early next mornin' to put de clothes out to dry." In contrast, men would "set 'round talkin' to other mens and den go to bed."[10] Women also sometimes sat up sewing. "When the work in the fields was finished women were required to come home and spin one cut a night," reported another Georgian. "Those who were not successful in completing this work were punished the next morning."[11] Women had to spin, weave, and sew in the evenings partly because slave owners bought few ready-made clothes, and when they did, the white family and single slave men were the most likely recipients. On one South Carolina plantation each male slave received a fall allotment of one cotton shirt, one pair of woolen pants, and one wooolen jacket. In the spring each man got one shirt and two pairs of cotton pants. Slave women, on the other hand, received six yards of woolen cloth and three yards of cotton shirting in the fall. In the spring they got six yards of cotton drillings and three yards of shirting. In both the spring and the fall women got one needle and a half dozen buttons.[12]

Perhaps a saving grace to this "double duty" was that women got a chance to interact with each other. On a Sedalia County, Missouri, plantation women looked forward to doing laundry on Saturday afternoons because, as Mary Frances Webb explained, they "would get to talk and spend the day together."[13] Quiltings, referred to by former slaves as female "frolics" and "parties," were especially convivial. South Caro-linian Sallie Paul explained that "when dey would get together den, dey would be glad to get together."[14]

Women also spent a lot of their nonworking hours with each other. Anna Peek recalled that when slaves were allowed to relax they gathered around a pinewood fire in Aunt Anna's cabin to tell stories. At that time "the old women with pipes in their mouths would sit and gossip for hours."[15] Missourian Alice Sewell told of women occasionally slipping away to hold their own prayer meetings. They cemented their mutual bonds at the end of every meeting when they walked around shak-ing hands singing "fare you well my sisters, I am going home."[16] Impromptu female religious services were a part of Minksie Walker's mother's life, too. Her mother, Walker testified, would stop and talk with other women after Sunday services on a Missouri plantation. "First thing I would know dey would be jumpin' up and dancin' around and pattin' their hands until all de grass was wore slick."[17]

Residential arrangements further reinforced the bonds

forged during work, social, and religious activities. The women of the slave quarters lived within a stone's throw of one another. Living at such close quarters could sometimes be unsettling since rumors, with or without foundation, spread faster in the confined environment. Yet, close living allowed for informal palavers during which females could share their joys, concerns, gossip, and heartbreak.

The organization of female slave work and social activities not only tended to separate women and men, but it also generated female cooperation and interdependence. It has already been noted that the pregnant female slave could usually depend on the company of her peers during delivery and convalescence.[18] The midwife or "doctor woman" who delivered the baby was often a member of that peer goup. One Virginia physician estimated that nine tenths of all deliveries among the black population in his state were conducted by midwives, most of whom were also black. Another Virginia physician set the number at five sixths.[19]

Slave women and their children could depend on midwives and "doctor women" to treat a variety of ailments. Menstrual cramps, for example, were sometimes treated with a tea made from the bark of the gum tree, and at least one woman treated colic by giving the fretting infant a syrup made from a boiled rat's vein.[20] Midwives and "doctor women" administered various other herb teas to ease the pains of many ailing slaves. Any number of broths, made from the leaves and barks of trees, from the branches and twigs of bushes, from turpentine, catnip, or tobacco were used to treat whooping cough, diarrhea, toothaches, colds, fevers, headaches, and backaches.[21]

Male slave herb "doctors" and professionally trained white doctors did play a limited role in female slave medical care but more often than not is was elderly and middle-aged black women who tended to the slave population.[22] William Howard Russell noted this phenomenon during his stay on a plantation outside of New Orleans where the cabin that served as a hospital for slaves was surpervised by an old woman.[23] While visiting an estate in Mississippi Frederick Olmsted overheard an elderly slave woman request medicines for a sick woman in her charge.[24] According to a Georgia ex-slave, "one had to be mighty sick to have the services of a doctor." On his master's plantation "old women were . . . responsible for the care of the sick."[25] This was also the case on Rebecca Hooks' former Florida residence. "The doctor," she noted, "was not nearly as popular as the 'granny' or midwife, who brewed medicines for every ailment."[26]

Female cooperation in the realm of medical care helped foster bonding that led to collaboration in the area of resistance. Frances Kemble could attest to the concerted efforts of the black women on her husband's Sea Island plantations. More than once she was visited by groups of women imploring her to get her husband to extend the lying-in period for child-bearing women. On one occasion the women had apparently prepared beforehand the approach they would take with the foreign-born and sympathetic Kemble, for their chosen spokeswoman took care to play on Kemble's own maternal sentiments, and pointedly argued that slave women deserved at least some of the care and tenderness that Kemble's own pregnancy had elicited.[27]

Usually, however, slave women could not be so outspoken about their needs, and covert cooperative resistance prevailed. Slaveowners suspected that midwives conspired with their female patients to induce abortions, and on Charles Colcock Jones' Georgia plantation such seems to have been the case. A woman name Lucy gave birth in secret and then denied that she had ever been pregnant. Although the midwife attended her, she too claimed not to have delivered a child, as did Lucy's mother. Jones had a physician examine Lucy, and the doctor confirmed what Jones had suspected, that Lucy had indeed given birth. Twelve days later, the decomposing body of a full-term infant was found, and Lucy, her mother, and the midwife were all hauled off to court. Another woman, a nurse, managed to avoid prosecution but not suspicion. Whether Lucy was guilty of murder and whether the others were accessories will never be known because the court could not shatter their collective defense that the child had been stillborn.[28]

The inability of slave owners to penetrate the private world of female slaves is probably what kept them from learning of many abortions. The secrets kept by a midwife named Mollie became too much for her to bear. When she embraced Christianity it was the first thing for which she asked forgiveness. As she recalled: "I was carried to the gates of hell and the devil pulled out a book showing me the things which I had committed and that they were all true. My life as a midwife was shown to me and I have certainly felt sorry for all the things I did, after I was converted."[29]

Health care is not the only example of how the organization of slave work and slave responsibilities led to female cooperation and bonding; slave women were also dependent on each other for child care. During his investigation of the domestic slave trade Eliza Andrews queried a slave trader as to how slave women could be expected to do a full day's work and raise their children, too. The trader dismissed the question as if it challenged the natural order of things: "Oh yes, they'll do a smart chance of work and raise the children besides."[30] Such expectations reveal that slave traders and slave owners either were not conscious of the time and energy child raising consumed or knew what efforts had to be expended and just did not care. In hindsight their demands, whether based on ignorance or callousness, seem unreasonable. Slave women had an intensive work day before child care was added. Few could satisfy the demands made by the master on the one hand and their children on the other. Fatigue was a hard enemy to conquer. Some women, like Booker T. Washington's mother, set aside time to spend with their children every evening, but others, like the parents of Laugan Shiphard, found their offspring asleep when they returned from the fields.[31]

Slave women had to have help if they were to survive the dual responsibilities of laborer and mother. Sometimes, especially on small farms or new plantations where there was no extra hand to superintend children, bondwomen took their offspring to the field with them and attended to them during scheduled breaks. Usually, however, infants and older children were left in the charge of an elderly female or females whose sole job was to baby-sit during working hours. These women did not assume the full maternal burden but they did spend as much or more time with a slave child than did the biological mother.

And they took their charge seriously. Said Robert Shepherd of the Georgia slave woman who looked after him: "Aunt Viney . . . had a big old horn what she blowed when it was time for us to eat, and us knowed better dan to git so fur off us couldn't hear dat horn, for Aunt Viney would sho' tear us up."[32] Josephine Bristow spent more time with Mary Novlin, the nursery keeper on Ferdinand Gibson's South Carolina plantation, than she spent with her mother and father who came in from the fields after she was asleep: "De old lady, she looked after every blessed thing for us all day long en cooked for us right along wid de mindin'."[33] In their complementary role as nurse, nursery superintendents ministered to the hurts and illnesses of infants and children.[34] It was not at all uncommon for the children's weekly rations to be given to the "grannies" rather than to the children's parents.[35] Neither the slaveowner nor slave society expected the biological mother of a child to fulfill all of that child's needs. Given the circumstances, the responsibilities of motherhood had to be shared, and this required close female cooperation.

Close female cooperation in this sphere helped slaves hurdle one of the most difficult of predicaments—who would provide maternal care for a child whose mother was either sold or deceased? Fathers sometimes served as both mother and father, but when slaves, as opposed to the master, determined child care it was usually a woman who became a child's surrogate mother. Most of the time that woman was a relative, usually an aunt or a sister, but in the absence of female relatives, nonkin women assumed the responsibility.[36] Sometimes, as in the case of Georgian Mollie Malone, the nursery superintendent became the child's substitute mother.[37] Sometimes, friends did. When her mother was killed by another Texas slave, Julia Malone, then just a small child, was raised by the woman with whom her mother shared a cabin.[38] On Southern plantations, the female community made sure that no child was truly motherless.

Because black women of a given plantation spent so much time together they inevitably developed some appreciation of one another's skills and talents. This intimacy enabled them to establish the criteria with which to rank and order themselves. The existence of certain "female jobs" that carried prestige created a yardstick by which bondwomen could measure their achievements. Some of these jobs allowed for growth and self-satisfaction, fringe benefits that were usually out of reach for the field laborer. A seamstress's work, for example, gave opportunities for self-expression and creativity. On very large plantations the seamstress usually did not do field work, and the particularly good seamstress, or "mantua maker," as she was known to contemporaries, might be hired out to others and even allowed to keep a portion of the money she earned.[39]

Other specialized jobs bestowed similar benefits upon the female slave. One of the spoils of the cook's office was privacy, since kitchens were usually located away from the slave owner's residence. In addition, cooks seldom worried about having enough to eat. In 1861, when Mary Chesnut asked her cook if the Civil War was making food scarce, the cook's indignant reply was: "I lack everything, what is cornmeal and bacon, milk and molasses? Would that be all you wanted? Ain't I bin living and eating exactly as you does all these years? When I cook for you didn't I have some of all?"[40] For reasons not too difficult to guess, midwives and female folk doctors commanded the respect of their peers, too. Midwives, in particular, often practiced their art away from their immediate plantation. This not only made them more mobile than most bondwomen, but they played an important role as couriers, carrying messages from one plantation to the next.

Apart from the seamstress, cook, and midwife, a few women were distinguished as work gang leaders. On most farms and plantations where there were overseers, managers, foremen, and drivers, these positions were held by men, either black or white. Occasionally, however, a woman was given a measure of authority over slave work, or a particular aspect of it. For instance, Louis Hughes noted that each plantation had a "forewoman who . . . had charge of the female slaves and also the boys and girls from twelve to sixteen years of age, and all the old people that were feeble."[41] Similarly, a Mississippi slave reported that on his master's Osceola plantation there was a "colored woman as foreman."[42]

Becoming a cook or seamstress or midwife sometimes involved more than just having the favor bestowed on one by the master or mistress. Skills were sometimes passed down from one generation to the next within a slave family. If a slave girl's mother was a cook, and the girl assisted her mother, then the daughter would, more than likely, assume her mother's role when the latter either was sold, grew too old, or died. Similarly, many midwives learned their skill from a female relative. The tightly guarded recipes for tonics and brews used by these "healers" were often transmitted to a younger generation by an elderly female relative. There were exceptions, of course. Clara Walker, for instance, was "apprenticed" at age thirteen by her master to a doctor who taught her how to deliver babies. According to Walker, once she learned the art, the doctor sat back and let her do his work for him.[43]

Like occupation, age also distinguished women. In fact, the female slave community could claim, as did Frederick Douglass in remarks about the slave community at large, that "there is not to be found, among any people, a more rigid enforcement of the law of respect to elders, than they maintain."[44] Absolute age was important in the slave community, but for women, age also corresponded to the number of children one had and one's stage in the childbearing cycle. Women called "Aunt" or "Granny" were either middle-aged or elderly but odds were that they also had had children, and in the case of a "Granny" might be past childbearing. By virtue of their greater experience, wisdom and number of children, old women commanded the respect of the young.

Clearly, a pecking order existed among bondwomen—one which they themselves helped to create. Either because of their age or occupation, association with the master class or personal achievements, certain women were recognized by other women and men as important people, even as leaders. Laura Towne met an aged woman who commanded such respect that other slaves bowed to her and lowered their voices in her presence. The old woman, Maum Katie, was, according to Towne, a "spiritual mother" and a woman of "tremendous influence over her spiritual children."[45] Sometimes two or three factors combined to distinguish a particular woman. Aunt Charlotte was the aged cook in John M. Booth's Georgia household. When Aunt Charlotte spoke, said Booth, "other colored people hastened to obey her."[46] Frederick Douglass's grandmother wielded influence because of her age and the skills she possessed. She made the best fishnets in Tuckahoe, Maryland, and she knew better than anyone else how to preserve sweet potato seedlings and how to plant them successfully. She had what Douglass called "high reputation," and accordingly "she was remembered by others."[47]

Older slave women sometimes used their position of authority to keep younger slave women in check. When Elizabeth Botume went to the Sea Islands after the Civil War she had as a house servant a young woman named Amy who performed her tasks slowly and sullenly until an older woman named Aunt Mary arrived from Beaufort. During slavery Amy and Aunt Mary had both worked in the house but Amy had learned to listen and obey Aunt Mary. After Aunt Mary arrived the once obstreperous Amy became "quiet, orderly, helpful and painstaking."[48]

The leadership of some women, however, had a disruptive effect on plantation operations. Bennet H. Barrow repeatedly lamented the fact that Big Lucy, one of his oldest slaves, had more control over his female hands than he did: "Anica, Center, Cook Jane, the better you treat them the worse they are. Big Lucy the Leader, corrupts every young negro in her power."[49] A self-proclaimed prophetess named Sinda was responsible for the cessation of all slave work on Butler Island in Georgia. According to a notation made by Frances Kemble in 1839, Sinda's prediction that the world would come to an end on a certain day caused the slaves to lay down their hoes and plows in the belief that their final emancipation was imminent. So sure were Sinda's fellow slaves of her prediction that even the lash failed to get them into the fields. When the appointed day of judgment passed uneventfully Sinda was whipped mercilessly. Yet, for a time she had commanded more authority than master and overseer alike.[50]

Bonded women did not have to go to the lengths Sinda did in order to make a difference in one another's lives. The supportive atmosphere of the female community was buffer enough against the depersonalizing regime of plantation work and the general dehumanizing nature of slavery. When we consider how much more confined to the plantation women were than men, that many women had husbands who visited only once or twice a week, and that on average slave women

outlived slave men by two years, we realize just how important
the female community was to its members.

The selling policies of slave masters underscore the point.
Raw economics dictated that a slave woman's value increased
in proportion to the number of children she had and nurtured as she grew older. A man was most valuable when he
was strong and energetic, qualities associated with youth. Male
tenure on a given plantation was, therefore, a bit more pre-
carious than female tenure. Cheryll Cody found that when
South Carolina cotton planter Peter Gaillard divided his estate
among his five sons and three daughters, he had, by 1825,
separated more young men from their family of origin than
young women. During the 1840s and 1850s, William J. Ball,
also of South Carolina, leased his male slaves to other planters
with the result that many young men were separated from
their families.[51]

Within the context of the reality of male slavery the female
slave community looms large. If we define a stable relationship as one of long duration then it was probably easier for
slave women to sustain stable emotional relationships with other
bondwomen than with bondmen. This is not to say that male-
female relationships were unfulfilling or of no consequence,
just that they were fraught with more uncertainty about the
future than female-to-female relationships. The female network and its emotional sustenance was always there—there
between an "abroad" husband's visits, there when a husband
or son was sent or sold off or ran away.

It could just be that in the slave community the most
enduring relationships were those existing between female
blood kin. In her study of ex-slave interviews Marth Goodson
found that of all the relationships slave owners disrupted, either
through sale or dispersal, they were least likely to separate
mothers and daughters.[52] Cody found that when Peter Gaillard divided his estate, slave women in their twenties and thir-
ties were twice as likely as men to have a sister with them, and

women over forty were four times more likely to have sisters with them than brothers. Similarly, daughters were less likely than sons to be separated from their mother. Over 60 percent of women aged twenty to twenty-four remained with their mothers when the estate was divided, as did 90 percent of those aged twenty-five to twenty-nine.[53] A slave song reflected the bonds between female siblings by indicating who took responsibility for the motherless female slave child. Interestingly enough, the one designated was neither the father nor the brother:

> A motherless chile sees a hard time.
> Oh Lord, help her on de road.
> Er sister will do de bes' she kin,
> Dis is a hard world, Lord, fer a motherless chile.[54]

If female blood ties did indeed make for the most enduring relationships, then we should probably assume that like occupation, age, and personal achievement, these relationships helped structure the female slave community. This should not, however, obscure the fact that in friendships and dependency relationships women often treated nonblood kin as if a consanguineous tie existed. This is why older women were called Aunt and Granny, and why unrelated women sometimes called each other sister.[55]

While the focus here has been on those aspects of the bondwoman's life that fostered female bonding, female-to-female conflict was not uncommon. It was impossible for harmony always to prevail among women who saw so much of one another and who knew so much about one another. Lifelong friendships were founded in the hoe gangs and sewing groups but the constant jockeying for "occupational" and social status created an atmosphere rife with smouldering jealousies and antipathies. In addition, women regularly vied for the attentions of men. When a husband or boyfriend switched his affection from one woman to another, an altercation between the women involved was likely to result. A master or overseer could precipitate a quarrel by playing favorites. Disputes over the possession of material goods such as a dress or kerchief were inevitable. Undoubtedly, women sometimes vented on each other anger that could not be directed at slave owners, overseers, and drivers. Discord, then, went hand-in-hand with close female ties.

Conflict among women was a matter many overseers and managers had to deal with. From Jesse Belflowers, the overseer of the Allston rice plantation in South Carolina, Adele Petigru Allston learned that "mostly mongst the Women" there was a "goodeal of quarling and disputing and telling lies."[56] The terms of a widely circulated overseer's contract advised rigorous punishment for "fighting, particularly amongst the women."[57] Some overseers followed this advice. According to Isaac Green of Georgia, "sometimes de women uster git whuppin's for fightin.' "[58]

On occasion, violence between women could and did get very ugly. Molly, the cook in James Chesnut's household, once took a red-hot poker and attacked the woman to whom her husband had given one of her calico dresses. In her jealous rage Molly tried to burn the dress off the woman's back.[59] As a young woman in Arkansas, Lucretia Alexander came to blows with another woman over a pair of stockings that the master had given Lucretia.[60] In yet another such incident on a Louisiana cotton plantation, the day's cotton chopping was interrupted when a feisty field hand named Betty lost her temper in the midst of a dispute with a fellow slave named Molly and struck Molly in the face with the hoe she was wielding at the time.[61]

Sometimes female conflict occurred within the idiom of witchcraft. While witchcraft beliefs are important in themselves, they also tell us how societies, and individuals within these societies, cope with their frustrations and anxieties.[62] In the slave community some people believed in witches and some did not; some believed half-heartedly, and others were absolutely without doubt. Those convinced of the presence and power of witches usually thought sorcery the root cause when an illness struck, an ailment lingered, or when insomnia made for a restless night.[63]

Persons thought to be witches were among the most feared in the slave quarters. The witch, usually a woman, was allegedly most active after the sun set. During the day she was flesh and blood, indistinguishable from other humans, but at night she shed her human skin and became a shadow who "rode" her victims. When she finished her evening "ride" she stepped back into her skin, assumed her human form, and left her victims puzzled as to the cause of their seemingly spontaneous ailment. The only recourse for the witch's victim was to wait until the witch took to "riding" again, find the skin she had shed, and sprinkle salt and pepper on it. The lore of the quarters held that a skin treated with these substances could not be reentered, and the shadow, or witch's spirit, would have to wander forever.[64]

Other bondwomen were reputed to be conjurers. Unlike witches, who were hardly ever associated with beneficent endeavors, conjurers were endowed with "powers" that could work good or evil. Their reputation tended to hinge on their ability to use herb and root medicines to prevent and cure illnesses, but they boasted of talents that included casting and removing spells, fortune telling, and brewing love and anti-love potions.[65]

It was not extraordinary for bondwomen to believe that some of their female adversaries used magic to gain revenge. In one Georgia slave community a woman, known to all as "old Aunty," was suspected of being a witch. Her fellow slaves called her a "cat witch." One morning another woman claimed, upon waking up, to be sore. She immediately accused "old Aunty" of "riding" her and beating her up in her sleep. With the aid of other slaves, this "victim" retaliated by thrashing a

black cat suspected of being "old Aunty" in disguise.[66] Cora
Shephard grew up believing witches would get to their female
adversaries by working through their husbands. "De witch come
in de house and crack de do' and she would see a woman
laying dere in de bed. 'Un hunh' say de ole witch, get outten
yo skin and come ridin' wid me." After the woman had shed
the skin the husband would find it, sprinkle salt and pepper
on it, and then stick forks in the bed so his wife could not lay
down.[67] Laura Steward of Georgia entertained similar beliefs.
A woman could even a lot of scores by sprinkling salt and
pepper on the skin of a woman who had gone "ridin wid de
ole witch." "When she come back . . . she say 'Skinny, Skinny,
don't you know me? De ole skin wouldn't jump up, so she
ain't had no skin a-tall."[68]

Caution dictated that such "powerful" individuals be treated
with deference. For instance, according to Ellen Crawley of
Arkansas, since slaves thought that Aunt Ellen could foretell
the future and cast a spell "she was much feared and respected
by the colored race."[69] Ned Channey's paternal grandmother
was known to all as a conjurer. The knowledge she had accumulated over her many years gave her such high status that,
according to Channey, "everybody set a heap of sto' by her."[70]
On Abner Parker's North Carolina plantation, Ann Parker's
mother was so feared by slaves that she was treated with the
utmost care: "Yes she was a queen, an' when she tol' dem not
to tell hit . . . dey doan tell, but when dey is out of sight of
de white folks dey bows down ter her an' does what she says."[71]
Such women commanded the respect of fellow slaves. But
unlike elderly or skilled women, conjurers and suspected
witches were treated circumspectly because they were feared.
If slaves bowed in their presence, the slave's motivation had
more to do with self-preservation than with admiration.

The presence of conflict within interpersonal relationships between female slaves should not detract from the more
important cooperation and dependence that prevailed among

women on Southern plantations and farms. Conflict occurred *because* women were in close daily contact with each other and because the penalties for venting anger on other women were not as severe as those for striking out at men, either black or white. It is not difficult to understand how dependency relationships could become parasitical, how sewing and washing sessions could become "hanging courts," how one party could use knowledge gained in an intimate conversation against another.

Just how sisterhood could coexist with discord is illustrated by the experience of the black women of the South Carolina and Georgia Sea Islands between 1862 and 1865. On November 7, 1861, Commodore S. F. Du Pont sailed into Port Royal Sound, quickly defeated the Confederates, and put Union troops ashore to occupy the Islands. Almost immediately after Du Pont's guns ceased firing, the entire white population left the islands for the mainland. A few house servants were taken by the fleeing whites, but most of the slaves remained on the islands. The following year they, and the occupying army, were joined by a host of government agents and Northern missionaries. There were several interest groups gathered in the Islands and each had priorities. As Treasury agents concerned themselves with the cotton, and army officers recruited and drafted black soldiers, and missionaries went about "preparing" slaves for freedom, the black Sea Islanders' world was turned upside down. This was true for young and middle-aged men who were forced to serve in the Union army against their will. It was true also for the women who had to manage their families, and do most of the planting and harvesting in the absence of the young and middle-aged men.[72] During the three years of upheaval black female life conformed in many ways to that outlined here. The comments of missionaries indicate that certain women were perceived as leaders by their peers. For instance, Harriet Ware identified a woman from Fripp Point on St. Helena Island named Old

Peggy as "the leader." This woman was important because she, along with another woman named Binah, oversaw church membership. As her housekeeper Flora told her, "old Peggy and Binah were the two whom all that came into the Church had to come through, and the Church supports them."[73]

On the Coffin's Point plantation on St. Helena Island, two women in particular stood out, Grace and Amaritta. At least twice Grace served her fellow women by acting as spokeswoman in disputes over wages paid for cotton production. On one occasion the women of the plantation complained to Mr. Philbrick, one of the plantation superintendents, that their wages were not high enough to permit them to purchase cloth at the local store. They were also upset because the molasses they bought from one of the other plantation superintendents was watered down. As Grace spoke in their behalf, the women shouted words of approval. At least part of the reason for Grace's ascendancy stemmed from the fact that she was among the older women of the island. She also proved to be a very diligent and forthright worker. Despite her advanced age she was able to plant, hoe, and harvest cotton along with the younger women.[74]

Amaritta, a younger woman than Grace, was also recognized by her peers as a leader. Throughout the entire period of Union occupation the blacks of the Islands were ill at ease because of the impressment operations of the army. Black women were never sure when their husbands and male relatives were going to be seized by soldiers and carried away. In April 1863 a rumor spread that the Union army was going to attack the plantations of St. Helena Island after Philbrick had promised to defend it with a battery of men. The anxious women of Coffin's Point confronted Philbrick to find out whether he really planned to endanger them so. As recorded by Harriet Ware, all the women came flocking around, "all talking at once to try and get at the truth of things." It was Amaritta who, according to Ware, "naturally stood forward as spokeswoman to get 'satisfaction.' " Only after she explained the cause of their anxiety was Philbrick able to dispel the rumor and put them at ease.[75] Along with Grace, Amaritta also played an important role in the dispute with Philbrick over low wages and watered molasses. Philbrick remained unmoved after Grace put forth the women's complaints. He stated his terms and left the women to think about it. While the rest of the women were shouting, Amaritta remained silent. She later led three or four other women to speak to Philbrick in private. With Amaritta as principal spokeswoman, they agreed to work for Philbrick under the terms he had previously specified.[76]

Besides the self-imposed pecking order, there was also ample evidence of dependency relationships and cooperation among the women on the Sea Islands throughout the war years. In slavery sick and lying-in women relied on their peers to help them, and plantation superintendents and missionaries alike found this to be the case on the Sea Islands during the Union occupation as well. For instance, Philbrick observed that it was quite common for the blacks to hire each other to hoe their assigned plots when sickness or other inconveniences kept an individual from it. In 1862 some of the men at Coffin's Point were recruited by government agents to pick cotton elsewhere in the Sea Islands. This left many of the women at Coffin's Point completely responsible for hoeing the land alloted to each. Women who were sick or pregnant stood to lose their family's allotment since neglected land was reassigned to others. However, the women saw to it that, according to Philbrick, "the tasks of the lying-in women are taken care of by sisters or other friends in the absence of their husbands." No doubt these "other friends" were women, since in the same letter Philbrick noted that the only men left on the plantation were those too old to work in the cotton.[77]

Missionaries, such as Elizabeth Hyde Botume, related similar episodes of female cooperation. Regardless of the circumstances surrounding a pregnancy, it was very common for the women of Port Royal to care for, and keep the company of, expectant and convalescing mothers. From time to time Botume was approached by spokeswomen seeking provisions for these females. She would sometimes agonize over the propriety of providing assistance because many of the lying-in women were not married. In the wake of a visit by one of these delegations on behalf of an unmarried woman named Cumber, Botume remarked abashedly: ". . . their readiness to help the poor erring girl made me ashamed."[78] Such encounters usually left her so impressed by the support that the pregnant women received from their peers that she suspended judgment and sent clothes and groceries for the mothers and infants. These were not the only instances of female-to-female cooperation. Some women moved in with each other and shared domestic duties; others looked after the sick together.[79] With so many of the men away women found ways of existing together and cooperating. But predictably, along with the "togetherness" went conflict.

There were few situations that did not provide the seeds of discord. Charles P. Ware, a missionary from Boston, once mused that the work in the crops would go much more smoothly if only he could get the women to stop fighting. At least some of the fights were caused by disputes over the distribution of the former mistress's wardrobe. Ware complained that when a woman said, " 'I free, I as much right to ole missus' things as you,' etc.," a fight was sure to erupt.[80] Harriet Ware once witnessed a fight where the women "fired shells and tore each other's clothes in a most disgraceful way." The cause of the fight was unknown to her but she was sure it was the "tongues of the women." Jealousy, she noted, ran rampant among the women, and to her mind there was "much foundation for it."[81]

The experiences of the Sea Islands women in the early 1860s formed a special episode in American history, but their behavior conformed to patterns that had been set previously by bonded women on large plantations. Few women who knew the pain of childbirth or who understood the agony and depression that flowed from sexual harrassment and exploitation survived without friends, without female company. Few lacked female companions to share escapades and courtship or older women to consult about the vicissitudes of life and marriage. Female slaves were sustained by their group activities. Historians have shown that the community of the quarters, the slave family, and slave religion shielded the slave from absolute dependence on the master; that parents, siblings, friends, and relatives served in different capacities as buffers against the internalization of infantile roles. The female slave network worked for black women in this way, but it did much more. Treated by Southern whites as if they were anything but self-respecting women, many bonded females could forge their own independent definition of womanhood through the female network, a definition to which they could relate on the basis of their own notions about what women should be and how they should act.

CHAPTER FIVE

Men, Women, and Families

. . . the domesticity in the enslaved cabin at the quarters was, ironically, about as close an approximation to equality of the sexes as the nineteenth century provided. An androgynous world was born, weirdly enough, not of freedom, but of bondage.[1]

RELATIONSHIPS BETWEEN SLAVE men and women defy simple description. They were varied and unpredictable, much as one would expect male-female interaction to be. Marital relationships were also multifaceted, but still very much dependent upon the compatibility of the personalities involved. What made slave male-female relationships unusual was the influence and power of the slave owner. Slaves helped to mold plantation realities but the right to make unsettling and life-threatening decisions remained with slave owners. Under the most rigorous controls the interaction between male and female slaves had to conform to the work and social patterns established by the system of slavery; in less demanding settings the interaction was easier but still could not conflict with them. In recent years historians have done much to debunk the myth of slave promiscuity and the absent slave family.[2] That territory, therefore, will not be explored here. Rather, this discussion of the bonded female and male will examine how women affected and were affected by men. It will also probe the slave woman's familial role and the likely family structure, given the circumstances under which slaves functioned.

One cannot say for sure what standards of femininity slave women observed but it is clear that they took pleasure in looking their best. The circumstances of the slave community, however, did not allow for many such opportunities. The dresses of field workers were tattered and dirty, and women did not change into their best clothes during the work week. Only on Sundays, religious holidays, and other festive occasions could they dress in their finest. Their finest usually consisted of just one dress that had been laid aside and worn sparingly. They used sweet-smelling flowers and herbs as perfume and often kept the good dress packed in the flowers and herbs so that the clothing would absorb the pleasant fragrance. Hoops were made out of grape vines and were worn to make the dress fall neatly away from the body. A bright-colored hat or headwrap made for the finishing touch. On the average, house servants dressed better than field hands since they had access to cast-offs from the master's family, but all slaves tried to dress up for religious services and parties.[3] According to Gus Feaster, "the gals come out in the starch dresses. . . . They took their hair down outen the strings," and "pulled off the head rags."[4]

If the Sunday religious activities on the plantation provided bondwomen with incentive to look their best so did the need to boost their self-esteem. The latter was related to a desire to be pleasing to the opposite sex, particularly for the single adolescents and young adults. "De gals charmed us wid honeysuckle and rose petals hid in dere bosoms. . . . Dey dried chennyberries and painted dem and wo' em on a string around dere necks," related South Carolinian Gus Feaster, a man who apparently paid a lot of attention to the young ladies. Young black "courting gals . . . tried to do just like the young white missus would do."[5]

Whether they followed the example of the white girls or not, young bondwomen had a receptive, indeed captive audience in young slave men, who often did all within their power to flatter their female companions. Henry Bibb was no exception. As a young man, Bibb found waiting on girls to be perfectly congenial to his nature. By his own admission, he wanted to be well thought of by them and went to great lengths to gain their affection. On two occasions he consulted conjurers on how to attract female attention. The advice he was given was questionable but he tried it nevertheless. On his first trip to his advisor he was instructed to take a certain bone out of a frog and touch a girl's neck with it. Bibb complied but frightened the girl so that she beat a hasty retreat. The second time, he was told to obtain a lock of a girl's hair and wear it in his shoe. Needless to say this was no more effective, partly because finesse was not one of Bibb's strong points. Instead of employing seductive persuasion or flattery he grabbed her and yanked her hair and, as he later reported, "never let go until I had pulled it out." These two attempts came to naught but Bibb later met and successfully courted Malinda, the woman he was married to while a slave.[6]

In situations where men outnumbered women there was fierce competition for female companionship. No man wanted to be edged out by another but sometimes the courtship ritual demanded abilities some men did not command. A case in point involved Sam, an antebellum Louisiana slave, and a woman, Miss Lively, for whom Sam had an ardent passion. At a Christmas party Sam attempted to impress Lively with his dancing talents, and she cooperated by giving him the honor of her first dance. While his rivals sat crestfallen Sam rose to demonstrate that he was worthy of her attention. His movements tested the strength of every muscle and ligament in his body, as his "legs flew like drumsticks down the outside and up the middle, by the side of his bewitching partner." While exhaustion proved the better of most couples, pride and passion drove Sam to superhuman exertions, which finally got the better of his agile body. One by one his rivals took their position by the side of Lively, who herself proved tireless. One by one they failed to make an impression on or to out-dance the coquette. In the end, all of Miss Lively's suitors had been turned away and she was left alone on the dance floor. She had proved that her reputation, as well as her name, was well deserved.[7]

If courtship tested the stamina of slave men it also sometimes drove them to hazard danger. Abraham, an antebellum Georgia house slave, put himself at risk when he "borrowed" his master's boots so that he could show himself off in them at a nearby frolic. As told by Neal Upsom, when Abraham arrived in his master's shiny footwear "he got all the gals' attentions. None of them wanted to dance with other Negroes." Abraham strutted and danced in high style until he was told that his horse, also "borrowed" from his master, had broken its neck. Then it was time for his rivals to gain their revenge. Since Abraham had taken their girl friends, they refused to help him get the dead horse back to the plantation. According to Upsom, Abraham escaped severe punishment because the master adhered to the same code of manhood as Abraham. All he ever said was, "Don't never let nobody beat your time with the gals."[8]

Machismo notwithstanding, love and affection played a large part in male-female relations. While conclusions regarding slave love and marriage should be tendered cautiously it is reasonable to assume that although men had much to gain from romantic liaisons they also had much to lose. Slave traders frequently perceived the slave family as a woman and her children.[9] Thus, when sale destroyed a slave family, wives lost husbands but husbands very often lost wives and children.

In addition, few men who had romantic relationships with

women escaped without wounded pride and an enduring anger. Louis Hughes stood stark still, blood boiling as his master choked his wife for talking back to the mistress. His wife was subsequently tied to a joist in a barn and beaten while he stood powerless to do anything for her.[10] Men who helped their wives in such situations sometimes had to behave like thieves in the night. Fearful of his master's retribution, a Georgia slave waited until dark before he cut his wife down from the tree she had been tied to for a whipping.[11] Dan Lockhart, a fugitive slave, found the hardest thing about slavery to be the abuse of his wife and child. Expressing a sentiment shared by countless slave men, Lockhart declared: "I don't want any man to meddle with my wife."[12]

Those who tried to protect their spouses were themselves abused. In revealing why some men waited until dark to aid their wives, Leah Garrett recalled that the men brazen enough to help them in sight of drivers, overseers, or masters "wuz beat afterwards."[13] Josiah Henson's father was beaten mercilessly after he tried to protect his wife. The whipping broke his spirit, leaving a hitherto good-natured and optimistic man listless and moody. He became an incorrigible runaway and his master, fearing financial loss, sold him.[14] The pain and indignity of a public assault on their lives, limbs, and pride were too much for many men to bear. Only the uncommon bondman mustered suicidal courage and took revenge on the white man who had whipped or raped his wife. More common, according to Linda Brent, was the man who slipped away and feigned ignorance of the attacks on his wife.[15]

Despite all the assaults on their manhood, most men married, and some even traded the quest of freedom for the love of a woman. Henry Bibb was such a man. Before he met Malinda, the woman he married and had a daughter with, he was bent on fleeing the South and slavery. But Malinda's affection temporarily supplanted his ultimate dream of freedom and for a long while he was satisfied to be the object of her attention and the father of their daughter, Frances. Malinda shared his dream of freedom and attempted to escape with him but the odds were against them. Bibb eventually escaped without Malinda and Frances. Although he had pleasant memories of his years with them he nevertheless regretted having permitted the "fascinating charms of a female to deter him from his goal of freedom" for a time. It was criminal of him, he thought, to become a husband and father of slaves.[16]

To avoid such feelings, some men refused to marry. When asked if he had a wife and child, J. W. Loguen replied: "I determined long ago never to marry until I was free. Slavery shall never own a wife or child of mine."[17] William Wells Brown shared a similar sentiment: "If I should have a wife, I should not be willing to leave her behind; and if I should attempt to bring her with me, the chances would be difficult for success."[18] Through no fault of their own, women held such men back. Brown and Loguen did not want to find themselves in the same situation as a North Carolina slave interviewed by James Redpath in Raleigh, North Carolina. The slave hired his time and apparently received a portion of the wages he earned for his master. "If I had not married . . . I would have been free now bekase I would have had a thousand dollars by this time to have bought myself with." He claimed that instead of saving his money and buying himself out of slavery, he spent it on his family. When Redpath asked him why he did not run away, his reply revealed an attitude slaveholders did much to cultivate: "I might be sold away from them [his family], which I won't be, if I don't try to run away—leastways till I'm old."[19]

While it was difficult for bondmen to initiate and preserve monogamous relationships slave sources show that slave men were as solicitous as they could be toward their women. There were men like Charles, a slave of President James Polk, who was suspected of running from Polk's Mississippi plantation to be with his wife on Polk's Tennessee estate.[20] There were

men like Sam, Debby's husband, who eternally teased yet
delighted his wife.[21] There were men like the slave of William
Black, who when put on the auction block pleaded with pro-
spective buyers to purchase himself, his wife, and his daughter as a family.[22] There were men like Anderson, Romeo, Pete,
Archy, and Gery who took their wives with them when, in
1864, they fled the Bayside Plantation in Louisiana for the
Yankee lines.[23] There were free black men who purchased
their wives and children from slavery, and some who would
have had their spouse's owner been willing.[24]

Although the preponderance of male-authored sources
makes the slave woman's feeling on this subject more difficult
to gauge, when love and respect were tendered by bonded
men, bondwomen usually returned it. When they were happy
with a relationship slave women did all within their limited
power to sustain it. Matilda Pugh Daniel of Alabama was married to Joe in the master's parlor and wore one of her mistress's dresses to the wedding. Daniel was grateful to her
mistress for keeping her as a house servant but after the war
when Miss Sara wanted her to go to Washington with her as
a paid housemaid, Daniel declined because, as she put it, "I
couldn't leave my ole man, Joe."[25] Susan and Ersey, slaves
belonging to proslavery novelist Nathaniel Tucker, did not
want to leave their husbands, either. They were devastated
when they heard that they might be forced to leave their mates
in St. Louis, Missouri, for a plantation in Texas. They begged
Tucker to reconsider his plans, claiming that "to be separated
from our husbands forever in this world would make us
unhappy for life."[26]

When slave owners separated slave spouses, women took
it just as hard as men. In a Richmond, Virginia, slave market
a bondwoman who had just recently been separated from her
husband told Frederick Olmsted that when her master took
her from him "my heart was a'most broke."[27] To keep her
heart from breaking, Julia, a slave of a Virginia man named

Freeland, fled Richmond with her husband. Julia was a house servant who was never allowed to be with her husband. Rather than submit to the separation demanded by Freeland she ran away.[28] However, Molly, a St. Simon's Island slave, was not so fortunate. Molly's husband was sold as a punishment for his repeated efforts to run away. Molly was given a new husband named Tony, with whom she had nine children and two miscarriages. When Molly introduced herself to Frances Kemble in 1839, she told Kemble that she was married to Tony but claimed that Tony "was not her *real* husband." In Molly's heart her *real* husband was the man sold away by their master eleven pregnancies ago.[29]

Molly's case prompts a close look at the statistics on slave marriages. Herbert Gutman's data show that slave marriages survived all sorts of problems, and that, contrary to conventional wisdom, separation of slave couples through sale was not universal. In North Carolina, for instance, he found that many former slaves registering continuing marriages at the end of the Civil War had been married for long periods. The registration records of 14 percent of North Carolina's entire adult slave population were available for scrutiny and, of those former slaves registering marriages in 1866, 25 percent had lived with their spouse between ten and nineteen years and a little over 20 percent had been together for twenty years. In Mississippi there was much evidence that slave marriages had often been disrupted by sale. Still, given the circumstances, slave unions proved to be remarkably long-lived. Among the registrants, 1,842 men and 1,911 women indicated the length of their earlier marriages. At least half of those aged twenty years or more reporting a terminated marriage in 1864–65 had lived with a spouse for a minimum of five years. According to Gutman, just over one in four men and women aged twenty to twenty-nine had been married between five and fourteen years. The older the slave the longer the marriage. Gutman also found evidence of long slave marriages in Virginia, the District of Columbia, South Carolina, and Louisiana.[30]

Statistics on long-lived slave marriages must be approached with caution. The length of a slave marriage does not necessarily indicate how voluntary it was, nor the circumstances under which it occurred. The St. Simon's Island woman, Molly, was "married" to Tony for at least nine years but still did not consider him her real husband. We can not possibly know how many slave women were like Molly but clearly slave owners were not above assigning slave women husbands. By itself the length of slave marriages also provides no indication that they were founded on romance. Slave romances existed, and courtship was one of the rites slave masters could not eliminate, if indeed they ever wanted to. However, for every marriage that was anchored in romantic love there was probably one that grew out of pragmatic considerations. Fannie's master, Ned Eppes of Florida, was going to sell Fannie to her husband's owner so that Fannie and her husband, Essex, would not be separated when Essex's master moved to Mississippi from Florida. Fannie, however, absolutely refused to go with her husband, preferring to stay with her mistress, the woman who had previously purchased her from a cruel owner. Fannie's experience with a mean master had taught her a lesson she took to heart: "I knows . . . dat it's mighty easy ter git a good husband, an' mighty hard ter git a good mistis." Fannie soon remarried, and when asked what she saw in her new husband, Henry Fort, Fannie replied: "Lord, . . . I knows Henry is might unlacky lookin' . . . but I needs somebody ter chop light 'ud splinters."[31] Jane, a slave whom Elizabeth Botume met in the Sea Islands, also married for utilitarian reasons. Botume wanted to know why Jane married so soon after her first husband, Martin, had been sold away. Jane explained: "You see, ma'am, w'en I come here I had no one to help me."[32] Men, it seems, were no more, nor less, practical. When Botume met Smart, his wife, Mary, had been dead for two months, hardly long enough, in Botume's opinion, to begin thinking about remarriage. Smart wanted to marry again though, and when Botume suggested he wait a while longer he proclaimed that he could not "live so." "I t'inks, ma'am, I mus' have some gal come to stay wid me an' keep my house."[33]

If statistics on long marriages are silent on the issues of voluntarism and romance they also do not address the question of marital disputes. Harmony did not always prevail in slave households. Aunt Rachel refused to tell her Louisiana master, Tolas Parsons, how she received the knot on her forehead, but that did not alter the fact that her husband, Jim, had hit her on the head with a poker.[34] Demps hit his wife, Hetty, before he locked her up to prevent her from participating in the 1838 New Year's parties on Bennet Barrow's Louisiana plantation.[35] Women, it seems, were no match for men in hand-to-hand combat but they might grab whatever weapon was available in the heat of an argument. During her visit to America, Harriet Martineau was told of a slave woman who, in a fit of jealousy, threw an ax at her husband and nearly killed him. The husband remained in a state of considerable anxiety until his wife died.[36]

Verbal aggression between slave spouses was not uncommon, and some women did not mince words in expressing their feelings. Years after slavery ended Susan Snow remembered that her mother was "wild and mean" and that her kind and gentle father was often the object of her mother's abuse; she was frequently heard to say "I can't tolerate you if you ain't got no backbone."[37] According to an Alabama woman, men often resorted to an antidote for verbal abuse called "hush water." It was "jes plain water what dey fixed so if you drink it you would be quiet an' patient. De mens would get it to give dey wives to make 'em hush up."[38]

Many a lovers' quarrel was precipitated by suspected infidelity. Mary Whitaker, a slave of James Chesnut, had a trying temper that her husband Jeems managed to tolerate until the

day she gave birth to twins. Since no one in his family had
ever had twins he was sure that the children were not his and
he threw Mary out of their cabin.[39] A few quarrels had tragic
endings. In 1848 a North Carolina slave was sentenced to death
for murdering the black man he suspected of seeing his wife.
The victim, also a slave, was beaten to death on the head with
an iron rod. Testimony revealed that the defendant often got
drunk, and on the evening when he committed the murder,
his wife, fearful of abuse at his hands, had fled from their
cabin to the victim's.[40]

Information on the abuse some female slaves suffered at
the hands of slave men is likely to remain elusive. While there
were slave women raped by black men, this abuse is overshad-
owed by white male exploitation of black women, and it is
overlooked because it hardly ever turned up in court since
there was no legal injunction against it. When George, a Mississippi slave, was convicted and sentenced to death in 1859
for the rape of a ten-year-old female slave, Judge Harris
reversed the decision and released George. According to Harris
the original indictment could not be sustained under common law or under the statutes of Mississippi because "it charges
no offence known to either system. . . . There is no act which
embraces either the attempted or actual commission of a rape
by a slave on a female slave."[41] A Tennessee judge made this
latter point when he remanded a slave named Grandison to
jail for attempting to rape a white woman named Mary Douglass. According to Judge Green, what gave "the offense its
enormity" was the fact that Douglass was white. "Such an act
committed on a *black woman,* would not," he noted, "be punished with death." In 1860, the Mississippi state legislature
passed an act making it a crime, punishable by death or whipping, for a black man to rape or attempt to rape a black female
under twelve years old.[42] Because the black female had to be
so young in order to have a black perpetrator punished, this

exception proved the rule of black female vulnerability to rape by black men.

This discussion of aggression, abuse, and disputes between slave men and women in no way suggests that the slave family, even those born of practicality, was not important to slaves. The family helped slaves resist total dependence on slave owners because it helped socialize bonded children, gave slaves familial roles to play, and thus enabled slaves to create an identity that went beyond that assigned by whites. Few definitive statements can be made about the slave woman's self-concept because they were an amorphous group. Yet, more than likely, it was not dissociated from the roles they played in slave families and the slave community nor was it dissociated from the harsh realities slavery imposed on them. The self-concept of the individual slave woman may be lost to us forever, but we should at least explore how certain variables affected their collective consciousness.

The nature of plantation life required that marital relationships allow slave women a large degree of autonomy. Marriage did not bring the traditional benefits to female slaves. As we have seen, slave women could not depend on their husbands for protection against whippings or sexual exploitation. Slave couples had no property to share, and essential needs like food, clothing, and shelter were not provided by slave husbands. Thus slave men could not use the provision of subsistence goods as leverage in the exercise of authority over women. In almost all societies where men consistently dominate women, their control is based on male ownership and distribution of property and/or control of certain culturally valued subsistence goods.[43] The absence of such mechanisms in slave society probably contributed to female slave independence from slave men.

The practice of marrying abroad could only have reinforced this tendency. As a South Carolina preacher who once was a slave explained: "There was two kinds of marriage, one was marrying at home and the other was called marrying abroad. . . . If a man married abroad it meant that he wouldn't see his wife [but] only about once a week."[44] The frequency of her husband's visits, however, was entirely dependent on the distance between plantations and on the disposition of masters, many of whom frowned on such marriages. Robert Shipherd, of Athens, Georgia, noted that men were allowed to see their wives on Wednesday and Saturday nights. "If it was a long piece off," he added, "he didn't git dar so often."[45] A Mississippi slave with a wife who lived twenty miles away left his plantation at twelve o'clock on Saturday and was allowed to spend the weekend with her.[46] On the other hand, Susan McIntosh of Georgia virtually grew up without her father, whom she saw only once or twice a month.[47]

Although an abroad marriage had its problems, many couples preferred this arrangement. Jealousies and suspicions were harder to deal with at a distance but spouses were also spared the misery of witnessing each other's abuse.[48] Fugitive slave John Anderson had a wife on a distant plantation but he wanted it that way because he could not bear to see her ill-treated.[49]

Abroad marriages usually contributed to the independence of women from their husbands. If men were not always present to fall back on, women were compelled to develop methods of dealing with domestic responsibilities and crises. Usually women who were separated from their spouses got along without outside help, or they relied on relatives and females who had similar problems and needs. When women depended mostly on other women, female solidarity usually increased while husbands and other men lost much of their control over the women involved.[50]

Whether or not she was half of an abroad relationship, the bonded women had to have a finely tuned instinct for survival. Her husband could at any time be sold away from her.

She herself might be sold to a plantation far from familiar male and female support. Whatever else slavery demanded of bondwomen, it forced them to develop instincts that ran counter to overdependence on any one individual.

Many bondwomen demonstrated their survival instincts by supplementing the food given their families by slave masters. So much has been made of the activities of slave men in this sphere that the role of slave women has been overlooked. Contemporary historians, including John Blassingame, Eugene Genovese, Robert Fogel, and Stanley Engerman, have emphasized the hunting and fishing done by men. "The slave who did such things for his family," wrote Blassingame, "gained not only the approbation of his wife, but he also gained status in the quarters."[51] According to Eugene Genovese, "The slaves would have suffered much more than many in fact did from malnutrition and the hidden hungers of nutritional deficiencies if the men had not taken the initiative to hunt and trap animals."[52] These things some men certainly did. But women, no less than men, also helped supplement the family diet.

Female house servants enjoyed special advantages. Sarah Fukke remembered that whenever the whites left the West Virginia plantation where she grew up the cook "had a habit of making cookies and handing them out to the slaves before the folks returned."[53] Linda Brent recalled that were it not for the food her grandmother, a house servant, gave her, she would have spent many a day hungry, working as a chambermaid for her South Carolina mistress.[54] Molly, the maid of Mary Chesnut, made no secret of the fact that she fed her children and other slave children in the Confederate politician's house. "Dey gets a little of all dat's going," she told Mrs. Chesnut.[55]

Women had other ways of providing for their families. Frederick Douglass remembered that his grandmother was not only a good nurse and "a capital hand at making nets for catching shad and herring," but she was "also somewhat famous for her good fortune in taking the fishes referred to."[56] Speaking of her mother, Eliza Overton of Missouri cited a specific incident that suggests she was both desperate and daring: "Many times we ran short of food so's one night mutuh went out to whar the hogs war. Mr. Coffman had so many hogs he didn't know how many he had. She had da water hot an' the hogs were a long ways from Mr. Coffman's house. So she hit a hog in de head with the ax an' killed it."[57] When circumstances demanded it, women even hunted. "My mamma could hunt good es any man," claimed Betty Brown of Arkansas. "She'd have 'coon hides n' deer n' mink, n' beavers, lawd."[58] Thus, without diminishing the male slave's role in procuring extra provisions for his family, it is important to understand that this was a shared responsibility and a further demonstration of female slave ingenuity and resourcefulness.

These attributes probably affected the way slave "divorce" was handled. Some slave women were indifferent to many of the concerns that plagued free women who pondered divorce. When James Redpath asked a slave woman why she had left her husband for another man she replied, "I didn't like him, and I neber did."[59] Another woman, whose husband preferred parties to prayer meetings, informed her owner that she had no objection to being taken into the country and separated from her husband.[60] Eophraim Beanland, one of James Polk's overseers, wanted to purchase the wife of his slave Caesar, so the two could live together on the same plantation. She, however, had different plans and informed Beanland that she was unwilling to join Caesar, who himself concluded that she had fallen out of love with him.[61] Some women left their husbands because their husbands abused them. A slave couple on George Noble Jones's Florida plantation provides a case in point. Rose refused to stay with her husband Renty "on account of his having so Many Children." It is not clear whether Rose was upset because Renty had children by other women while he was married to her, or whether he paid too much attention to children he had with a previous wife, but the two quarreled so much that the overseer was glad when they agreed to separate.[62] Yet another couple separated after a quarrel. When the husband had second thoughts and sought a reconciliation his wife would not take him back "cause he drawed back to hit her with a chair."[63]

Clearly the slave woman's set of restraints in matters of divorce was different from the free woman's. Slave marriages were not recognized by the courts, and slave women were not dependent on their husbands for food, shelter, or clothing. These legal and economic restraints did not keep slave women in a marriage. Nor do there appear to have been many social impediments. Slave community condemnation of slave marital separation is conspicuous by its absence from antebellum slave sources.[64] Slave owners did not always force married couples to stay together, either. In cases of incompatibility, most either gave up after unsuccessful efforts or never bothered at all.[65]

However, slave masters did make decisions affecting the bonded woman's concerns about divorce. Female slaves had to fear separation resulting from sale, and the possibility that they would have a new husband assigned to them. Beyond that a major impediment was the slave owner's concern about the realization of the full potential profit from a bonded woman of childbearing age. Given what we know to be true in this realm, if a woman of childbearing age who desired separation could find another mate with whom to have children, slave masters probably had little objection to her separation and remarriage. If she was beyond childbearing age there was probably no objection at all. If, however, the pool of eligible men was limited and the slave woman was not past childbearing, she was probably stuck.

Integrated with other information we have about female slaves, the manner in which women voluntarily separated from their husbands says something about female slave identity and about slave families. As noted previously, revisionist historians have had difficulty reconciling the slave woman's reality with Western cultural mores that dictate a subordinate familial role for women within the family. They have ignored the fact that slave women played important provider roles and that, short of brute force, bondmen lacked the leverage by which to impose subordinate status on their wives. The extensive female network has also gone unrecognized by those who have assumed that the slave woman's primary source of emotional support came from bonded men. Admittedly, part of the cultural bias that crept into the literature was aimed at countering negative images of slave women as unnaturally strong and domineering. However, the stark reality is that slave women were not sheltered from life's ugliness nor dependent on their men for subsistence goods and services. Their society did not discourage them from taking initiatives in the quest for survival. Slave women brought to the marriage relationship about as much as men and, by virtue of their ability to contribute resources to the family economy, they had as much influence in that family as men.[66] To the extent that slave owners made few decisions affecting her everyday marital life the slave woman had considerable autonomy within the slave marriage. This does not mean that she dominated her husband. It means that in her relationships with a lover or a husband she was an equal partner.

Therefore, slave families were unusually egalitarian. Equality could not have been based on sameness because, while slave men and women often did the same kinds of work and provided similar services, many jobs and responsibilities still belonged by definition to one sex or the other. This suggests that equality within the slave family was founded on complementary roles, roles that were different yet so critical to slave survival that they were of equal necessity. Support for these conclusions can be found in recent anthropological literature concerning societies—mainly among peasants—where non-formalized roles are extremely important. Whether the society under study is a Greek or Portuguese peasant village or an aboriginal group in Australia, it appears that women exert power equal to that of men when they are able to make substantial contributions to the economic health of the household, when social and economic segregation is such that each sex functions in its own domain, and when exclusion of one sex group from the domain of the other does not necessarily have negative implications for the excluded group.[67] Antebellum sources indicate that in terms of these criteria slave families were egalitarian.

Nevertheless, relationships between mother and child still superseded those between husband and wife. Slaveholder practices encouraged the primacy of the mother-child relationship, and in the mores of the slave community motherhood ranked above marriage. In fact, women in their role as mothers were the central figures in the nuclear slave family. Women earned for the slave family some security against sale and separation when they had and nurtured children. Mothers helped supplement the family diet, and they served as the critical information link when fathers were sold or ran away. By itself, the fact that slave society did not condemn "illegitimacy" indicates the centrality of the mother role, a role which was presumed legitimate independent of the father's or husband's role.[68]

It may seem that we have come back full circle to the conclusions of black sociologist and historian E. Franklin Frazier, who was among the first to point out the central role slave women played in slave families. But in fact we have come only halfway. When Frazier wrote that slave women were self-reliant and that they were strangers to male slave authority he evoked an image of a domineering woman. The effect of his conclusions was to malign slave women for struggling to pull their families together. Yet, slave women did what American pioneer women did on the frontier: they mustered their reserves, persevered, and helped others survive. What black women did was very much in the pattern of their female African ancestors who had for generations stood at the center of the African family. Slave women did not dominate slave marriage and family relationships; they did what women all over the world have done and been taught to do from time immemorial. Acting out a very traditional role, they made themselves a real bulwark against the destruction of the slave family's integrity.

CHAPTER SIX

From Slavery to Freedom

"... and ar'n't I a woman?"[1]

IN OCTOBER 1858 Sojourner Truth gave a series of lectures in Silver Lake, Indiana, on the abolition of slavery. During the course of the talks a rumor circulated in the audience that Truth was actually a man posing as a woman. At her final talk, a man from the audience challenged her to prove the rumor false by having her breasts examined by some of the women present. When his challenge was put to a vote it passed with such a resounding "aye" that a "nay" vote was not even called for. Many of the women in the audience were appalled by the demand, but Truth herself appeared undaunted. She told the men that her breasts had suckled many a white babe, to the exclusion of her own offspring, and that many of these babies had grown to be better men than those in the audience. From her place in front of the congregation Sojourner Truth bared her breasts and told the men that it was not to her shame that she did so but to theirs.[2]

Truth's experience serves as a metaphor for the slave

woman's general experience. To the question "Ar'n't I a woman?" the Silver Lake audience answered "No." It was an answer given daily to the millions of enslaved women who worked on Southern plantations. They were the only women in America who were sexually exploited with impunity, stripped and whipped with a lash, and worked like oxen. In the nineteenth century, when the nation was preoccupied with keeping women in the home and protecting them, only enslaved women were so totally unprotected by men or by law. Only black women had their womanhood so totally denied.

The Civil War soon stirred hopes of freedom, however, and emancipation promised change. Black women knew what freedom meant. It meant not working for white men who could beat and rape them. It meant being able to raise and care for their families, especially their children, away from abusive white masters, mistresses, and overseers. Freedom meant moving around at will and owning one's own labor. It meant being able to do, act, dress, and say what one wanted, and above all it meant having the protection of law. Like freedmen, freedwomen wanted literacy, and they wanted land. In short, they wanted all the rights of citizenship, and the right to define themselves as women on their own terms.

The Civil War had barely begun, though, before enslaved women learned the same lesson Sojourner Truth learned in Silver Lake. The nation was not prepared to respect their citizenship, much less their womanhood. During the war and after, they endured incredible hardship. They were targets of brutality, the butt of jokes and ridicule, and their womanhood was denied over and over. It was a struggle just to stay free, and an even greater struggle to define womanhood. And yet slavery had prepared them for this contest. They had not survived enslavement to succumb to freedom. The strategies devised under slavery became the blueprint for life in freedom.

The shots that marked the opening of the Civil War on April 14, 1861, had different meaning for blacks and whites. Southern whites heard the cannon fire as a call to arms to defend slavery, the foundation of their distinctive "civilization" and the domestic institution around which their states' rights ideology congealed. At stake for most Northern whites was the preservation of a government they thought the world's best at protecting property and elevating the condition of man. For a year and a half after the start of the war Lincoln held fast to this position—that the war was necessary to preserve the Union. He had no "lawful right" to interfere with slavery where it existed, he declared during his first inaugural address, and "no inclination to do so."[3]

Unlike white Americans, black people were of one mind regarding the war. Though disappointed by Lincoln's determination to preserve slavery, free and enslaved African-Americans cheered the firing on Fort Sumter as the beginning of the end of bondage. One African-American complained, "Our union friends say the[y] are not fighting to free negroes. . . . we are fighting for the union. . . . very well let the white fight for what the[y] want and we negroes fight for what we want." Of course, what they wanted was freedom. In Mississippi, when a young domestic slave named Dora Franks overheard whites talking about the war, she "started praying for freedom" and reported that "all the rest of de women did the same thing."[4]

And indeed, enslaved women had a lot to pray for. Just as they had had difficulty running away during slavery, women and children found it hard to accompany the men that were impressed into, or escaped to the Union army. As men left, women's work expanded and they did more "men's work" than ever before. Like the Sea Island women noted in chapter 4, throughout the war women all over the South managed all aspects of cotton production and plantation maintenance without male help.[5] Even teenage girls found themselves doing extremely heavy labor. One recalled that she "plowed a mule an' a wild un at dat." Her hands got so cold that she "jes' cry."[6]

Life on the plantation also got dangerous. Union soldiers were unpredictable and unsympathetic to blacks, who they blamed for the war. Hardly eager liberators, they left both blacks and whites homeless and hungry when they destroyed plantation property, raided both the big house and slave quarters for food and supplies, and seized black men for involuntary service in the Union army.[7] "Us all thought de Yankees was some kin' of debils an' we was skeered to death of 'em," recalled Mollie Williams, who was just a child during the war.[8] Indeed they had reason to be. Sam Word's mother met her first Yankee soldier as he was in the process of stealing her quilts, walking out of the yard with them. "Why, you nasty, stinking rascal," she shouted, "you say you come down here to fight for the niggers, and now you're stealing from 'em." His response no doubt reflected the feelings of most white Union soldiers, especially those who were drafted. "You're a goddamm liar," he retorted, "I'm fighting for $14 a month and the Union."[9]

Women, in fact, had as much to fear of Union soldiers as they did of Confederates. The soldiers "insult women both white and black," reported elderly ex-slave Eliza Handy.[10] Usually they did more than that. Nearly everywhere the Union army left a trail of violence against black women and the men who tried to protect them. In Fortress Monroe, Virginia, two soldiers seized the father and son-in-law of a slave woman while two others raped her. Another black woman was raped "after a desperate struggle" in the "presence of her father and grandfather."[11] On the Jenkins plantation in the South Carolina Sea Islands, after Union soldiers burned ten slave cabins, robbed its residents of food and fowl, furniture, and cooking utensils, they tried to rape the slave women. When husbands and brothers tried to protect them the men were cruelly beaten and threatened with instant death.[12] Some women, like "old Mom Rosetta," escaped rape by a gang of Union soldiers by disguising herself as a sick, old, disabled woman. A Haines Bluff, Mississippi, woman who was raped by a white Union Army cavalryman in front of her grandchildren was not so fortunate.[13]

As much as women feared Union soldiers, Southern whites

still proved their most ardent enemies. Women whose menfolk had fled to Union lines were particularly vulnerable to the vengeance of anguished white men and women who saw their way of life slipping away. Frances Johnson was a Kentucky slave whose husband joined the army. She reported that in 1864 her master had told her "all the 'niggers' did mighty wrong in joining the Army." Her master had his son whip and kick her for refusing to do work she was unable to perform.[14] In Missouri, an enslaved woman wrote her soldier husband that "you do not know how bad I am treated. They are treating me worse and worse every day."[15]

But clearly, risks had to be taken if freedom was to be won. Rather than wait until the end of the war to be liberated, black people liberated themselves. From the beginning of the conflict they refused to do certain kinds of work and argued over matters of discipline and the management of the plantation.[16] "The negroes seem very unwilling to work," a young white woman confided to her journal, as men, women, and children slowed their work pace to a crawl.[17] They left weeds in the cotton fields, burned the food they cooked for whites, and let the cows trample the corn.[18] When a slave owner greeted one of his workers with "Howdy, Uncle," the indignant slave responded, "Call me Mister."[19]

Whenever the opportunity arose, slaves left—women less easily than men—but women whenever they could. Despite their misgivings about Union soldiers, most fled to Union army lines. Naturally, African-Americans expected to be freed once they reached Mr. Lincoln's army. But at the beginning of the war neither Lincoln nor the army were inclined to make the war a fight against slavery. Northern soldiers actually returned fleeing blacks to their masters, and when Union generals issued orders freeing all slaves in territories under their command, Lincoln overrode them.[20] The sheer numbers of escaping slaves, however, forced a reconsideration of army policy.[21] In 1861, General Butler, stationed in Virginia, declared escaping slaves "contraband"—property taken during war—and allowed them to stay with the army. That same year Congress passed the first Confiscation Act, which kept slave owners from reenslaving runaways. In March 1862, Congress passed a law forbidding Union soldiers from returning escaped slaves, and four months later, it passed the second Confiscation Act, which more broadly freed the slaves of any master helping the Confederacy.[22]

Once escaping slaves had forced the issue on liberation, the army faced the practical problem of housing and caring for thousands of liberated African-Americans. They put men to work as drivers, cooks, blacksmiths, and construction workers.[23] Men also served as soldiers. Once the Union army changed its policy in July 1862 by allowing blacks into the Union army, more than 93,000 black men from the Confederate states, or 14 percent of the black male population aged eighteen to forty-five, served as soldiers.[24] These men wanted to fight for freedom, but they were justifiably concerned that slaveowners would take revenge on the women and children they left behind. Some, therefore, had to be wrenched involuntarily from their families. Others volunteered and brought their loved ones with them. As still other women with children fled plantations for Union lines, the army faced an unprecedented problem of caring for women and children in war zones.

It "solved" the problem by housing women, and men who were unable to serve, in contraband camps behind Union lines, and by putting them to work as wage-laborers on Union-controlled plantations. For black women, the living conditions might not be better than on their old plantation. The camps were crowded and often lacked food, shelter, and medicine.[25] Historian Jacqueline Jones found that the camps offered little in the way of refuge from abuse and callousness. Black women were denounced as prostitutes and "idle lazy vagrants" by military officials. Although some found jobs as cooks and laundresses in and around the camps, gainful employment was unavailable, and most were forced to live in wretched conditions throughout the war. Life could be made even more intolerable by Union soldiers. At Camp Nelson, Kentucky, in late 1864, while the black men of the camp were on the battlefield fighting Confederates, white soldiers leveled the makeshift shantytown erected by black women to house their children and left four hundred people homeless in bitterly cold weather.[26]

Women who worked as free laborers on Northern-controlled plantations fared little better. They were supposed to be paid, but they often received low wages and sometimes got no compensation at all. Food and clothing were usually in short supply, and women were charged for their food and that of their children. Northern plantation managers had pledged not to whip or use physical punishment against former slaves, but reminiscent of slavery, labor contracts often required women to get permission and a pass to leave the plantation. Worse still were the Confederate soldiers who reenslaved captured workers.[27]

Early on, escaping slaves could not be sure of the future, but as the war dragged on, especially after Lincoln's September 1862 Emancipation Proclamation, the conflict turned into a war against slavery, and blacks escaped in droves. Their owners felt betrayed. As often as enslavers had heard the words to spirituals like "Steal Away" and "Go Down, Moses," they had never let themselves believe the songs to be more than the innocent chants of contented inferiors. Few realized that the songs expressed a heartfelt yearning for earthly freedom, that black people really meant it when they sang "Let my people go." As some of the most "trusted" slaves left, and as the masks fell off the faces of those who remained, African-Americans forced masters and mistresses to confront the traumatic reality that white people had not been benevolent civilizers, and that black subservience and faithfulness had been the product of white power and imagination.

Most shattering to slaveowners during and immediately after the war was the departure of women they had thought of "like one of the family"[28]—their black "mammies." In Virginia, Aunt

Polly, a long-time family favorite for whose services her master said he could set no price, left as soon as she heard Northern troops in the distance.[29] During the war, Eliza Andrews confided to her diary that so many blacks had turned into Yankee spies that even Mammy could not be trusted.[30] Andrews was as distressed as North Carolinian Catherine Edmundson. She could not understand why Fanny, a confidante who had nursed her in "the most devoted and affectionate manner," who during a long sickness actually "wept over me," abandoned her "without provocation or reason" and "without the slightest notice."[31]

Other trusted slaves left, including the men who served as house slaves and drivers, but Mammy's leaving had special significance. As we have seen, Mammy personified the ideal slave and the ideal woman, the centerpiece in the antebellum Southerner's perception of the perfectly organized society. She was at once black and female, and thus in reality and mythology was subservient to white men.[32] For men whose honor and manhood ultimately depended on their ability to control women and slaves, Mammy's leaving was just as surely as emasculating as defeat on the battlefield. More significant, even though few black house servants had been what masters and mistresses perceived them to be, many of the women *had been experienced* as surrogate mothers. For white men and women who had never questioned their black maid's devotion—even maternal love—Mammy's departure was felt as deeply as a mother's abandonment or rejection. This Florida woman's diary reveals an unbearable anguish:

> I hardly know how to tell it, my dear black Mammy has left us. . . . I feel lost, I feel as if someone is dead in the house. Whatever will I do without my Mammy? When she was going she stopped on the doorstep and, shaking her fist at Mother [with whom she had had an altercation], she said: I'll miss you—the Lord knows I'll miss you—but you'll miss me, too—you see if you don't.[33]

Prophetic words, for like a child who has lost a mother, the South hardly knew how to manage without its eternally loyal, nurturing, and humble Mammy. Southerners had created this icon as proof to themselves and the world that slavery was benign, that its regenerative powers could domesticate Jezebel. Before the Civil War slaveowners had held the naked power to make their fantasy mother a reality for themselves. Emancipation shattered the fantasy and slammed them into a world full of fist-shaking women walking out on them. As buffers between themselves and the black female world came tumbling down, white men and women faced a black woman they did not recognize. Similar to Jezebel, this new antithesis to Mammy seemed menacing and threatening. So aggressive in defense of her freedom, she hardly seemed a woman. In reality she was a new African-American citizen who had dreamed about freedom and who was now intent on making her dreams come true. But to Southerners she was too resourceful and brazen. As Sojourner Truth had been to the audience at Silver Lake, she was too much like a man to have breasts. It was inevitable that slavery's demise would explode the Mammy myth; it was tragic that black women had to start their new lives in a society mourning the passing of the archetype whose very title grew from that part of the body whites believed black women had lost.

But start their freedom they did. What to black women was proof of a new status was to whites evidence of a demon let loose. They could not, for example, understand that black people needed to test their freedom by moving around. For all African-Americans a real mark of liberty was to come and go at will—without white permission, without a pass, without fear of dogs on their trail. Black women had been especially confined by slavery[34] and few passed up the right to move. They were like the South Carolina woman who left her position as cook and traveled only a short distance to do the same work—now for wages—for a different white family. Her former enslavers offered her twice what her new employers were paying, but to their chagrin she opted to go. When pressed for an explanation, she was direct and purposeful: "I must go," she said. "If I stay here I'll never know I am free."[35]

Like black men, black women used their newfound mobility to search for loved ones separated by force. Many elicited help from the Freedman's Bureau, established by Congress in 1865 to help freedpeople make the transition from slavery to freedom.[36] Francis Bell, for example, wrote the bureau asking about her children because she had "great anxiety regarding their welfare." Peggy Kelly also wrote requesting information about her parents, sisters, and brothers: "Any information given of any of the whereabouts of them will be thankfully rec'd. Let me know if they are dead or alive," she pleaded.[37] Tragically, many, like twenty-eight-year-old Martha Showvely, found their loved ones dead. Separated from her mother when she was only seven years old, she traveled to the county where her mother reportedly resided only to find that she had been dead for three years.[38] Equally tragic was the reunion of a mother with her eighteen-year-old daughter who had been torn from her in infancy. As she embraced her long lost baby she cried and pined over the marks on the child's body: "See how they've cut her up. From her head to her feet she is scarred just as you see her face."[39]

Even when parents knew their children's whereabouts, reunion was not always guaranteed. In what amounted to legal reenslavement, apprenticeship laws allowed whites to keep and employ black children under the age of twenty-one whose parents or relatives were deemed by a court to be either unfit or unable to be kept off the public dole.[40] As often as did men, women fought for custody of their children and other kin. Historian Leslie Schwalm found that women's struggles were complicated by stereotypical notions that black women were incompetent, if not abusive, mothers.[41] The notion that black women lacked maternal sense, especially potent now that black women could lavish attention on their own children rather than whites, made the black mother's actions appear sinister. In reality, countless black mothers risked life and limb rescuing their children. A South Carolina woman named Sue, for example, was beaten, then shot and killed at point-blank range by her former owner because she opposed his apprenticeship of her nephew. In another example, South Carolinian Susan Johnson, mother of three children, contracted for herself and her two oldest children a year's work at twenty-five dollars at the plantation of Elisha Durr. When Johnson found she could do better at a neighboring plantation, she returned to the Durrs, where she had left her children, only to have the Durrs threaten to set their dogs on her. First she took her complaint to the local Freedman's Bureau agent, who sent her to the local magistrate. When he dismissed her complaint as trivial and sent her back to the Durrs, she returned to the bureau and with the help of an armed guard got her children. Her persistent efforts cost her a year's wages and the money to travel between the bureau, the magistrate, and the Durrs. None of it was recovered.[42]

Black women faced other challenges, particularly when impressionable children were involved. The story of Franke Goole is a case in point. Goole had been raised by her mistress after her mother was sold away. She had slept in the same room with her mistress and was very attached to her. She was twelve when her mother came for her, but Goole was bewildered. When asked by a judge if the woman who claimed to be her mother was truly so, she replied: "I dunno, she sezs she ez." Reflecting back, years later, Goole recalled her confusion: "W'at did I know ob a mammy dat wuz tuk fum me at six weeks ole."[43] Cases like this brought black and white women into direct conflict. Dispossessed of slavery's naked power, white women mixed meanness with their economic advantage to steal black children away from their mothers. Sarah Debro's mistress had taken Sarah as a house servant, and given her white sheets, clean clothes, and plenty to eat. When Sarah's mother came to get her after the war, Sarah and her white "mother" clung to each other, neither wanting to give the other up. Despite the mistress's pleas and Sarah's wailing, Sarah's mother was resolute. Tearing her daughter from the mistress's arms she reminded the white woman of her cruelty: "You took her away from me an' didn' pay no mind to my cryin', so now I'se

takin' her back home. We's free now, Mis' Polly, we ain't gwine be
slaves no more to nobody." While Sarah followed her mother
and traded her clean sheets and comfortable accommodations
for a straw mattress and a broken-down cabin, others, like Lizzie
Hill, ran away three times from her mother, returning to the
Alabama mistress who had given her the same food and clothes
as the white children.[44]

As much as black women demanded the rights of motherhood, they also insisted on the right to redefine their work. This
too put them at odds with whites intent on reinstating black subservience. As Leslie Schwalm has brilliantly demonstrated, black
women sought a new level of dignity as wage earners. Women
hired as field workers refused to do "double duty," or domestic
production—work like spinning and weaving, butchering and
preserving meat—for their white employers. To make this point,
women on one of the Allston plantations in South Carolina put
an end to after-harvest wool production by slaughtering and eating the sheep.[45] Freedwomen also rejected particularly demean-
ing work like washing white women's menstrual rags, and especially arduous work like ditch digging and repair in knee-deep
mud.[46] In defining their new status as free workers, women and
men rejected slavery's brutal hours and refused to work under
former drivers and overseers. By taking their children with them
and caring for them during the workday, household workers
avoided the slavelike conditions that kept them separated from
their children for long hours. Domestic workers also broke down
domestic tasks into specific chores so that their work would not
be so overwhelming. Hagar, for example, would clean but would
not do laundry nor beat mattresses. When women did not get
their way they quit and sold their labor somewhere else.
Sometimes they resorted to work slowdowns and stoppages. In
1866, for example, the "colored washerwomen" of Jackson,
Mississippi, organized themselves, established a price code for
their services, and threatened to fine women who violated the
code.[47] The strike underscored black women's determination to

define their freedom. Predictably, it fueled white anger and resentment.[48]

So too did black women's expressions of femininity. During slavery, they had been forced to wear dirty and tattered clothing, subjected to indecent examinations, and sexually exploited. In truth, they could not even claim their sexual organs as their own. With emancipation they reclaimed their bodies, pampered and adorned them. With freedom black women did what Gus Feaster remembered they did only on Sundays and special occasions— they came out "in starch dresses," "took their hair down outen the strings," and "pulled off the head rags."[49] Sometimes the starched dresses had been taken from white mistresses who had abandoned their homes and possessions when Union troops conquered an area. Of course, it infuriated white women to see black women in dresses once theirs, but they were equally galled to see black women in their own spruced-up modest attire, women who refused to bow or pay deference to white people. At the heart of it was black appropriation of the trappings that had for centuries been the exclusive mark of white femininity. Emma Holmes, a white woman of Camden, South Carolina, could not bear to see blacks dressed in "round hats, gloves and even lace veils." This twenty-six-year-old thought that freedwomen would do better to adopt "a plain, neat dress for the working classes, as in other countries, and indeed among our country negroes formerly." Rather than hats and veils, she thought black women looked better in "the respectable and becoming handkerchief turban."[50] This preference put Holmes in direct opposition to African-American women who now openly rejected the appellations "Aunt" or "Mammy," and claimed the long-denied "Miss" and "Mrs." Such was the case with a young female whose master called her a "nigger." "I ain't no nigger," she replied. "I'se a Negro and I'm Miss Liza Mixon."[51]

Such dignity carried a price. Like black men, women were ridiculed and scorned, murdered and terrorized for exercising their rights. White Southerners wanted them back in their fields and kitchens; they wanted their Jezebels and their Mammies, and they would beat, rape, and kill to turn back the clock. As Catherine Clinton, Laura Edwards, Eric Foner, Leon Litwack, Leslie Schwalm, and others have argued, black women's gender did not protect them from white terror. Mixon's master chased her with a switch, but others did much worse. Angered by Hagar Barnwell's threat to leave the plantation rather than work in his kitchen, her former master took Hagar to a shed at pistol point and strung her up by her thumbs so that her feet barely touched the ground.[52] Another planter similarly brutalized a pregnant woman named Sarah. As a consequence of being suspended for two hours, Sarah delivered a stillborn child, and those who reported the crime to a Freedman's Bureau agent did not expect her to live. Sarah's crime? To visit someone on the planter's property "against orders."[53] Margaret Martin of Athens, Georgia, also suffered greatly for moving around at will. In 1868, when Martin returned to her plantation from a visit to her niece she was "badly beaten and choked" by her employer.[54] As harrowing as the experience must have been, Martin was luckier than George Band's wife, who was hung to a tree and hacked to death with knives.[55]

Historian Catherine Clinton has argued that such violence escalated in the postwar era because emancipation removed the landowners' economic motivation to keep their workers alive and healthy.[56] Her observations seem confirmed by the sheer barbarity of the crimes. For example, when Rhoda Childs and her husband tried to keep their share of the crop they had farmed for the better part of a year, white men took Childs, threw her to the ground, and raped her: "One of the two men stood upon my breast, while two others took hold of my feet and stretched my limbs as far apart as they could while the man standing upon my breast applied the strap to my private parts until they were satisfied that I was more dead than alive. Then a man supposed to be an ex-confederate soldier, as he was on crutches, fell upon me and ravished me. During the whipping one of the men had run his pistol into me, and said he had a great mind to pull the trigger."[57] Childs escaped with her life, but Jane Twyman, of Culpepper County, Virginia, was shot and killed by her employer, Isiah Perry. Twyman was tortured and murdered because she accused Perry's wife and daughter of sleeping with other men. When Isiah Perry heard the accusation, he grabbed his gun, confronted Twyman, and shot her as she fled his house. Perry later apologized to Twyman, saying that he only wanted to scare her. But while the bullet was being removed, Perry's son pistol-whipped and "stomped" Twyman to death.[58] In yet another tormenting episode, Sarah Barnett, of Granville County, North Carolina, was shot in the shoulder by Richard Pines for defending herself when Pines's wife hit her with a stick. Barnett, "bathed in her own blood," was convicted of assaulting a white woman and fined forty dollars. Unable to pay the fine she was imprisoned in the county jail.[59]

Barnett's case reveals that black women, like black men, could expect no justice in a court of law, nor could they look to authorities for protection. For example, when Patience Thompson took her case against Thomas Gross, a white man, to court for beating her after she refused to sell him soap, the court forced *her* to pay court costs and told *her* to "make up" with him.[60] In Richmond, Virginia, "the most likely looking negro women" were regularly rounded up, "thrown into cells, robbed and ravished at the will of the guard." The people in the vicinity of the jail testified "to hearing women scream frightfully almost every night."[61] And in July of 1866, in Clinch County, Georgia, a black woman was arrested and given sixty-five lashes for addressing a white woman with abusive language. A month later Viney Scarlett, another black woman, was similarly arrested, tried, fined sixteen dollars, and given sixty lashes for the same "offense."[62]

How do we explain this relentless assault upon black women? The Clinch County magistrates made it clear that emancipation had not erased the perceived inequality of black and white women. In fact, the message the unmitigated violence delivered was that black women were not women at all. Freedom brought wage labor but no legal protection against exploitation. It gave black women their bodies back but brought no laws and courts that recognized the crime of murder or rape against them. Male relatives who tried to protect black women risked brutal beatings and even death. As during slavery, black women had to rely upon survival instincts that ran counter to dependence. They had to bargain for the best wage, aggressively resist white attempts to steal their children, and be strong-willed in negotiating the kind of house and field work they would and would not do. Still in need of strength for backbreaking field labor, they never knew when they would have to defend themselves against physical or sexual attack. In short, life still challenged them to a different kind of womanhood, nothing like that of white women.

This reality, however, escaped post–Civil War whites in whose minds the image of Sapphire congealed long before it got a name in the mid-twentieth century.[63] As a stereotype, Sapphire is a domineering female who consumes men and usurps their role. Her persona is not sexual but is as indomitable as Jezebel's and equally emasculating in effect. While Jezebel emasculates men by annulling their ability to resist her temptations, and thus her manipulations, Sapphire emasculates men by usurping their role. Her assertive demeanor identifies her with Mammy, but unlike Mammy she is devoid of maternal compassion and understanding. Sapphire is as tough, efficient, and tireless as Mammy. Mammy operates, however, within the boundaries prescribed for women, while Sapphire is firmly anchored in a man's world. This image helps explain attacks on black women. As Sapphires, black women were placed beyond the pale of womanhood and violated with impunity.

The demonization of black women forces a reinterpretation of African-American history that long ignored the brutalizing of black women while emphasizing the plight of black men.[64] Historian Elsa Barkley Brown has argued that such male-centeredness has led to the assumption that black women were violated less often and therefore were less threatening to whites than black men. This focus on men led naturally to an emphasis on lynching as *the* major form of racial violence and limited attention to black women who were lynched (at least fifteen between 1889 and 1898; at least seventy-six between 1882 and 1927).[65] Brown might have added that rape has very often been interpreted not as a violent crime but as the crime of emasculation against black men, preventing them from protecting their women. Closer attention to fact demonstrates that whites sought not only to emasculate black men but also to defeminize black women. In sum, the vast killing, maiming, and ridicule of black men *and* women, and the rape of black women, was designed to reenslave black people and neuter the race.

Clearly, freedom, then, demanded as much courage as had slavery. Indeed, the first years of freedom forced freedpeople to draw on the lessons learned in slavery. With all blacks under assault, both men and women had to be providers. Both had to protect their children, fight for their rights as citizens, and aggressively protect their bodies and the integrity of the black family. Women as much as men had to make shrewd and difficult choices, and as they did they reinterpreted the meaning of self-respecting womanhood.

One of the most difficult choices for married women was whether to legalize their marital relationships. This decision was fraught with as much jubilation as anxiety. Jubilation because they could now choose their husbands without slavemaster interference, consecrate their wedding vows in church, and have them recognized under law; agony because freedom required wrenching decisions. Like the exuberant mother of a large family who declared, "My husband and I have lived together fifteen years and we wants to be married over again now," thousands of black couples presented themselves to authorities to be married. Virginia Graves, a former house servant who had been given a broomstick ceremony and her mistress's cast-off wedding dress, rushed to formalize her relationship. "We had a real sho nuff' wedding' wid a preacher. Dat cost a dollar," she reported triumphantly.[66] Less expensive were the mass wedding ceremonies involving as many as seventy couples at a time.[67]

Whites might ridicule these marriages as all form and no substance, but decisions regarding marriage posed dilemmas that required depressing deliberation. So many husbands and wives had been separated that the first step was to find each other. The odds were against reuniting, but once together again former slaves faced a curious dilemma: which marriage should take precedence?[68] Numerous spouses had of course remarried since their forced separation. In one case, Nathan Williams, after nine years of marriage to Louisa, went away and married again, leaving her with a child and no means of support.[69] Louisa must have felt as horrible as another freedwoman who when queried about her husband, replied, "I had one . . . but he ran away one day with another woman. . . . Feel like it most killed me at first. I get over it now."[70] In freedom just as many couples rushed to legalize their relationship as took the opportunity to divorce. A case that epitomizes the various dilemmas involved Jane, a woman noted earlier.[71] When missionary Elizabeth Botume met Jane in the Sea Islands, Jane's former husband, Martin, had been sold away and she was currently married to Ferguson, not because she loved him but because, as she put it, "w'en I come her I had no one to help me."[72] Emancipation brought her true love Martin back into her life, and when asked what would happen to Ferguson, she replied: "Martin Barnwell is my husband, . . . I am got no husband but he. W'en de secesh sell him off we nebber 'spect to see each odder more. He said, 'Jane take good care of our boy, an' w'en we git to hebben us will lib togedder to nebber part no more." Ferguson knew of Jane's love for Martin, and when they married it was understood that if Martin came back "he would be my husband above all others." Martin did come back, and Jane remained faithful to her promise. When asked about her plans, she replied: "Martin is my husband, ma'am, an' the father of my child, and *Ferguson is a man.*" Ferguson pleaded for Jane: "Martin has not seen you for a long time. He *cannot* think of you as I do. O Jane! Do not go to Charleston. Come to Jacksonville. I will get a house and we will live here. Never mind what people say. Come to me Jane." Jane, however, chose Martin. To Ferguson, she dictated her response: "Tell him, I say I'm sorry he finds it so hard to do his duty. But as he does, I shall do mine, an' I shall always pray de Lord to bless him. . . . I shall never write to him no more. But tell him I wish him well."[73]

Some black women made the very calculated choice to live with a man out of wedlock. As historian Noralee Frankel has observed, some refused to marry because a new marriage would jeopardize the women's pension from the U.S. government. When Union soldiers died, whether during or after their service, their widows were entitled to a widow's pension of at least eight dollars a month. Federal laws forbade women who remarried or lived with a man from claiming a military pension. Many women, feeling they could more easily hide live-in arrangements than a formal marriage, did as Louisa Smith, who explained: "I have never married Speers because I understood that by marrying I would lose my right to pension."[74] For other women the considerations were different. Mary Nesbit married "to insure my honor," but Charlotte Washington refused to marry Frank Grant, whom she lived with for a year, because "he drank so much whiskey and was so no account I picked up and left him and never had anything to do with him after that."[75] Ellen Cooper's consideration was her ill sister. Her husband, Mingo, had secured employment in a distant town and wanted her to move with him. Ellen, however, stayed and nursed her ailing sister. While Regina Toney left James Bracey, her husband, and married another man, "because James didn't shew me proper respect—I heard he had another woman," Amy Deas preferred to cultivate her land on Edisto Island, rather than accompany her husband, Robert, back to the plantation where they had lived and worked as slaves.[76]

White people considered these relationship decisions haphazard, evidence of promiscuity; but black people, especially women, understood their gravity. Women could hardly ignore the attempts of the government, planters, and some black men to impose a patriarchal structure on the black family and the penalty they would pay for nonconformity. The Freedman's Bureau designated the husband as head of the black household and insisted that he sign contracts for the labor of the entire family. One example: a black man in Cuthbert, Georgia, was forced to sign a contract that promised he would "work faithfully and keep his wife in subjection."[77] Women lost all agency in this kind of arrangement. The Bureau also set wage scales that paid women less than men for identical plantation labor, and its agents sometimes doled out less land to families headed by women. Women were also treated unequally under the Southern Homestead Act of 1866. Its provisions allowed women to claim a portion of the public domain only if unmarried.[78] These policies amounted to an attempt to subordinate black women and make black families conform to the "proper" relationship between men and women.

Women who resisted were demonized, risking abuse and poverty. Motherhood now structured black women's freedom as it had differentiated their slavery. Single black women with children were among the poorest in the South. Indeed, as Jacqueline Jones and Catherine Clinton have argued, freedwomen with children found that economic necessity bred its own kind of slavery. Responsible for their own survival, they had to feed, shelter, and clothe children who were regarded by landowners as a liability. Some women wanted to farm without a male partner, but landowners were reluctant to hire them as farm hands or to rent land to them. "There is little call for female help, and women with children are not desired," reported a Freedman's Bureau agent from King Williams County, Virginia.[79] Discrimination against single women and especially single mothers forced women to work for pitiful wages and left them vulnerable to being run off the land before they got paid. In fact, the largest category of grievances initiated by black women under the

Freedman's Bureau "complaint" procedures concerned non-payment of wages.[80] In one Alabama county in 1867 the petitions for relief revealed almost 90 percent of the heads of households were women. Domestic workers who refused to leave their children at home were equally oppressed. Resenting the attention young children demanded from their mothers, employers preferred women without young children.[81]

The burden of sex discrimination fell heavily on black women who struggled to meet its challenges. Some single women were forced to work on the same plantation and work for their former masters as if slavery had not ended. Economic necessity forced others to enter utilitarian relationships with men they found compatible and helpful. Most former slave women eventually found some kind of work but on new terms. Significantly, they worked at least fourteen hundred hours less than they had during slavery.[82] Their partial withdrawal from field and domestic labor did not lead to lives of leisure. On the contrary, they still worked harder and longer than most women in the United States. Freedom, however, made the difference between always working for white people and sometimes working for themselves.

Working for themselves was crucial. By 1867 black people knew that their dreams of land ownership were dashed. President Andrew Johnson and most Americans were unwilling to confiscate land from ex-Confederates, and legislatures enacted laws that made it difficult, if not illegal, for African-Americans to purchase land. Property that might have been bought was gobbled up by Northern speculators before cash-poor ex-slaves could earn enough money to buy it. Rather than work for landowners who methodically cheated them out of wages after they had planted and harvested crops, freedpeople found working for a share of the crop preferable to working for cash. Sharecropping allowed ex-slaves to live on a rented plot in a family group, away from lecherous landowners and whip-wielding overseers. Where enslaved blacks had worked in gangs at a pace set by drivers, sharecropping families now worked as a unit with adult family members setting the pace and content of their own and their children's labor. Sharecropping carried an advantage and a disadvantage: it allowed black people to earn a living doing what they did best; conversely, it kept them in a never-ending cycle of debt to landowners and merchants who had advanced food, supplies, and equipment for a share of the family's meager crop. Since interest rates were usuriously high, and since neither landowners nor merchants had any interest in making black tenants independent, year after year black people worked for landowners without making a profit from their share of the crop.

According to historian Sharon Ann Holt, household production kept many African-Americans from being overwhelmed by the debilitating credit system.[83] Household or home-based production was work sharecroppers did for their family, not the landowner. Take the Clark and May families of Beaufort County, North Carolina. From 1880 to at least 1903, Elias Clark did contract work for Rufus W. Wharton, but his wife, Nicy, and their children worked for Wharton only at harvest time. At other times they worked directly for their own and their family's benefit. They earned extra wages, worked in the family crop, grew vegetables in the family garden, took in laundry, raised chickens, and produced baskets, shoes, hats, and clothing for use or sale. In 1889 Nicy Clark and her two daughters earned over eleven dollars from extra harvest-time labor. Elias also worked in the family crop whenever he could, and did extra wage work and hunting to increase the family's surplus resources.[84]

Rodin May had a similar arrangement with Wharton. He contracted to cultivate twelve acres, and like Elias, when time allowed, he did extra work for his family. His wife and four daughters, however, worked mostly for the family, laboring for Wharton only during harvest season.[85] Anderson Scales also counted on his wife's work for the family. While he ran a small hauling business in Madison, North Carolina, his wife and children worked on their "acre homestead" fertilizing soil, tending a vegetable garden and fruit trees, and taking in washing.[86]

As the family became the center of black women's lives, kinship networks replaced the female network as a source of strength and identity.[87] Women now did household work and quiltings with female relatives more than with unrelated women. Girls were now more likely to be socialized by their mothers, fathers, and other relatives than by the trash gangs found on large plantations. For North Carolinian Elizabeth Harris, life as a nine-year-old girl was a lot different than it would have been in slavery. Her mother worked in town as a full-time laundress and sent Elizabeth to the country to live with her grandparents. This relieved her of Elizabeth's care while she worked, and it added another laborer to her grandparents' household. Elizabeth sold the produce her literate grandfather grew in their garden, and in their spare time he tutored her. Elizabeth also helped her grandmother with the sewing and quilt-making. At her mother's house she cooked, cleaned, and took care of the house because, as she sensitively noted, after a week's work her mother "was too tired for these little extras."[88] Had Elizabeth grown up in slavery on a sizable plantation, she might have done the same chores. Perhaps she would have worked as hard, if not harder. But her early years would have been spent more in the company of unrelated females; these women might have been as loving and as interested in Elizabeth as her family. They could not, however, shelter her from abuse or plan for her future as her mother and grandparents now did.

The elevation of the family and breakup of the female network would seem to have helped establish patriarchy, reducing women's status. Some historians have argued that women's partial withdrawal from field work, the Freedman's Bureau's preferential treatment of men, and landowner policy of making men responsible for women's work, all indicate a new subordinate status for women in the black family and in black society at large.[89] Their arguments are boosted by the fact that the Fifteenth Amendment awarded the vote to black men alone and by the pronouncements of black men themselves. "When I married my

wife," a Tennessee freedman told his employer, in rejecting the
employer's request for his wife's services, "I married her to wait
on me and she has got all she can do right here for me and the
children."[90] In one part of Louisiana black men told employers
that "whenever they wanted their wives to work they would tell
them themselves: and if [they] could not rule [their] own domestic affairs on that place [they] would leave it."[91] Planters were
also convinced that men were behind women's partial withdrawal
from the field. An Alabama planter claimed that he had lost one-
fourth of his labor because the men regarded it as "a matter of
pride" to exact from their employers a new division of labor that
would exempt their women from field work. Accentuating the
point, a Georgia newspaper reported in 1869 that "the freedmen have almost universally withdrawn their women and children from the fields, putting the first at housework and the latter at school."[92]

Such is one side of the story. But did emancipation substitute
one kind of subordination for another? Did black women escape
racial slavery only to become "slaves" to their husbands? Clearly
the answer is "no." True, freedom did give men a greater opportunity to act as husbands and fathers, to serve as protectors of
women and children, and as providers for their kinship network.
But it also freed women from some of the burdens they had
shouldered during slavery, and it demanded of husbands and fathers a more equitable sharing of responsibility for the family's
survival. Women now cooperated with kin instead of the female
network, but neither this nor men's increased responsibility
made wives and mothers dependent on husbands and fathers or
subordinate to them. Survival, as we have seen, was too dependent on the work and contributions of every household member
for men to dismiss women's work. Too many women found themselves heading impoverished households without male support,
and women were still victims of the worse kind of violence.
Instead of women becoming dependent and subservient to men,

freedom made black men and women more dependent on each other.

This disturbed white people. They could not see that black cutback on women's work in the fields and white households was calculated to limit white men's abusive access to black women. They could not believe black women would object to their oppressive work regimens because they still believed black women coveted relations with whites, either as Jezebels or Mammies.[93] They were equally blind to husband and wife equalitarianism, thinking that black people were merely mimicking white familial forms. Myopically, they ridiculed black women's work for their own families as "playing the lady." "The women have got rather lazy and try your patience severely," complained South Carolina planter E. B. Hayward. "If you chide them they say 'Eh ch! Massa, aint I mus' mind de fowl, and look a' me young corn aint I mus' watch um.' And to do this, the best hand on the place will stay at home all day and every day." Heyward chose to ignore the difference that chicken and corn made in this woman's and her family's life. So did an Alabama landowner who complained "the black women do not like to work, it is not ladylike."[94] Of course, black women were still working, just not as much for white people. Like the many landowners who complained about "female loaferism,"[95] the problem was that "ladydom" was the reserve of white women alone; black women were mere parodies. During slavery when black women had been sick and "laid-up," masters had similarly complained that they were "playing the lady." No concession to their gender could be made. Emancipation brought no change. White women were paragons of femininity and domesticity; black women were Amazons and Sapphires. Black women, as Sojourner Truth learned in Silver Lake, were outcasts of femininity.

But white women would have done well to imitate black women. As Drew Gilpen Faust notes, the war ended Southern white women's celebration of helplessness. The war forced them to manage slaves and farms, control children, and even work to provide their own basic support. The poverty that accompanied the war and its aftermath forced white women into the wage-earning labor force and public arena of reform in greater numbers than ever before. During the war, overworked and underfed farmwomen led petition campaigns against the Confederacy to release their husbands from military service so the men could return home and assist with farm production. When Jefferson Davis's government proved insensitive to their despair they led protest movements that in cities such as Richmond, Wilmington, and Mobile broke out into full-scale bread riots. So widespread was poverty that states established public assistance programs and distributed surplus food or provided cash payments to those in need. In light of the lessons the war taught Southern white women about the folly of absolute dependence, they could have used an ideology of womanhood that celebrated female self-support, strength, resilience, and assertiveness. Instead, white women, especially those of the middle and upper classes, retreated to the race-grounded gender ideology that required them to hide their personal strength under a veil of femininity in order to claim the "ladydom" that was the privilege of whiteness.

Black women, on the other hand, etched out a womanhood that demanded respect for their abilities and recognition of their roles as survivors and defenders of black rights. Postbellum economic necessity certainly forced black women into the labor force, but so did their search for self-fulfillment. Tom Thorton did not want his wife to work, but Margaret earned wages year-round as a wet nurse and laundress. Her nursing gave her a sense of accomplishment: "I wus brung up ter nurse," she boasted to her interviewer. "I has nursed 'bout two thousand babies. . . . I has nursed gran'maws an' den dere gran'chiles."[96] Like Margaret Thorton, many women wanted to feel as free as their men. Thus, despite the patriarchal policies of landowners and Freedman's Bureau agents, many women objected to their husbands' signing labor contracts for them, demanded separate payment of their wages, and refused to be liable for their husbands' debts at country stores. Some married women even followed the example of single women who opened individual accounts at the Freedman's Saving's Bank.[97]

Some freedwomen also had to seek protection from abusive black men. Under slavery they had had little to no protection against assault from any men. Now that they theoretically had recourse to the courts they attempted to use it as protection. Thus Laney, a freedwoman in Orangeburg, South Carolina, complained to a regional bureau agent of being "beat about 30 lashes, with a leather strap, over her back and shoulder, by her husband Cesar." Cesar's defense was that Laney was lazy. She had failed to do his wash and mend his clothes and had generally neglected his "comfort and welfare." Silvy also complained to the Orangeburg bureau about being beaten. John Gardner, her assailant, felt justified by Silvy's behavior. She, he claimed, "was acting very unchastely and sleeping with a man without being married." For a while at least, black women felt safe in taking their complaints against black men to white officials, who were somewhat more responsive in these cases than when black women sought protection against white men. In sentencing Leah Perry's husband for choking and beating her, a Beaufort, South Carolina, judge noted that "the matter of beating their wives is so common among the freedmen that pretty stern action is necessary to put a stop to it."[98] In Granville, North Carolina, a black man named Jack Allen was indicted for the rape of Clarissa Wortham, despite his self-righteous defense that Wortham had instigated the sexual relations between them.[99]

Black women also pursued the rights of their people. They did not get the vote in 1870 when the Fifteenth Amendment was ratified. Still African-American women participated in the mass meetings, parades, and conventions where decisions were made about black people's future. Women took off work on voting days as readily as men, going along to the polls to insure a properly cast vote.[100] As Elsa Barkley Brown has observed, African-

American women and men viewed the vote as a collective right, not an individual possession. In Richmond, Virginia, for example, both black men and women attended the August 1867 Republican state convention, and from the gallery loudly joined in debates held on the convention floor. The black women of Richmond also belonged to black political societies like the all-female Rising Daughters of Liberty and the Daughters of the Union Victory. These political societies were not unique to Richmond but also common in South Carolina, Louisiana, other areas of Virginia, and throughout the South in general.[101]

Also not unique to Richmond was African-American women's armed defense of political meetings and polling places. No sooner had black people attained rights of citizenship than white people tried to take them away. Vigilante groups like the Ku Klux Klan organized a reign of terror. So widespread was white intimidation, fraud, and violence that both men at the polls and women and children at home feared white vengeance. Women's presence at polling places, therefore, was probably, as Elsa Barkley Brown notes, "a sign of the need for collective protection.[102] If the women were like those in Charleston, South Carolina, they carried weapons, for there black women were spied "carrying axes or hatchets in their hands hanging down at their sides, their aprons or dresses half-concealing the weapons."[103]

Such behavior only confirmed the white idea of black women as a sort of female hybrid, capable of being exploited like a woman but otherwise treated like a man. They therefore continued to treat them as Jezebels, and this perception left them vulnerable to sexual crimes. From emancipation through more than two-thirds of the twentieth century, no Southern white male was convicted of raping or attempting to rape a black woman. Yet the crime was widespread. In 1969, the staff of the National Commission on the Causes and Prevention of Violence admitted that the poverty of complaints reflected not the crime's low incidence but the fact that "white males have long had nearly institutionalized access to Negro women with relatively little fear of being reported."[104] Black women had almost as little recourse to justice when the perpetrator was black. As the nineteenth century faded into the twentieth and lynching of black men and women became a hallmark of Southern race relations, courts became less receptive to black women's pleas for protection against black men. For their part, black women, afraid that their men would be lynched, became increasingly reluctant to seek help from white authorities.[105] Meanwhile African-American women ranked among the hardest working women in the United States. More common than not, they worked from age seven to seventy and still died poor.[106]

And white people got their Mammies back. As the Old South's last white generation penned memoir after memoir, the nation came to accept the South's point of view about plantation slavery before the Civil War. In the pictures painted by Americans, Mammy towered behind every orange blossom, mint julep, erring white child, and gracious lady. She was immortalized in D. W. Griffith's popular antiblack film, *Birth of a Nation,* and eight years after its 1915 debut, the United Daughters of the Confederacy petitioned Congress to erect a granite monument to Mammy. American films, pancake boxes, and syrup bottles imprinted Mammy on the American psyche more indelibly than ever before. So entrenched was she that for most of the century following emancipation black women were virtually locked out of every occupation except work in white people's fields or homes. On the eve of the modern Civil Rights Movement white Americans could feel that all was well with the world: Sapphire was still in their fields, and Mammy was back in their kitchens.

Thank God black women were never what white people perceived us or wanted us to be. There is no question that we have suffered tremendously from historic racism and sexism. We were never superwomen. Disease, mortality, and depression—the perils of adversity—have taken their toll. But African-American women's lives have been salvaged by sustained psychological and physical resistance to white exploitation and terror. In slavery and in freedom we practiced an alternative style of womanhood. A womanhood that persevered in hardship but revered overt resistance. A womanhood that celebrated heroism but accepted frailty. A womanhood that could answer a confident and assertive "yes" to the persistent question: *"Ar'n't I a woman?"*

Notes

REVISITING *AR'N'T I A WOMAN?*

1. For example, the autobiographical narrative of Harriet Brent Jacobs's *Incidents in the Life of a Slave Girl* was dismissed as nonauthentic until Jean Fagan Yellin's discovery of original transcripts established it as a bonafide autobiography written by an escaped female slave. See Jean Fagen Yellin, "Written by Herself: Harriet Jacobs' Slave Narrative," *American Literature* (November 1981), 53: 479–486. Jean Fagan Yellin comments extensively on the invisibility of black women in history and the failure to take black women's sources seriously in "Afro-American Women, 1800–1910: Excerpts from a Working Biography," in *All the Women Are White, All the Blacks Are Men, but Some of Us Are Brave: Black Women Studies*, Gloria T. Hull, Patricia Bell Scott, and Barbara Smith, eds. (New York: Feminist Press, 1982) pp. 221–244.

2. Chap. five, "On the Dilemmas of Scholarship in Afro-American History," in August Meier and Elliot Rudwick's *Black History and the Historical Profession, 1915–1980* (Urbana: University of Illinois Press, 1986), Nathan Huggins's "Integrating Afro-American History into American History" and Vincent Harding's "Responsibilities of the Black Scholar to the Black Community," both in *The State of Afro-American History: Past, Present, and Future,* Darlene Hine, ed. (Baton Rouge: Louisiana University Press, 1986) remind us that in the mid-1980's the objectivity of black historians in the field of African-American history was not taken for granted but was a much debated topic.

3. Thus, even though plantation records seldom revealed the thoughts and feelings of enslaved women, early evaluators of *Ar'n't I a Woman?* insisted that more weight be given to them than to the interviews and narratives. As all historians of this period know, the Works Progress Administration interviews are problematic. They were recorded long after enslavement ended, the interviewers were far from objective recorders, and depression influenced both the questions and responses. Nevertheless, I maintained then, and continue to argue, that they are

a less problematic source than plantation records, which were recorded mostly by white males who had very distorted and self-serving ideas about African-American women.

4. This story is told in Nancy Weiss Malkiel's "Invincible Woman," in *Visible Women: New Essays on American Activism*, Nancy A. Hewitt and Suzanne Lebsock, eds. (Urbana: University of Illinois Press, 1993), pp. 388–389.

5. See, for example, Elizabeth Spellman, *Inessential Women: Problems of Exclusion in Feminist Thought* (Boston: Beacon Press, 1988); Patricia Hill Collins, *Black Feminist Thought: Knowledge, Consciousness, and the Politics of Empowerment* (New York: Routledge, 1991); Elsa Barkley Brown, " 'What Has Happened Here': The Politics of Difference in Women's History and Feminist Politics," *Feminist Studies* (Summer 1992), 18: 295–312, and "Womanist Consciousness: Maggie Lena Walker and the Independent Order of Saint Luke," *Signs* (Spring 1989), 14(3): 610–633; Evelyn Brooks Higginbotham, "African-American Women's History and the Metalanguage of Race," *Signs* (Winter 1992), 17: 251–274; Tessie Liu, "Teaching the Differences among Women from a Historical Perspective: Rethinking Race and Gender as Social Categories," *Women's Studies International Forum* (1991), 14(4): 265–276.

6. See pp. 15, 162.

7. Kathleen M. Brown, *Good Wives, Nasty Wenches, and Anxious Patriarchs: Gender, Race, and Power in Colonial Virginia* (Chapel Hill: University of North Carolina Press, 1996), pp. 119, 122, 133.

8. Jennifer Lyle Morgan, "Laboring Women: Enslaved Women, Reproduction, and Slavery in Barbados and South Carolina, 1650–1750" (Ph.D. dissertation, Duke University, 1995).

9. Elizabeth Fox-Genovese, *Within the Plantation Household: Black and White Women of the Old South* (Chapel Hill: University of North Carolina Press, 1988), pp. 101, 135, 192, 193.

10. Brenda Stevenson, "Gender Convention, Ideals, and Identity among Antebellum Virginia Slave Women," in *More Than Chattel: Black Women and Slavery in the Americas*, Darlene Clark Hine and David Barry Gaspar, eds. (Bloomington: Indiana University Press, 1996), p. 181.

11. Brenda E. Stevenson, *Life in Black and White: Family and Community in the Slave South* (New York: Oxford University Press, 1996), p. 236.

12. See p. 25.

13. See p. 25.

14. Melton A. McLaurin, *Celia, A Slave* (New York: Avon Books, 1991); Dorothy Roberts, *Killing the Black Body: Race, Reproduction, and the Meaning of Liberty* (New York: Pantheon, 1997).

15. Nell Irvin Painter, "Soul Murder and Slavery: Toward a Fully Loaded Cost Accounting," in *U.S. History as Women's History: New Feminist Essays*, Linda Kerber, Alice Kessler-Harris, and Kathryn Kish Sklar, eds. (Chapel Hill: University of North Carolina Press, 1995) p. 130.

16. J. Marion Sims, *The Story of My Life*, ed. H. Marion Sims (New York: D. Appleton & Co., 1886), pp. 230–246; Seale Harris, *Woman's Surgeon: The Life Story of J. Marion Sims* (New York, Macmillan Company, 1950), pp. 82–108; *New Orleans Medical and Surgical Journal* (June 1879), pp. 933–942.

17. See, for example, Dorothy Roberts, *Killing the Black Body;* Darlene Clark Hine, "Rape and the Inner Lives of Black Women in the Middle West: Preliminary Thoughts on the Culture of Dissemblance," *Signs* (Summer 1989), 14: 912–920

18. See, for example, Sharla Fett, "African American Healing and Southern Antebellum Plantations, 1800–1860" (Ph.D. dissertation, Rutgers University, 1995).

19. Carlton Mabee, *Sojourner Truth: Slave, Prophet, Legend* (New York: New York University Press, 1993), pp. 67–82; Nell Irvin Painter, *Sojourner Truth: A Life, A Symbol* (New York: W. W. Norton, 1996), pp. 164–178.

20. Painter, *Sojourner Truth*, pp. 281–287.

21. *Ibid.*, p. 273.

22. See pp. 14, 162.

23. Painter, *Sojourner Truth*, p. 171.

INTRODUCTION

1. *Narrative of Sojourner Truth, A Bondwoman of Olden Time*, Olive Gilbert, comp. (New York: Arno, 1968 [1878]), pp. 131–133.

2. *Ibid.*, p. 133.

3. *Ibid.*, pp. 133–134. Truth's 1851 speech is widely quoted. Usually, however, the word "ain't" is substituted for "ar'n't." I have chosen to use the word as it appeared in her 1878 narrative.

4. Statement made by Lucy Stone at a national women's rights convention in Cincinnati in October 1855, quoted in Aileen S. Kraditor, ed., *Up From the Pedestal* (Chicago: Quadrangle, 1968), p. 71.

5. John Stuart Mill and Harriet Taylor Mill, *The Subjection of Women* in *Essays of Sex Equality*, Alice Rossi, ed. (Chicago: Univeristy of Chicago Press, 1970, [1869]), pp. 137–144, 155, 158.

6. C. Vann Woodward, ed., *Mary Chesnut's Civil War* (New Haven: Yale University Press, 1981), p. 729.

7. Sarah Grimké, "Letters on the Equality of the Sexes and the Condition of Women," in *The Feminist Papers*, Alice S. Rossi, ed. (New York: Bantam Press, 1978), pp. 314–315; Angelina Grimké, "An Appeal to the Women of the Nominally Free States," in *Root of Bitterness, Documents of the Social History of American Women*, Nancy F. Cott, ed. (New York: Dutton, 1972), p. 194–195.

8. Several excellent studies can be used to verify these general statements. Among them are Eugene D. Genovese, *Roll, Jordan, Roll, The World the Slaves Made* (New York: Vintage, 1974), and Leslie Howard Owens, *This Species of Property, Slave Life and Culture in the Old South* (Oxford: Oxford University Press, 1976).

9. One of the first scholars to give the subject of female slavery serious attention was Angela Davis. See "Reflections on the Black Woman's Role in the Community of Slaves," *Black Scholar* (December 1971), 3: 3–15. See also Genovese, *Roll, Jordan, Roll*, pp. 494–501; Martia Graham Goodson, "An Introductory Essay and Subject Index to Selected Interviews From the Slave Narrative Collection" (Ph.D. dissertation, Union Graduate School, 1977); Jacqueline Jones, " 'My Mother was Much of a Woman': Black Women, Work, and the Family Under Slavery," *Feminist Studies*, (Summer 1982), 8(2): 235–267.

10. Stanley M. Elkins, *Slavery, A Problem in American Institutional and Intellectual Life*, 2nd ed. (Chicago: University of Chicago Press, 1968 [1959]), pp. 130.

11. *Ibid.*, pp. 81–82, 94.
12. *Ibid.*, pp. 82, 132.
13. *Ibid.*, pp. 97–98.
14. *Ibid.*, p. 100; See also Elizabeth Donnan, ed., *Documents Illustrative of the History of the Slave Trade to America*, 4 vols. (Washington: Carnegie Institute of Washington, 1930), 2: 358,595.
15. Elkins, *Slavery*, p. 136.
16. *Ibid.*, pp. 137–138.
17. *Ibid.*, p. 130; see also Kenneth Stampp, *The Peculiar Institution, Slavery in the Ante-Bellum South* (New York: Random House, 1957), p. 344, and E. Franklin Frazier, *The Negro Family in the United States* (Chicago: University of Chicago Press, 1939), p. 125.
18. W. E. B. DuBois, *The Gift of Black Folk: The Negroes in the Making of America* (Boston: Stratford, 1924), p. 339.
19. John W. Blassingame, *The Slave Community, Plantation Life in the Ante-bellum South* (New York: Oxford University Press, 1972), pp. 80, 85, 88, 92–93, 100, 102.
20. Robert William Fogel and Stanley Engerman, *Time on the Cross, The Economics of American Negro Slavery* (Boston: Little, Brown, 1974), pp. 141.
21. Genovese, *Roll, Jordan, Roll*, pp. 491–492, 500.
22. Herbert G. Gutman, *The Black Family in Slavery and Freedom, 1750–1925* (New York: Pantheon Books, 1976).
23. See Denise Paulme, ed., *Women of Tropical Africa* (Berkeley: University of California Press, 1963), p. 4.
24. Gerda Lerner, *Black Women in White America: A Documentary History* (New York: Vintage Books, 1972), p. 14.
25. See Gerda Lerner, *The Majority Finds Its Past, Placing Women in History* (New York: Oxford University Press, 1979), pp. 75–82.
26. See John Dollard, *Caste and Class in a Southern Town*, 3d ed. (New York: Doubleday, 1957 [1937]), p. 303; Daniel Patrick Moynihan, *The Negro Family: The Case for National Action* (Washington, D.C.: United States Department of Labor, 1965), p. 16.
27. Simone de Beauvoir, *The Second Sex* (New York: Vintage Books, 1974 [1952]), p. 192.
28. Paul Lawrence Dunbar, *Lyrics of Lowly Life; Complete Poems* (London: Chapman and Hall, 1897), pp. 112–113.
29. Ulrich B. Phillips, *American Negro Slavery, A Survey of the Supply, Employment, and Control of Negro Labor as Determined by the Plantation Regime* (Baton Rouge: Louisiana State University Press, 1966 [1918]), p. 309.

1. JEZEBEL AND MAMMY:
THE MYTHOLOGY OF FEMALE SLAVERY

1. Michelle Wallace, *Black Macho and the Myth of the Superwoman* (New York: Dial, 1979), p. 107.
2. William H. Chafe, *Women and Equality, Changing Patterns in American Culture* (Oxford: Oxford University Press, 1977), pp. 49–50.
3. Winthrop D. Jordan, *White Over Black, American Attitudes Toward the Negro, 1550–1812* (Chapel Hill: University of North Carolina Press, 1968), pp. 1–43.

4. William Bosman, *A New and Accurate Description of The Coast of Guinea* (London: Frank Cass, 1967 [1705]), pp. 208–211.

5. William Smith, *A New Voyage to Guinea* (London: Frank Cass, 1967, [1744]), pp. 51–52, 146, 221–223; Ashley Montagu, "Edward Tyson, M.D., F. R. S., 1650–1708," in *Memoirs of the American Philosophical Society* (1943), 20: 249–253.

6. Smith, *A New Voyage to Guinea*, p. 52.

7. Quoted in Jordan, *White Over Black*, p. 150. From Bryan Edwards, *The History, Civil and Commercial of the British Colonies in the West Indies*, 3 vols. 3d ed. (London: Bradbury and Evans, 1801), 2: 32–38.

8. *South Carolina Gazette*, July 10, 1736.

9. Merrill D. Peterson, ed., *The Portable Thomas Jefferson* (New York: Viking, 1975), p. 187.

10. William Howard Russell, *My Diary North and South (Canada, Its Defenses, Condition, and Resources)*, 3 vols. (London: Bradbury and Evans, 1863), 1: 135; Alexander B. Groshart, ed., *The Poems and Literary Prose of Alexander Wilson*, 2 vols. (Paiseley: Alex Gardner, 1876), 1: 167–168.

11. Johann David Schoepf, *Travels in the Confederacy, 1783–1784*, 2 vols. (Philadelphia: Campbell, 1911), 1: 101.

12. James Redpath, *The Roving Editor, or Talks With Slaves in Southern States* (New York: Burdick, 1859), p. 141.

13. Samuel Cartwright, "Slavery in the Light of Ethnology," in *Cotton Is King and Pro-Slavery Arguments*, E. N. Elliot, ed. (Augusta, Ga.: Pritchard, Abbott, and Loomis, 1860), p. 714; Frederick Law Olmsted, *A Journey in the Seaboard Slave States* (New York: Dix and Edwards, 1856), p. 602.

14. Frederick Law Olmsted, *A Journey in the Back Country, 1853–1854* (New York: Putnam's Sons, 1907), p. 153, 113.

15. Frederick Law Olmsted, *The Cotton Kingdom*, David Freeman Hawke, ed. (New York: Bobbs-Merrill, 1971), p. 163; Olmsted, *Seaboard Slave States*, pp. 49–50; Olmsted, *Back Country*, p. 59; *Plantation Manual*, p. 3, Southern Historical Collection (SHC), The University of North Carolina at Chapel Hill, Chapel Hill, North Carolina; *DeBow's Review* (1857), 22: 376–77; *DeBow's Review* (1856), 21: 617–620.

16. Ophelia S. Egypt, J. Masouka, Charles S. Johnson, eds. *Unwritten History of Slavery: Autobiographical Accounts of Negro Ex-Slaves*, in Goerge Rawick, ed., *The American Slave, A Composite Autobiography*, 19 vols. (Westport, Conn.: Greenwood, 1972 [1945]), 18:92. All references to the Rawick series will be cited with the foregoing construction.

17. N.C., 15(2): 229. See also B. A. Botkin, ed., *Lay My Burden Down: A Folk History of Slavery* (Chicago: University of Chicago Press, 1945), p. 155.

18. Thomas Hamilton, *Men and Manners in America*, 2 vols. (Edinburgh: William Blackwood, 1833), 1: 216–217; see also Frederika Bremer, *Homes of the New World*, 2 vols. (New York: Harper and Brothers, 1853), 2: 201.

19. Frederic Bancroft, *Slave Trading in the Old South* (New York: Frederick Ungar, 1931), p. 112.

20. Solomon Northup, *Twelve Years A Slave, Narrative of Solomon Northup* in *Puttin' On Ole Massa*, Gilbert Osofsky, ed. (New York: Harper and Row, 1969), p. 264. Hereafter cited as Northup in Osofsky, ed., *Ole Massa.*

21. Schoepf, *Travels in the Confederacy*, p. 147; see also Frances Anne Kemble, *Journal of a Residence on a Georgian Plantation*, John A. Scott, ed. (New

York: Knopf, 1961), pp. 180, 227–228; Olmsted, *Seaboard Slave States*, p. 391; Olmsted, *Cotton Kingdom*, p. 79; Ga., 12(2): 269.

22. Olmsted, *Cotton Kingdom*, p. 63.

23. Drew, *The Refugee*, pp. 48–49, 92.

24. Henry Bibb, *Narrative of the Life and Adventures of Henry Bibb* in Osofsky, ed., *Ole Massa*, p. 120.

25. Bibb in Osofsky, ed., *Ole Massa*, p. 115.

26. Helen T. Catterall, ed., *Judicial Cases Concerning American Slavery and the Negro*, 5 vols. (Washington, D.C.: Carnegie Institute of Washington, 1936), 3: 55–56.

27. Northup in Osofsky, ed., *Ole Massa*, p. 321.

28. William Wells Brown, *Narrative of William Wells Brown* in Osofsky, ed., *Ole Massa*, pp. 194–195. Hereafter cited as Brown in Osofsky, ed., *Ole Massa*.

29. Bibb in Osofsky, ed., *Ole Massa*, pp. 162–163. See also Linda Brent, *Incidents in the Life of a Slave Girl*, Lydia Maria Child, ed. (New York: Harcourt Brace Jovanovich, 1973 [1861]), pp. 53, 56, 85. This work, first published in 1861, is the autobiographical narrative of fugitive slave Harriet Jacobs. Jacobs wrote it under the pseudonym Linda Brent to protect herself and those who had illegally helped her to escape. The authenticity of the narrative has been challenged but the recent discovery of a cache of Jacobs' letters has established the work as a well-documented pseudonymous autobiography. This work uses Jacobs' fictitious name, Linda Brent, throughout. See Jean Fagan Yellin, "Written By Herself: Harriet Jacobs' Slave Narrative," *American Literature* 53(3): 479–486.

30. C. Vann Woodward, ed., *Mary Chesnut's Civil War* (New Haven: Yale University Press, 1981), p. 15.

31. Northup in Osofsky, ed., *Ole Massa*, p. 255.

32. Olmsted, *Seaboard Slave States*, p. 28; Levi Coffin, *Reminiscences of Levi Coffin* (Cincinnati, Ohio: Robert Clarke, 1898), p. 518. See also Woodward, ed., *Chesnut's Civil War*, p. 588.

33. Bremer, *Homes of the New World*, 1: 492–493.

34. Coffin, *Reminiscences*, p. 467.

35. Northup in Osofsky, ed., *Ole Massa*, pp. 246–248, 264–269, 280, 310–311.

36. Olmsted, *Cotton Kingdom*, p. 60.

37. For a discussion of the "Fancy Trade" see Frederic Bancroft, *Slave Trading in the Old South* (New York: Frederick Ungar, 1931), pp. 217–218, 328–334.

38. Bremer, *Homes of the New World*, 1: 373; *Ibid.*, 2: 535; see also Kemble, *Journal of a Residence on a Georgian Plantation*, p. 282.

39. Northup in Osofsky, ed., *Ole Massa*, p. 268.

40. Dr. [William Gilmore] Simms, "The Morals of Slavery," in Elliott, ed., *Pro-Slavery Arguments*, p. 329; Chancellor [William] Harper, "Harper on Slavery," *Ibid.*, pp. 41–46; Governor [James] Hammond, "Hammond's Letters on Slavery," *Ibid.*, pp. 119–120.

41. Harper, "Harper on Slavery," *Ibid.*, pp. 41–46.

42. Quoted in Olmsted, *Seaboard Slave States*, p. 403; see also J. H. Easterby, ed., *The South Carolina Rice Plantation as Revealed in the Papers of Robert F. W. Allston* (Chicago: University of Chicago Press, 1945), p. 146; Harriet

Martineau, *Society in America,* 3 vols. (London: Saunders and Otley, 1837), 2: 138, 309, 338 and 3: 117.
43. Woodward, ed., *Chesnut's Civil War,* 168–169, 309; see also p. 243.
44. Quoted in Olmsted, *Seaboard Slave States,* p. 403.
45. Woodward, ed., *Chesnut's Civil War,* p. 29.
46. Brent, *Slave Girl,* p. 34.
47. S.C., 2(1): 150.
48. Botkin, ed., *Lay My Burden Down,* pp. 122–123; see also Coffin, *Reminiscences,* p. 518; Brent, *Slave Girl,* p. 35.
49. Catterall, *Judicial Cases,* 3: 181–182; *Ibid.,* 2: 139, 281; see also *Ibid.,* p. 188, 253, 272.
50. Fla., 17:95. See also S.C., 2(1):150, and *Ibid.,* 2:14.
51. Northup in Osofsky, ed., *Ole Massa,* p. 333.
52. William and Ellen Craft, *Running a Thousand Miles for Freedom, or the Escape of William and Ellen Craft From Slavery* (London: William Tweedie, 1860), p. 2.
53. Fla., 17:174; *Reminiscences,* p. 419, 421.
54. Brent, *Slave Girl,* pp. 31–32.
55. J. C. Nott and George R. Gliddon, *Types of Mankind,* 7th ed. (Philadelphia, Penn.: Lippincott, Grambo, 1854), pp. 372–374, 397–399, 401–402, 403, 407–408; John H. Van Evrie, *Negroes and Negro Slavery* (New York: Van Evrie Horton, 1861), pp. 143–168.
56. Olmsted, *Seaboard Slave States,* p. 602.
57. *Southern Cultivator,* (June 1855), 13: 173–174; see also Emily Burke, *Reminiscences of Georgia* (Oberlin, Ohio; James M. Fitch, 1850), p. 152.
58. William Drayton, *The South Vindicated from the Treason and Fanaticism of Northern Abolitionists* (Philadelphia: H. Manley, 1836), p. 104.
59. George Fitzhugh, *Sociology for the South; or The Failure of Free Society* (Richmond, Va.: A. Morris, 1854), p. 213.
60. George Fitzhugh, *Cannibals All! or Slaves Without Masters* (Cambridge: The Belknap Press of Harvard Univeristy Press, 1960 [1857]), p. 29.
61. George S. Sawyer, *Southern Institutes or, An Inquiry into the Origin and Early Prevalence of Slavery and the Slave Trade* (Philadelphia: J. B. Lippincott, 1858), p. 221.
62. *A Defense of Southern Slavery Against the Attacks of Henry Clay and Alex'r Campbell* in *A Defense of Southern Slavery and Other Pamphlets* (New York: Negro Universities Press, 1969 [n.d.]), p. 40.
63. Thomas R. R. Cobb, *An Inquiry into the Law of Negro Slavery in the United States of America to which is prefixed An Historical Sketch of Slavery* (New York: Negro University Press, 1968 [1858]), p. ccxvii. See also Edward Pollard, *Black Diamonds Gathered in the Darky Homes of the South* (Washington, D.C.: Pudney and Rusell, 1859), p. 95.
64. Mrs. Nicholas Ware Eppes, *The Negro of the Old South* (Chicago: Joseph G. Branch, 1925), p. 74.
65. Louisa Campbell Sheppard, "Recollections" (typescript, 1892), SHC., p. 7.
66. Susan Dabney Smedes, *Memorials of a Southern Planter,* Fletcher M. Greene, ed. (New York: Knopf, 1968), p. 60.
67. Eliza Ripley, *Social Life in Old New Orleans, Being Recollections of My Girlhood* (New York: Appleton, 1912), pp. 209–213.

68. Smedes, *Southern Planter*, p. 71.

69. *Recollections of the Daughter of Charles Friend*, White Hill Plantation Books, SHC p. 5, 41.

70. Eppes, *The Negro of the Old South*, p. 76.

71. Smedes, *Southern Planter*, p. 60.

72. Eppes, *The Negro of the Old South*, pp. 74–76.

73. White Hill Plantation Books, p. 5, 41 SHC.

74. Smedes, *Southern Planter*, p. 48. For another description of Mammy see Marion Alexander Boggs, ed., *The Alexander Letters* (Athens: The University of Georgia Press, 1980), pp. 108–109, 129, 168–169, 223.

75. Ark., 10: 243–244.

76. Ala., 6: 120.

77. Botkin, ed., *Lay My Burden Down*, p. 125.

78. Martineau, *Society in America*, 2:309.

79. *Meta Morris Grimball Diary, 1860–1866*. Typescript, SHC, pp. 5, 38, 112–114.

80. Susan Strasser, *Never Done. A History of American Housework* (New York: Pantheon Books, 1982), pp. 1–125.

81. *Mrs. Isaac Hilliard Diary*, 1849–1850, Department of Archives, Louisiana State University, in *Southern Historical Manuscripts* (Westport, Conn.: Greenwood, Microcard Division, 1973), p. 58.

82. Ok., 7:36; See also *Ibid.*, 97.

83. Miss., 7:140, 158–159.

84. Ga., 13(3):157. See also George Rawick, ed., *The American Slave: A Composite Autobiography, Supplement, Series, 2,* 10 vols., (Westport, Conn.: Greenwood, 1977), Texas, Supplement 2, 2:161. Hereafter, references from the Rawick Series 2, Supplement will be cited with the foregoing construction.

85. S.C., 2:89; See also Catherine Clinton, *The Plantation Mistress. Woman's World in the Old South* (New York: Pantheon Books, 1982), pp. 22–29.

86 Texas, Supplement 2, 2:161, 294.

87. Ala., 6:77; Ok., 7:128–129, 135.

88. Miss., 7: 49–50.

89. Ala., 6:56.

90. Tenn., 16:20–21.

91. Woodward, ed., *Chesnut's Civil War*, p. 250.

92. Robert Manson Myers *Children of Pride, A True Story of Georgia and the Civil War* (New Haven: Yale University Press, 1972), pp. 543, 592, 596.

93. Beth G. Crabtree and James W. Patton, eds., *The Diary of Catherine Ann Devereaux Edmondston* (Raleigh: North Carolina Division of Archives and History, 1979), p. 146. See also Olmsted, *Back Country*, p. 36, and *Hilliard Diary*, p. 8.

94. Frederick Douglass, *My Bondage and My Freedom* (New York: Mulligan, New York and Auburn, 1855), p. 180.

95. Jacob Stroyer, *My Life in the South* (Salem, Mass.: New Comb and Gavs, 1898), pp. 78–80.

96. Eugene Genovese, *Roll, Jordon, Roll, The World the Slaves Made* (New York: Random House, 1974), pp. 360–361.

97. Ruth H. Bloch, "American Feminine Ideals in Transition: The Rise of the Moral Mother, 1785–1815," in *Feminist Studies* (June 1978), 4(2):101.

98. D. Harland Hagler, "The Ideal Woman in the Antebellum South: Lady or Farmwife" *The Journal of Southern History* (August 1980), 46(3):410.

99. *Southern Cultivator*, (May 1855), 13(5):159.

100. John Pendleton Kennedy, *Swallow Born or Sojourn in the Old Dominion* (New York: Harcourt, Brace, 1929 [1832]), pp. 31–33, 192–193. See also Francis Pendleton Gaines, *The Southern Plantation, A Study of The Development and the Accuracy of a Tradition* (Gloucester, Mass.: Peter Smith, 1962), pp. 18–22.

101. H. B. Tucker, *George Balcombe, A Tale of Missouri*, 2 vols. (New York: Harper and Brothers), p. 278.

102. Caroline Gilman, *Recollections of a Southern Mistress* (New York: Harper and Brothers, 1838), pp. 24–25.

103. Tucker, *George Balcombe*, 2:166.

104. Margaret Isabella Weber, *Reminiscences of Margaret Isabella (Walker) Weber*, SHC., p. 13.

105. Sheppard, "Recollections," p. 17.

106. Pollard, *Black Diamonds*, pp. 22-23.

107. Bloch, "American Feminine Ideals," p. 118–120.

108. Pollard, *Black Diamonds*, pp. 23, 33, 94–95.

109. Thomas Butler King Papers, 9:10, 24, SHC.

110. Mary H. Eastman, *Aunt Phyllis's Cabin; or Southern Life As It Is* (Philadelphia: Lippincott, Grambo, 1852), p. 137.

111. Bloch, "American Feminine Ideals," p. 101.

112. Thomas Nelson Page, *Social Life in Old Virginia Before the War* (New York: C. Scribner's Sons, 1897), pp. 57–58.

2. THE NATURE OF FEMALE SLAVERY

1. Linda Brent, *Incidents in the Life of a Slave Girl*, Lydia Maria Child, ed. (New York: Harcourt Brace Jovanovich, 1973 [1861]), p. 79.

2. Elizabeth Donnan, ed., *Documents Illustrative of the History of the Slave Trade to America*, 4 vols. (Washington: Carnegie Institute of Washington, 1930), 2:595, 353.

3. Charles H. Nichols, *Many Thousand Gone, The Ex-Slaves' Account of Their Bondage and Their Freedom* (Bloomington: Indiana University Press, 1963), p 9.

4. George Francis Dow, *Slave Ships and Slaving* (Salem, Massachusetts: Marine Research Society, 1927), p. 145.

5. Donnan, ed., *Slave Trade*, 2:266.

6. Helen T. Catterall, ed., *Judicial Cases Concerning American Slavery and the Negro*, 5 vols. (Washington, D.C.: Carnegie Institute of Washington, 1936), 1:19.

7. Donnan, ed., *Slave Trade*, 3:323.

8. *Ibid.*, 2:69, 78, 100.

9. Russell R. Menard, "The Maryland Slave Population, 1658 to 1730: A Demographic Profile of Blacks in Four Counties," *William and Mary Quarterly* (January 1975), 32:33.

10. Allan Kulikoff, "The Beginnings of the Afro-American Family in Maryland," in *The American Family in Social-Historical Perspective*, Michael Gordon, ed., 2nd ed. (New York: St. Martin's, 1978), p. 446.

200   NOTES

11. Peter H. Wood, *Black Majority, Negroes in Colonial South Carolina from 1670 through the Stono Rebellion* (New York: Norton, 1974), p. 160. See also pp. 134–155. For further discussion of the colonial black sex ratio see Wesley Frank Craven, *White Red and Black, The Seventeenth-Century Virginian* (Charlottesville: The University Press of Virginia, 1971), pp. 98–100. Craven believes the sex ratio in Virginia to have been between 180.5 and 200 to 100.

12. See Kulikoff, "The Beginnings of the Afro-American Family," pp. 446–448; Menard, "The Maryland Slave Population," p. 354. For a general discussion of slave family life in colonial America see Herbert Gutman, *The Black Family in Slavery and Freedom 1750–1925* (New York: Vintage, 1975), pp. 327–360.

13. Kulikoff, "The Beginnings of the Afro-American Family," pp. 446–448; Menard, "The Maryland Slave Population," p. 354.

14. See notes 56 through 64 of chap. 3.

15. Daniel C. Littlefield, *Rice and Slaves, Ethnicity and the Slave Trade in Colonial South Carolina* (Baton Rouge: Louisiana State University Press, 1981), pp. 63–65.

16. William Waller Hening, ed., *The Statutes At Large Being A Collection of all the Laws of Virginia* (Richmond: Samuel Pleasants, 1823), 1:144, 242, 292, 454; *Ibid.*, 2:170, 187, 296.

17. Thomas Nairne, *A Letter From South Carolina Giving an Account of the Soil, Air Products, Trade, Government, Laws, Religion, People, Military Strength, etc. of that Province* (London: J. Clarke, 1732), pp. 50–60.

18. Edmund S. Morgan, *American Slavery, American Freedom, The Ordeal of Colonial Virginia* (New York: Norton, 1975), pp. 295–315. Morgan argues that it was well into the eighteenth century before slavery became more profitable than servitude. Planters did not immediately realize that slave women would be profitable as both a worker and childbearer. Once planters recognized the benefit, it became one of several reasons why they preferred slavery. Frank Craven makes a similar argument for the seventeenth century. See Craven, *White, Red and Black*, pp. 100–101.

19. Menard, "The Maryland Slave Population," pp. 43, 47, 53; Kulikoff, "The Beginnings of the Afro-American Family," pp. 448–50; Winthrop D. Jordan, *White Over Black, American Attitudes Towards the Negro, 1550–1812* (Baltimore, Ma.: Penguin, 1968), p. 175; Allan Kulikoff, "A 'Prolifick' People: Black Population Growth in the Chesapeake Colonies, 1700–1790," *Southern Studies* (Winter 1977), 16(4):398–414.

20. See the discussion presented in Carl N. Deglar, *Neither Black Nor White, Slavery and Race Relations in Brazil and the United States* (New York: Macmillan, 1971), p. 61–67; see also Michael Crabon, "Jamaican Slavery," and Richard Sheridan, "Mortality and the Medical Treatment of Slaves in the British West Indies," both in Stanley Engerman and Eugene Genovese, eds., *Slavery in the Western Hemisphere: Quantitative Studies* (Stanford: Stanford University Press, 1975); see also Orlando Paterson, *Sociology of Slavery*, (London: MacGibbon and Kee, 1967), chaps. 4 and 6.

21. See Henry Bibb, *Narrative of the Life and Adventures of Henry Bibb, An American Slave*, in *Puttin' On Ole Massa*, Gilbert Osofsky, ed. (New York: Harper & Row, 1969), pp. 74, 80, 81 (hereafter cited as Bibb in Osofsky, ed., *Ole Massa*): William Wells Brown, *A Fugitive Slave*, in Osofsky, ed., *Ole Massa*, p.

180, 213; Ga. 12(1):25; *Ibid.*, 2:12–13; Josiah Henson, *An Autobiography of the Reverend Josiah Henson*, in *Four Fugitive Slave Narratives* (Reading, Mass.: Addison Wesley, 1969), pp. 13–14; John Anderson, *The Story of the Life of John Anderson, A Fugitive Slave* (London: William Tweedie, 1863), p. 129; Gerda Lerner, *Black Women in White America, A Documentary History* (New York: Random House, 1972), p. 172.

22. A lengthy discussion of this topic in the text would take us far afield of the point being made in this chapter. However, literary evidence on this point abounds. According to J. D. DeBow, women made up the nucleus of any estate. Once a plantation was well stocked with women, it was only a matter of time before there would be more Negroes to work more land. A Virginia legislator explained the rudiments of slaveholding this way: ". . . the master forgoes the service of the female slave, has her nursed and attended during the period of gestation and raises the helpless infant offspring. The value of the property justifies the expense; . . . in its increase consists much of our wealth." Young girls, therefore, were valuable for their progeny as well as for the labor they would be expected to do in the field. If handled properly, females made for their masters a "mine of wealth." A Louisiana planter told William Howard Russell just how to get the most from them: "The way to get them right," he explained, "is not to work the mother too hard when they are near their time; to give them plenty to eat and not to send them to the fields too soon." A Mississippian, though, had different ideas: "Labor is conducive to health, a healthy woman will rear the most children." He got the most yield from his female slaves by giving them good and fair work, but not so much as to "tax the animal economy."*

Southerners bragged about their "breeding wenches" the way they bragged about their horses, cows, and mules. A Virginia planter was certain he had the most prolific "brood" in the state. His women, he proudly proclaimed, were "uncommonly good breeders"; no women on earth bred faster. A rice planter in South Carolina would have disagreed. As evidenced by the 5 percent annual increase on his plantation, his women were better still. Even James Madison did not conceal his pride in his slave women. As reported to Harriet Martineau, one-third of his slaves were under five years of age. Since planters figured that at least 5 or 6 percent of their profit would result from natural increase of the slave population it is no wonder that Frederick Olmsted so frequently heard people boast of the breeding potential of female slaves. Before he left the South he was convinced that "a slave woman is commonly esteemed least for her working qualities, most for those qualities which give value to a brood mare."†

Many farmers made their first investment not in a male slave, but in a young childbearing woman. This was probably not the case in the Southwest where basic land clearing demanded the strength and endurance of a male. But many listened to J. D. B. DeBow who advised perspective slave buyers that women became heirlooms. DeBow himself knew of a plantation where fifty or sixty of the slaves were the descendants of a single female, all realized in the lifetime of the original purchaser! As an ex-slave explained: "A white man start out wid a few womenfolk slaves, soon him have a plantation full of little niggers runnin' 'round in deir shirt tales and a kickin' up deir heels, whilst deir mammies was in de field a hoeing and geeing at the plow handles, workin lak a man." A woman, therefore, had double value. As explained to E. A. Andrews, she could not only be counted on to "do a smart chance of work," but she would "raise the children besides." This was Eophraim Beanland's line of reasoning. Beanland, one of President James Polk's overseers, purchased a slave woman while employed by Polk and subsequently hired her out to Polk for a fee which he collected with his wages. This indeed was smart business because the woman could "marry" any one of Polk's slaves and the child would still belong to Beanland. Another of Polk's overseers, Charles Bratton, did the same and in 1839 he wrote to Polk requesting that Polk "buy me a negro woman, young and likely and be sering that she is sound on the best terms you can bring down." Bratton had decided to follow Beanland's example, for he too informed Polk that the woman would work with Polk's slaves.**

Sound business sense notwithstanding, even the best plans could go awry, as this conversation between two Louisiana gentlemen demonstrates:

> "I hear you were very unlucky with that girl you bought of me last year?" "Yes, I was, very unlucky. She died with her first child, and the child died too." "Well, that was right hard for you. She was a fine girl. I don't reckon you lost less than five thousand dollars, when she died." "No, sir, not a dollar less." "Well, it came right hard upon you—just beginning so." "Yes, I was foolish, I suppose, to risk so much on the life of a single woman."

Many a lesser man would have been discouraged, but this gentleman was not to be beaten. He began again, but improved his odds by buying two women. At the time of the conversation, one of them had a fine baby boy and the other, "as hearty as ever," was pregnant.††

See the following:*DeBow's Review (1857), 30:74; Frederick Law Olmsted, A Journey in the Seaboard Slave States (New York: Dix and Edwards, 1856), p. 282; Louis F. Tasistro, Random Shots and Southern Breezes, 2 vols. (New York, Harper and Brothers, 1842), 1:88–92; William Howard Russell, My Diary North and South (Canada, Its Defenses, Condition, and Resources), 3 vols. (London: Bradbury and Evans, 1863), 1:397; Frederick Olmsted, A Journey Through the Back Country 1853–1854 (New York: Putnam's Sons, 1907), p. 59. †Frederick Olmsted, The Cotton Kingdom, David Freeman Hawke, ed. (New York: Bobbs-Merrill, 1971), pp. 12, 72; Harriet Martineau, Society in America, 3 vols. (London: Saunders and Otley, 1837), 2:327–328; Industrial Resources of the Southern Western States, 3 vols. (Washington, D.C.: U.S. Government Printing Office, 1854), 1:163. **DeBow's Review (1857), 30:74; George P. Rawick, ed., The American Slave: A Composite Autobiography, 19 vols. (Westport, Conn.: Greenwood, 1972), S.C., 2(1):173. Hereafter this work will be cited with the foregoing construction); E. A. Andrews, Slavery and the Domestic Slave Trade in the United States (Boston: Light and Stearns, 1836), p. 149; John Spencer Bassett, ed., The Southern Plantation Overseer as Revealed in His Letters (Northhampton, Mass.: Southworth, 1925), pp. 89–90, 119. ‡‡Olmsted, Cotton Kingdom, p. 153.

23. Reynolds Farley, Growth of the Black Population, A Study of Demographic Trends (Chicago: Markham, 1970), pp. 21, 34. See also Reynolds Farley, "The Demographic Rates and Social Institutions of the Nineteenth-Century Negro Population: A Stable Population Analysis," in Demography (1965), 2:389, 390;

Melvin Zelnick, "Fertility of the American Negro in 1830–1850," *Population Studies* (1966), 20:82.

24. It is important to note that this particular topic has stimulated heated debate and involves some controversial issues. Among them is the subject of interregional slave sales. Some historians have argued that the older Southern states of Virginia, Maryland, Delaware, and North Carolina "bred" slaves for the "buyer" states of the Southwest and that slave fertility was more important to slave owners in the older regions than in the newer regions. See Kenneth Stampp, *The Peculiar Institution, Slavery in the Ante-Bellum South* (New York: Random House, 1956), pp. 245–258, and Frederic Bancroft, *Slave Trading in the Old South* (New York: Frederick Ungar, 1931). Conrad and Meyer also supported the "slave-breeding" thesis. They found that slave owners in the older South realized a greater profit on slave women than slave men. See Alfred Conrad and John R. Meyer, "The Economics of Slavery in the Ante-Bellum South," *The Journal of Political Economics* (April 1958), 66:106–115. William Calderhead was not as convinced as Stampp, Bancroft, and Conrad and Meyer. See William Calderhead, "How Extensive Was the Border States' Slave Trade: A New Look," *Civil War History* (March 1972), 18:42–85. Richard Sutch concluded that "slave owners in the American South systematically bred slaves for sale." Slave breeders located in the border and Atlantic coast slave states held "disproportionally large numbers of women in the childbearing age group . . . , fostered polygamy and promiscuity among their slaves and then sold the products of the breeding operation to southwestern slave states." See Richard Sutch, "The Breeding of Slaves for Sale and Westward Expansion of Slavery 1830–1860," in Engerman and Genovese, eds., *Race and Slavery*, pp. 173–210; Fogel and Engerman argue that slave fertility was more highly valued in the newer regions than in the older ones. They claim that the higher fertility rate in the latter is explained by the fact that there was a higher proportion of single women without children in the interregional migration than in populations that remained behind. See Robert William Fogel and Stanley L. Engerman, *Time on the Cross, The Economics of American Negro Slavery* (Boston: Little, Brown, 1974), pp. 44–52, 78–84. For a rebuttal of the Fogel and Engerman position see Herbert Gutman, *Slavery and the Numbers Game, A Critique of Time on the Cross* (Urbana: University of Illinois Press, 1975), pp. 102–113.

25. Peter H. Wood, *Black Majority: Negroes in Colonial South Carolina* (New York: Knopf, 1974) p. 244. Wood quotes the unpublished paper of Russell L. Blake, "Slave Runaways in Colonial South Carolina," prepared for Kenneth Lockridge, University of Michigan, 1972, p. 22.

26. Gerald W. Mullin, *Flight and Rebellion, Slave Resistance in Eighteenth-Century Virginia* (London: Oxford University Press, 1972), p. 40.

27. James Sellers, *Slavery in Alabama* (University, Ala.: University of Alabama Press, 1950), p. 292.

28. Genovese, *Roll, Jordan, Roll*, p. 798. Genovese quotes Professor Paul Gaston.

29. Judith Kelleher Schafer, "New Orleans Slavery in 1850 as Seen in Advertisements," in *Journal of Southern History* (February 1981), 46:43. For further evidence see Charles Sackett Sydnor, *Slavery in Mississippi* (Gloucester, Mass.: Peter Smith, 1965), p. 126. These statistics form a consistent pattern despite the fact that not all runaways were advertised for in local

newspapers. See also John W. Blassingame, *The Slave Community. Plantation Life in the Antebellum South*, 2nd ed. (New York: Oxford University Press, 1979), pp. 201–202.

30. Stampp, *The Peculiar Institution*, p. 110; Genovese, *Roll, Jordan, Roll*, p. 648; Joe Gray Taylor, *Negro Slavery in Louisiana* (Louisiana: Louisiana Historical Association, 1963), p. 179; Lorenzo J. Greene, "The New England Negro as Seen in Advertisements for Runaway Slaves," *Journal of Negro History*, (April 1944), 29:131.

31. S.C., vol. 2, pt. 2. Kipple and King estimate that slave mothers nursed their infants for about one year. See Kenneth F. Kipple and Virginia Himmelsteib King, *Another Dimension to the Black Diaspora. Diet, Disease, and Racism* (Cambridge: Cambridge University Press, 1981), p. 97.

32. See Bancroft, *Slave Trading*, pp. 186–187.

33. Schafer, "New Orleans Slavery," p. 47.

34. Brent, *Incidents in the Life of a Slave Girl*, p. 97.

35. Catterall, ed., *Judicial Cases*, 1:411.

36. Josiah Henson, *Autobiography of the Reverend Josiah Henson in Four Fugitive Slave Narratives* (Reading, Mass.: Addison Wesley, 1969), p. 60.

37. Bibb, in Osofsky, ed., *Ole Massa*, pp. 126–128.

38. E. A. Andrews, *Slavery and the Domestic Slave-Trade in the United States* (Boston: Light and Stearns, 1836), p. 153.

39. William Still, *The Underground Railroad, A Record of Facts, Authentic Narratives, Letters, etc.* (Philadelphia: Porter and Coates, 1872) pp. 50.

40. *Ibid.*, p. 188.

41. *Ibid.*, p. 80.

42. Harriet Beecher Stowe, *Uncle Tom's Cabin* (New York: Washington Square Press, 1962 [1852]), p. 74; Levi Coffin, *Reminiscences of Levi Coffin* (Cincinnati, Oh.: Robert Clarke, 1898), pp. 147–149; Marion Gleason McDougall, *Fugitive Slaves [1619–1865]* (New York: Bergman, 1967 [1891]), p. 47.

43. Coffin, *Reminiscences*, p. 114. Coffin thought it best to conceal the identity of this woman so as to prevent her recapture.

44. Still, *Underground Railroad*, p. 68; Brent, *Slave Girl*, pp. 151–164. See also Still, *Underground Railroad*, p. 264.

45. Still, *Underground Railroad*, p. 264.

46. *Ibid.*, p. 37.

47. *Ibid.*, p. 158.

48. Benjamin Drew, *The Refugee: A North-Side View of Slavery*, in *Four Fugitive Slave Narratives* (Reading, Mass.: Addison Wesley, 1969), p. 49.

49. Brent, *Slave Girl*, pp. 93, 104. See also OK., 6:317, and Ala., 6:73.

50. Mullin, *Flight and Rebellion*, pp. 103–104, 187; Wood, *Black Majority*, p. 241; Catterall, ed., *Judicial Cases*, 5:220.

51. Ga., 12 (2):324.

52. Frances Anne Kemble, *Journal of a Residence on a Georgian Plantation*, John A. Scott (New York: Knopf, 1961), pp. 215–216.

53. Solomon Northup, *Twelve Years a Slave, Narrative of Solomon Northup*, in Osofsky, ed., *Ole Massa*, pp. 360–361. See also, S.C., 2(2):145; Bassett, *The Southern Plantation Overseer*, p. 129.

54. Louis B. Wright and Marion Tinling, eds., *The Secret Diary of William Byrd of Westover, 1709–1712* (Richmond, Va.: Dietz, 1941), pp. 196, 197, 199,

202, 205, 206, 215, 257. See also, Ark., 10(7):90.

55. See for instance Bancroft, *Slave Trading*, pp. 156–161; Fogel and Engerman, *Time on the Cross*, p. 43; Genovese, *Roll, Jordan, Roll*, pp. 390, 392–398; Mullin, *Flight and Rebellion*, p. 36; Shafer, "New Orleans Slavery," pp. 54–55; Sydnor, *Slavery in Mississippi*, pp. 6–7, 11.

56. For example, in her escape from Washington, D.C., in 1855, Maria Weems donned a pair of pantaloons, changed her name to Joe, and pretended to be a coachman. Clarissa, a slave who fled to Portsmouth, Virginia, in 1854 also dressed in male attire to make good her escape, as did Linda Brent who dressed as a sailor when she escaped. See Still, *Underground Railroad*, p. 182; Coffin, *Reminiscences*, p. 347; Brent, *Slave Girl*, p. 114. See also Mullin, *Flight and Rebellion*, pp. 113–114, 191.

57. See the discussions in the following: Stanley Elkins, *Slavery, A Problem in American Institutional and Intellectual Life*, 2nd ed. (Chicago: University of Chicago Press, 1959), pp. 136–137; George M. Frederickson and Christopher Lasch, "Resistance to Slavery" in *The Debate Over Slavery, Stanley Elkins and His Critics*, Ann J. Lane, ed. (Urbana: University of Illinois Press, 1971), pp. 223–244; Genovese, *Roll, Jordan, Roll*, p. 587–598.

58. Susan Dabney Smedes, *Memorials of a Southern Planter*, Fletcher M. Greene, ed. (New York: Knopf, 1965), p. 180. Resistant behavior was exhibited by many eighteenth-century slaves. Whenever Landon Carter's spinners thought he was away they slacked off. One day he caught them by surprise and had them whipped. Suckey, one of Robert Carter's slave women, used Carter's absence to her advantage. When the overseer demanded that she report to work, she calmly sent word that Carter had excused her so she might wash clothes and "go to any meeting she pleased, any time in the weke." The overseer was thrown into a quandary and wrote Carter requesting that he separate Suckey from the rest of the slaves if she was to be given special privileges. See Jack P. Greene, ed., *The Diary of Colonel Landon Carter of Sabine Hall, 1752–1778*, 2 vols. (Charlottesville: Virginia Historical Society, 1965), 2:762; Ulrich B. Phillips, *Plantation and Frontier: Documents, 1649–1863*, 2 vols. (Cleveland: Arthur H. Clarke, 1909), 1:325.

59. See *DeBow's Review* (1851), 11:333–334.

60. Henson, *Autobiography of the Reverend Josiah Henson*, p. 116.

61. See Olmsted, *Cotton Kingdom*, p. 153; Olmsted, *Seaboard Slave States*, p. 194; B. A. Botkin, ed., *Lay My Burden Down, A Folk History of Slavery* (Chicago: University of Chicago Press, 1945), p. 174; Harriet Martineau, *Society in America*, 3 vols. (London: Saunders and Otley, 1837), 2:318–319; *South Carolina Gazette*, August 1, 1769; Joshua Coffin, ed., *An Account of the Principal Slave Insurrections*, in *Slave Insurrections, Selected Documents* (New York: American Anti-Slavery Society, 1968), p. 15; Catterall, ed., *Judicial Cases*, 2:15–16 and 3:162; Henry Muhlenberg, *The Journals of Henry Melchior Muhlenberg*, Theodore Tappert and John W. Doberstein eds. and trans., 3 vols. (Philadelphia: The Evangelical Lutheran Ministerium of Pennsylvania and Adjacent States and the Muhlenberg Press, 1941), 2:585.

62. *Ibid.*, p. 174–175.

63. Ark., 10(7):193; see also Ok., 6:161, 346; Botkin, ed., *Lay My Burden Down*, p. 174.

64. Rev. J. W. Loguen, *The Rev. J. W. Loguen as a Slave and as a Free Man* (Syracuse, N.Y.: by the author, 1859), pp. 20–21.

65. S.C., 2(2):65–66. See also Bibb, in Osofsky, ed., *Ole Massa*, p. 112.

66. Joshua Coffin, ed., *An Account of the Principal Slave Insurrections*, p. 15; *South Carolina Gazette*, August 1, 1769.

67. C. Vann Woodward, ed., *Mary Chesnut's Civil War* (New Haven: Yale University Press, 1981), pp. 218–219.

68. Olmsted, *Seaboard Slave States*, p. 190.

69. Greene, *Diary of Colonel Landon Carter*, 2:604, 610, and 1:371–372.

70. See Ulrich B. Phillips, *American Negro Slavery, A Survey of the Supply, Employment, and Control of Negro Labor as Determined by the Plantation Regime* (Baton Rouge: Louisiana State University Press, 1966 [1918]), pp. 258–286.

71. Newstead Plantation Books, March 23, 1857, Southern Historical Collection (SHC), University of North Carolina at Chapel Hill, Chapel Hill, North Carolina.

72. Ferguson to Richard J. Arnold, July 1832, in Chas. Arnold and Screven Family Papers, Series B, 1811–1869, SHC.

73. Bayside Plantation Book, March 5, 1880, Bayside Plantation Records, SHC.

74. Bassett, ed., *The Plantation Overseer*, pp. 35, 59, 77, 119, 139, 142, 144, 150, 151, 156, 157.

75. See Mullin, *Flight and Rebellion*, p. 55.

76. Olmsted, *Back Country*, p. 79.

77. Leslie Howard Owens, *This Species of Property, Slave Life and Culture in the Old South* (Oxford: Oxford University Press, 1976), p. 57; see also pp. 50–69. For other discussions of slave health see: Kipple and King, *Diet, Disease, and Racism;* William Desite Postell, *The Health of Slaves on Southern Plantations* (Baton Rouge: Louisiana State University Press, 1951); Todd L. Savitt, *Medicine and Slavery, The Diseases and Health Care of Blacks in Antebellum Virginia* (Urbana: University of Illinois Press, 1978), pp. 49–148; Felice Swados, "Negro Health on the Antebellum Plantation," *Bulletin of the History of Medicine* (1941), 10:460–472.

78. Savitt, *Medicine and Slavery*, pp. 115, 119–120; see also Postell, *The Health of Slaves*, pp. 111–128; Swados, "Negro Health," p. 470.

79. Farley, *Growth of the Black Population*, p. 33.

80. The Seventh Census, *Report of the Superintendent of the Census* (Washington, D.C.,: Robert Armstrong, 1853), p. 13. These statistics were based on an aggregate of 244,786 slaves and 17,537 free colored. See also E. M. Pendleton, "On the Susceptibility of the Caucasian and African Races to the Different Classes of Disease," in *Southern Medical Reports* (1949 [1856]), 2:340; George Tucker, *Progress of the United States in Population and Wealth in Fifty Years* (New York: Augustus M. Kelley, 1964 [1855]), pp. 68–69; J. D. B. DeBow, *Statistical View of the United States, Compendium of the Seventh Census* (Washington, D.C.: Senate Printer, 1854), p. 92. It should be mentioned that DeBow felt the 1850 slave mortality statistics were underreported. See p. 92.

81. Fletcher M. Greene, ed., *Ferry Hill Plantation Journal*, in *The James Sprunt Studies in History and Political Science* (Chapel Hill: University of North Carolina Press, 1961), p. 25–56.

82. E. M. Pendleton, "On the Susceptibility of the Caucasian and African races to the different classes of Disease," p. 338.

83. John H. Morgan, "An Essay on the Production of Abortion Among Our Negro Population," in *Nashville Journal of Medicine and Surgery*, (August

1860), 19:117–118. See also Robert Manson Myers, ed., *The Children of Pride, A True Story of Georgia and the Civil War* (New Haven: Yale University Press, 1976), pp. 528, 532–533.

84. Catterall, ed., *Judicial Cases*, 2:475.

85. Botkin, ed., *Lay My Burden Down*, pp. 130–131.

86. Mo., 10(7):135.

87. Cheryll Ann Cody, "Slave Demography and Family Formation. A Community Study of the Ball Family Plantations, 1720–1896," (Ph.D. dissertation, University of Minnesota, 1982), pp. 122–123.

88. Morgan, "The Causes of the Production of Abortion," pp. 117, 122.

89. *Ibid.*, p. 122–123.

90. Pendleton, "On the Susceptibility of the Caucasion and African Races to the Different Classes of Disease," p. 338.

91. Evidence that white women were fearful of childbearing can be found in the following: Anne Firor Scott, *The Southern Lady, From Pedestal to Politics, 1830–1930* (Chicago: University of Chicago Press, 1970), pp. 37–39; Linda Gordon, *Woman's Body, Woman's Right, A Social History of Birth Control in America* (New York: Penguin, 1974), p. 106; Ann Douglas Wood, " 'The Fashionable Diseases': Women's Complaints and Their Treatment in Nineteenth-Century America," in *The Journal of Interdisciplinary History* (Summer 1973), 4(1):34–35.

92. See for instance, Savitt, *Medicine and Slavery*, p. 128.

93. See note 22 of this chapter; Gutman, *Black Family*, p. 50; Kipple and King, *Diet, Disease, and Racism*, p. 65.

94. Kipple and King, *Diet, Disease, and Racism*, p. 65. One wonders how slave fertility would have compared to Southern white fertility if pregnant slave women had not resisted slave owner work demands. More demographic information is needed before we can draw more precise conclusions. Cheryll Cody's study of the Ball plantations in South Carolina suggests the kind of questions that need to be asked. Cody has shown how slave conceptions, births, and infant deaths correlated positively with the slave woman's work regimen and access to mates. She has also compared the fertility rates of the Ball family's slaves to other fertility populations. Although limited to a few South Carolina plantations, her work is extremely valuable. See Cody, "Slave Demography and Family Formation."

95. See note 91.

96. Gordon, *Woman's Body, Woman's Right*, p. 153–154; Daniel Scott Smith, "Family Limitation, Sexual Control, and Domestic Feminism in Victorian America," in *Clio's Consciousness Raised, New Perspectives on the History of Women*, Mary S. Hartman and Louis Banner, eds. (New York: Harper and Row, 1974), p. 48.

97. Farley, *Growth of the Black Population*, p. 57; Gordon, *Woman's Body, Woman's Rights*, p. 48.

98. Catterall, ed., *Judicial Cases*, 2:59.

99. *Ibid.*, 5:139; Bassett, ed., *Plantation Overseer*, p. 59.

100. Olmsted, *Seaboard Slave States*, p. 601.

101. Ok., 6:302.

102. Michael P. Johnson, "Smothered Slave Infants: Were Slave Mothers at Fault?" in *The Journal of Southern History* (November 1981), 47(4):495.

103. Savitt, *Medicine and Slavery*, p. 122; Savitt quotes from Abraham B.

Bergman, J. Bruce Beckwith, and C. George Ray, eds., *Sudden Infant Death Syndrome: Proceedings of the Second International Conference on Causes of Death in Infants* (Seattle, 1970), p. 18.
104. Johnson, "Smothered Slave Infants," 501–506; Savitt, *Medicine and Slavery*, p. 124.
105. Johnson, "Smothered Slave Infants," p. 509; Savitt, *Medicine and Slavery*, p. 127.

3. THE LIFE CYCLE
OF THE FEMALE SLAVE

1. George Rawick, ed. *The American Slave, a Composite Autobiography*, 19 vols. (Westport, Conn: Greenwood, 1972); Va., 16:2. (Hereafter cited with the foregoing construction.)
2. Arnold van Gennep, *The Rites of Passage* (Chicago: University of Chicago Press, 1960), pp. 2–3.
3. For more information on the life of children and the age-segregated world they lived in see Eugene Genovese, *Roll, Jordan, Roll, The World the Slaves Made* (New York: Vintage, 1974), pp. 508–509.
4. Ala., 6:33.
5. Ark., 10 (5):155.
6. Frances Anne Kemble, *Journal of a Residence on a Georgian Plantation*, John A. Scott, ed. (New York: Knopf, 1961), p. 156. See also Beth G. Crabtree and James W. Patton, eds., *"Journal of a Secesh Lady" The Diary of Catherine Devereux Edmondston 1860–1866* (Raleigh, N.C.: Division of Archives and History, 1979), p. 45.
7. B. A. Botkin, ed., *Lay My Burden Down: A Folk History of Slavery* (Chicago University of Chicago Press, 1945), p. 62.
8. Ophelia S. Egypt, J. Masuoka, Charles S. Johnson, eds., *Unwritten History of Slavery, Autobiographical Accounts of Negro Ex-Slaves* (Nashville, Tenn.: Fisk University Press, 1945), p. 15.
9. Ala., 6:197.
10. Linda Brent, *Incidents in the Life of a Slave Girl*, Lydia Maria Child, ed. (New York: Harcourt Brace Jovanovich, 1973 [1861]), p. 7.
11. Botkin, ed., *Lay My Burden Down*, pp. 63, 90, 141–142; Frederick Olmsted, *The Cotton Kingdom*, David Freeman Hawke, ed. (New York: Bobbs-Merrill, 1971), p. 152; William Howard Russell, *My Diary North and South (Canada, its Defenses, Condition, and Resources)*, 3 vols. (London: Bradbury and Evans, 1863), 1:387.
12. Ga., 13(3):160; Louis Hughes, *Thirty Years a Slave* (Milwaukee: South Side, 1897), p. 41; Mo., 10(7):255; Frederick Olmsted, *A Journey in the Seaboard Slave States* (New York: Dix and Edwards, 1856), p. 430; *Plantation Manual*, Southern Historical Collection, University of North Carolina at Chapel Hill, Chapel Hill, North Carolina. Hereafter cited as SHC; Olmsted, *Cotton Kindgom*, pp. 78, 175; Kemble, *Journal of a Residence on a Georgian Plantation*, pp. 87, 197; Hughes, *Thirty Years a Slave*, pp. 22, 41; Benjamin Drew, *The Refugee: A North-Side View of Slavery*, in *Four Fugitive Slave Narratives* (Reading, Mass.: Addison, Wesley, 1969), p. 128; Adwon Adams Davis, *Plantation Life in the Florida Parishes of Louisiana 1836–1846 as Reflected in the Diary of Bennet*

H. Barrow (New York: Columbia University Press, 1943), p. 127; Crabtree and Patton, eds., *"Journal of a Secesh Lady"*, p. 46.

13. James Trussel and Richard Steckel, "The Age of Slaves at Menarche and Their First Birth," *Journal of Interdisciplinary History* (Winter 1978), 8:504.

14. Miss., 7(2):44; Olmsted, *Seaboard Slave States*, pp. 27–28, 112; S.C., 2(2):47; Botkin, ed., *Lay My Burden Down*, p. 80, 113.

15. S.C., 2(2):47; Botkin, ed., *Lay My Burden Down*, p. 145.

16. Ala., 6:243.

17. Brent, *Incidents in the Life of a Slave Girl*, p. 57.

18. Ga., 12(4):292; Ga., 13(3):69.

19. Brent, *Incidents in the Life of a Slave Girl*, p. 17.

20. Egypt, ed., *Unwritten History*, pp. 68.

21. *Ibid.*, p. 167; see also S.C., 2:201.

22. Norman Yetman, *Voices from Slavery* (New York: Holt Rhinehart, and Winston, 1970), p. 102.

23. Ark., 8(2):319.

24. Fisk University, *Unwritten History*, p. 10.

25. Va., 16:15.

26. Fisk University, *Unwritten History*, p. 8; Va., 16:25.

27. C. Vann Woodward, ed., *Mary Chesnut's Civil War* (New Haven: Yale University Press, 1981), p. 307.

28. Olmsted, *Back Country*, p. 169.

29. Ok., 6:280.

30. S.C., 2(2):51–52.

31. Although historian Robert Fogel and Stanley Engerman cite the slave woman's age at first birth at 22.5, other historians, including Herbert Gutman and Richard Dunn, have found the age to be substantially lower. Dunn found the average age at first birth on the Mount Airy Virginia Plantation to be 19.22 years. Gutman found the range to be from 17 to 19. Economists James Trussell and Richard Steckel have found the age to be 20.6 years. See Robert Fogel and Stanley Engerman, *Time on the Cross, The Economics of American Negro Slavery* (Boston: Little, Brown, 1974, pp. 137–138); Richard Dunn, "The Tale of Two Plantations: Slave Life at Mesopotamia in Jamaica and Mount Airy in Virginia, 1799–1828," *William and Mary Quarterly* (January 1977), 34:58; Herbert Gutman, *The Black Family in Slavery and Freedom, 1750–1925* (New York: Pantheon Books, 1976), pp. 50, 75, 124, 171; James Trussell and Richard Steckel, "Age of Slaves at Menarche and First Birth," p. 504; the term marriage is used in this text with the understanding that legal marriage among slaves was prohibited.

32. *Industrial Resources of the Southern and Western States* 3 vols. (Washington, D.C.: Government Printing Office, 1854), 1:163.

33. Mo., 10(7):310; Fisk University, *Unwritten History*, 61–62; Ga., 13(3):79, 262; Ark., 10(7):14; Letter, Richard J. Arnold to Mr. Swanson, May 22, 1937, in Arnold Screven Family Papers, Series B, 1811–1869, SHC; Frederick Olmsted, *A Journey in the Back Country 1853–1854* (New York: Putnam's Sons, 1907), p. 154.

34. *Plantation Manual*, SHC.

35. Susan Dabney Smedes, *Memorials of a Southern Planter*, Fletcher M. Green, ed. (New York: Knopf, 1965), p. 42.

36. Henry Bibb, *Narrative of the Life and Adventures of Henry Bibb, an American Slave,* in *Puttin' on Ole Massa,* Gilbert Osofsky, ed. (New York, Harper and Row, 1969), p. 79.

37. N.C., 2:32. See also Ga., 12(1):165.

38. John Spencer Basset, ed., *The Southern Plantation Overseer as Revealed in His Letters* (Northampton, Mass.: Southworth, 1925), pp. 31, 139, 141; Ulrich Bonnell Phillips, ed., *Plantation and Frontier Documents, 1649–1863,* 2 vols. (Cleveland: Arthur H. Clarke, 1909), 1:312; Kemble, *Journal of a Residence on a Georgian Plantation,* p. 179.

39. Phillips, ed., *Plantation and Frontier Documents,* 1:109.

40. Kemble, *Journal of a Residence on a Georgian Plantation,* pp. 95, 127.

41. Ga., 13(4):8.

42. Helen T. Catterall, ed., *Judicial Cases Concerning American Slavery and the Negro,* 5 vols. (Washington, D.C.: Carnegie Institute of Washington, 1936), 2:151–152.

43. Bassett, *Plantation Overseer,* p. 32. See also Raymond and Alice Bauer, "Day-to-Day Resistance to Slavery," *Journal of Negro History* (October 1942), 27:415.

44. Catterall, ed., *Judicial Cases,* 3:65, 204. See also *Ibid.,* 69, 79, 164, 195, 213, 523, 541; *Ibid.,* 2:214, 392.

45. Olmsted, *Seaboard Slave States,* p. 55.

46. Ga., 12(1):191.

47. Botkin, ed., *Lay My Burden Down,* p. 119.

48. Dunn, "Two Plantations," p. 58; Mo., 10(7):253.

49. Botkin, ed., *Lay My Bruden Down,* pp. 160–162.

50. William Wells Brown, *Narrative of William Wells Brown, a Fugitive Slave,* in Osofsky, ed., *Ole Massa,* p. 214.

51. Bibb in Osofsky, ed., *Ole Massa,* p. 119. See also Harriet Martineau, *Society in America,* 3 vols. (London: Saunders and Otley, 1837), 2:156; Fla., 17:168; Miss., 6:114; Va., 16:11.

52. Trussell and Steckel, "The Age of Slaves at Menarche and First Birth," p. 492.

53. *Ibid.*

54. Cheryll Ann Cody, "Slave Demography and Family Formation. A Community Study of the Ball Family Plantations, 1720–1896" (Ph.D. dissertation, University of Minnesota, 1982), pp. 59, 155, 156.

55. See, for example, what historian Leslie Howard Owens says about the slave family: Leslie Howard Owens, *This Species of Property, Slave Life and Culture in the Old South* (Oxford: Oxford University Press, 1976), pp. 200–202; see also Genovese, *Roll, Jordan, Roll,* pp. 450–458.

56. Gutman, *The Black Family,* pp. 14, 17, 31–33, 67.

57. Niara Sudarkasa, "Female Employment and Family Organization in West Africa," in Filomina Chioma Steady, *The Black Woman Cross-Culturally* (Cambridge, Mass.: Schenkman, 1981), p. 53.

58. Agnes Akousua Aidoo, "Ashante Queen Mothers in Government and Politics in the Nineteenth Century," in Steady, *The Black Woman Cross-Culturally,* p. 65. See also Monique Gessain, "Coniagui Women," in Denise Paulme, ed., *Women of Tropical Africa* (Berkeley: University of California Press, 1963), p. 17.

59. Paulme, ed., *Women of Tropical Africa,* pp. 11–12. Gessain, "Coniagui

Women," p. 17. Melville Herskovits, *The Myth of the Negro Past* (Boston: Beacon, 1978 [1941]), p. 186–187.

60. Gessain, "Coniagui Women," p. 28; Marguerite Dupire, "The Position of Women in a Pastoral Society (The Fulani Wo Daa Be, Nomads of the Niger)," in Paulme, ed., *Women of Tropical Africa*, p. 58, 62.

61. Gessain, "Coniagui Women," p. 42; Dupire, "The Position of Women in a Pastoral Society," pp. 56, 72.

62. Niara Sudarkasa, "Interpreting the African Heritage in Afro-American Family Organization," in Harriete Pipes McAdoo, ed, *Black Families* (Beverly Hills, Calif.: Sage, 1981), p. 42–43.

63. *Ibid.;* Nancy Tanner, "Matrifocality in Indonesia and Africa and Among Black Americans," in Michelle Zimbalist Rosaldo and Louise Lamphere, eds., *Woman, Culture and Society* (Stanford: Standford University Press, 1974), p. 147; Sylvia Leith-Ross, *African Women: A Study of the Ibo of Nigeria* (London: Routledge and Kegan Paul, 1939), p. 127; Herskovitz, *Myth of the Negro Past*, p. 64.

64. Gessain, "Coniagui Women," p. 43; Dupire, "The Position of Women in a Pastoral Society," p. 73.

65. In researching links to the African past it is probably unwise to look for one-to-one correlations between African societies and black American society. It seems best to take the approach of anthropologists Sidney Mintz and Richard Price. They argue that the African-American's adaptation to Western cultural mores was governed by "unconscious 'grammatical' principles," which provided the framework for the development of new institutions and served as a catalyst in their development. This approach recognizes African influences in black culture while realizing the imprint of the black experience in the Americas. See Sidney W. Mintz and Richard Price, *An Anthropological Approach to the Afro-American Past: A Caribbean Perspective* (Philadelphia: ISHI, 1976).

66. Gutman, *The Black Family*, pp. 60–67, 78–79, 114, 163.

67. *Ibid.*, p. 191.

68. Kemble, *Journal of a Residence on a Georgian Plantation*, p. 169; Egypt, ed., *Unwritten History*, pp. 41–42; Elizabeth Hyde Botume, *First Days Amongst the Contrabands* (New York: Arno, 1968 [1893]), p. 125.

69. Botume, *First Days Amongst the Contrabands*, p. 163

70. George P. Rawick, Jan Hillegas, Ken Lawrence, eds., *The American Slave: A Composite Autobiography: Supplement, Series 1*, 12 vols., (Westport, Conn.: Greenwood, 1978); N.C., 11:41; Ark., 8(2):333; Kentucky, 16(1):91–92.

71. Catherine M. Scholten, "On the Importance of the Obstetric Art: Changing Customs of Childbirth in America, 1760–1825," in *William and Mary Quarterly* (1977) 34(430, 443, 444.

72. See, for example, Fla., 17:175; Ga., 12(2):112; N.C., Supplement, 2:137. Bayside Plantation Records SHC, vol. 2, 1864.

73. Carolyn Mitchell, "Health and the Medical Profession in the South," *Journal of Southern History* (1944), 10:433–436; Scholten, "Changing Patterns of Childbirth," pp. 430, 443, 444.

74. Olmsted, *Back Country*, p. 78.

75. Catterall, *Judicial Cases*, 3:503.

76. See Catterall, *Judicial Cases*, 2:85–86; Kemble, *Journal of a Residence on a Georgian Plantation*, pp. 76–77, 114, 170, 214. See also note 43.

77. Kemble, *Journal of a Residence on a Georgian Plantation*, p. 296; Ga., 12(2):260–261; S.C., 2(2):68; Fla., 17:213.
78. Botkin, ed., *Lay My Burden Down*, p. 85.
79. Fla., 17:143.
80. Brown in Osofsky, ed., *Ole Massa*, p. 187.
81. N.C., 15(2):144; Ga., 12(1):64; Ronnie C. Tyler and Lawrence R. Murphy, eds., *The Slave Narrative of Texas* (Austin, Tex.: Encino, 1974), p. 36.
82. Hughes, *Thirty Years a Slave*, p. 85.
83. On the Ball plantations in South Carolina the mean age at last birth from colonial times through the Civil War was 39.8 to 40. This mean age at last birth is close to that of other historical natural fertility populations. See Cody, "Slave Demography and Family Formation," p. 198.
84. Crabtree and Patton, eds, *"Journal of a Secesh Lady,"* p. 20.
85. For a few descriptions of the work which women did see J. H. Easterby, ed., *The South Carolina Rice Plantation as Revealed in the Papers of Robert F. W. Allston* (Chicago: University of Chicago Press, 1945), p. 346; Kemble, *Journal of a Residence on a Georgian Plantation*, p. 65; Olmsted, *The Cotton Kingdom*, pp. 67, 81; Drew, *The Refugee*, p. 92; Ga., 13(4):357; Oklahoma, 6:270; Miss., 6:151, 158.
86. Historians Fogel and Engerman claim that work was segregated by sex, with women never having to plow or do heavy labor. Eugene Genovese thinks otherwise. See Fogel and Engerman, *Time on the Cross*, p. 141, and Genovese, *Roll, Jordan, Roll*, pp. 319, 767.
87. See, for instance, Ga., 12(2):58; Ala., 6:2.
88. Olmsted, *Seaboard States*, p. 425.
89. Phillips, *Plantation and Frontier Documents*, 1:27.
90. Ga., 12(2):112.
91. S.C., 2(2):55;
92. Fla., 17:174; see also Olmsted, *Back Country*, p. 76.
93. Cody has found that when Peter Gaillard's estate was distributed among his children, daughters were twice as likely as sons to stay with their mothers. Cody argues that the higher proportion of parents who continued to live on the same plantation with their daughters suggest that the care of elderly parents was entrusted more frequently to daughters than to sons. See Cheryll Ann Cody, "Naming, Kinship, and Estate Dispersal: Notes on Slave Family Life on a Southern Carolina Plantation, 1786–1833," in *William and Mary Quarterly* (1982), 39(1):207–209.
94. Brent, *Slave Girl*, p. 14.
95. Kemble, *Journal of a Residence on a Georgia Plantation*, p. 228.
96. Ira Berlin, *Slaves Without Masters, The Free Negro in the Antebellum South* (New York: Random House, 1974), pp. 151–152, 177–178.
97. Easterby, *The South Carolina Rice Plantation*, p. 316.

4. THE FEMALE SLAVE NETWORK

1. Michelle Zimbalist Rosaldo, "Woman, Culture, and Society: A Theoretical Overview," in *Woman, Culture, and Society*, Michelle Zimbalist Rosaldo and Louise Lamphere, eds. (Stanford: Stanford University Press, 1974), p. 39.
2. Fredericka Bremer, *Homes of the New World*, 2 vols. (New York: Harper

and Brothers, 1853), 2:519; Frances Anne Kemble, *Journal of a Residence on a Georgian Plantation*, John A Scott, ed. (New York: Knopf, 1961 [1863]), p. 66. See also Harriet Martineau, *Society in America*, 3 vols. (London: Saunders and Otley, 1837), 2:243, 311–312.

3. Benjamin Drew, *The Refugee: A North-Side View of Slavery*, in *Four Fugitive Slave Narratives* (Reading, Mass.: Addison Wesley, 1969), p. 92.

4. George Rawick, ed., *The American Slave, A Complete Autobiography*, 19 vols., (Westport, Conn.: Greenwood, 1972); Ga., 13(4):139. All subsequent references to this work are cited with the foregoing construction.

5. Frederick Law Olmsted, *A Journey In the Seaboard Slave States*, (New York: Dix and Edwards, 1856), pp. 430, 431, 432; and *The Cotton Kingdom*, David Freeman Hawke, ed. (New York: Bobbs-Merrill, 1971) p. 176; William Howard Russell, *My Diary North and South (Canada, Its Defenses, Condition, and Resources)*, 3 vols. (London: Bradbury and Evans, 1865), 1:379–380; Solomon Northup, *Twelve Years a Slave, Narrative of Solomon Northup*, in *Puttin' on Ole Massa*, Gilbert Osofsky, ed. (New York, Harper & Row, 1969), pp. 308–309 (hereafter cited as Northup in Osofsky, ed., *Ole Massa*); Ark., 10(5):54; Ala., 6(46):336; Newstead Plantation Diary 1856–58, entry Wednesday, May 6, 1857, Southern Historical Collection (SHC), University of North Carolina at Chapel Hill, Chapel Hill, North Carolina; Adwon Adams Davis, *Plantation Life in the Florida Parishes of Louisiana 1836–1846 as Reflected in the Diary of Bennet H. Barrow* (New York: Columbia University Press, 1943), p. 127; Frederick Law Olmsted, *A Journey in the Back Country* (New York: Putnam's Sons, 1907), p.152; *Plantation Manual*, SHC, p.4; Eugene Genovese, *The Political Economy of Slavery, Studies in the Economy and Society of the Slave South* (New York: Random House, 1961), p. 133; Stuart Bruckey, ed., *Cotton and the Growth of the American Economy: 1790–1860* (New York: Harcourt, Brace, and World, 1967), pp. 176, 177, 179, 180.

6. See note 5.

7. J. A. Turner, ed., *The Cotton Planters Manual* (New York: Orange Judd, 1865), pp. 97–98; Guion B. Johnson, *A Social History of the Sea Islands* (Chapel Hill: University of North Carolina Press, 1930), pp. 28–30; Jenkins Mikell, *Rumbling of the Chariot Wheels* (Columbia: University of South Carolina Press, 1923), pp. 19–20; Bruchey, *Cotton and the Growth of the American Economy*, pp. 176, 177, 179, 180.

8. Texas, 4(2):p. 292.

9. S. C., 2(2):114. See also Ala., 6:297, 360; Ok., 7:315.

10. Ga., 13(4):157.

11. Ga., 13(3):186.

12. *Plantation Manual*, SHC, p. 1.

13. Ok., 7:315.

14. S. C., 3(3):244.

15. George P. Rawick, Jan Hillegas, Ken Lawrence, eds., *The American Slave: A Composite Autobiography, Supplement, Series 1*, 12 vols., (Westport, Conn.: Greenwood, 1978), Ga., Supplement 1, 4:479. All subsequent references to this work are cited with the foregoing construction.

16. Mo., 11:307.

17. *Ibid.*, 11:366. Women did not always wait until after services to "get religion." Shouting and mourning is an activity almost impossible to quantify from a 150-year distance yet most testimony suggests that during religious

services women were far more expressive than men. It could very well be that men found excessive emotional outbursts unmanly. Whatever the reason, while most slave preachers were male, it seems it was woman's ordained role to show "the spirit" most dramatically.*

All the shouters recalled by one ex-slave were female. As if compelled by her name, Aunt Bellow was a "great shouter." Aunt Charlotte "use to cry most all the time," and when Aunt Kate, "a shouter," started "it took some good ones to hold her down." No one, however, could match the shouting of his grandmother Eve, "when she called on God she made heaven ring." According to Gus Feaster, slaves sometimes were called upon to sing spirituals for the whites. So moving was the singing, reported Feaster, that "now and then some old mammy would fall outen . . . a-shoutin Glory and Hallelujah! and Amen!" Martha Colquitt remembered that her Grandma was a "powerful Christian woman" who loved to sing and shout. "Grandma would git to shouten' so loud and she would make such a fuss nobody in de church could her de preacher."†

Women took up their shouting roles during baptizings, and during funerals women assumed the chief mourning roles. Remembering the first baptizing she attended, Lina Hunter recalled an old woman who emerged from the crick "a-shoutin' bout she was walkin' through de pearly gates and wearin' golden slippers." Since she was just a child at the time, the metaphor was lost on Hunter who could see no more than "brogans" on the woman's feet. According to Henry Barnes, "when a nigger die, dey was buried in de graveyard lak dey do now, an' dey shouted and hollered an' sometimes a 'oman she faint an hab to be tote home." On a Florida plantation funeral ceremonies were conducted by a woman. According to the woman's daughter, her mother "boss all de funerals on de plantation an' she got a long white veil for wearin." Explaining further she noted that the veil worn by her mother "kept the hants away."**

*Many anthropologists would not find this odd at all. Michelle Rosaldo finds that while men mourn and cry during religious rituals, it is women who cry longest and loudest, or who in some other way must show suffering at death. In some societies women are considered more attuned to those mysterious forces involved in death because they are associated with the mysterious miracle of birth. They are perceived as intermediaries, as links between the living, thinking world of human beings and the seemingly caprious ways of nature. See Sherry B. Ortner, "Is Female to Male as Nature Is to Culture?" in Rosaldo and Lamphere, ed., *Woman, Culture, and Society*, pp. 67–87, and Michelle Zimbalist Rosaldo, "Woman, Culture, and Society: A Theoretical Overview," in *Ibid.*, pp. 30–31, 33.

†Charles S. Johnson, ed., *God Struck Me Dead. Religious Conversion Experiences and Autobiographies of Negro Ex-Slaves* (Nashville, Tenn.: Fisk University Press, 1945), pp. 156–157; Botkin, ed., *Lay My Burden Down*, p. 146; Ga., 12(2):247. See also Robert Manson Myers, ed., *The Children of Pride. A True Story of Georgia and the Civil War* (New Haven: Yale University Press, 1972), p. 483.

**Ga., 12(2):263; Ala., 6:22; Fla., 17:191. See also Ala., 6:341.

18. See chapter 3 in this work.

19. Todd L. Savitt, *Medicine and Slavery: The Diseases and Health Care of Blacks in Antebellum Virginia* (Urbana: University of Illinois Press, 1978), p. 182.

20. Miss. Supplement 1, 8:1027; N. C., 15(2):134.
21. For examples of cures see Ark., 10(5):21, 125; Ala., 6:256, 318; Ga., 13(3):106.
22. Savitt, *Medicine and Slavery*, p. 180.
23. Russell, *Diary North and South*, 1:373.
24. Olmsted, *Back Country*, p. 76.
25. Ga., 12(1):303.
26. Fla., 17:175; see also Miss. Supplement 1, 6:317; Ga. Supplement 1, 4:444; John Spencer Bassett, *The Southern Plantation Overseer, as Revealed in His Letters* (Northamptom, Mass.: Southworth Press, 1923), p. 31; see also p. 28.
27. Kemble, *Journal of a Residence on a Georgian Plantation*, p. 222.
28. Myers, ed., *Children of Pride*, pp. 528, 532, 542, 544, 546.
29. Charles S. Johnson, ed., *God Stuck Me Dead*. in Rawick, ed., *The American Slave*, 19:74.
30. E. A. Andrews, *Slavery and the Domestic Slave-Trade in the United States*, (Boston: Light and Stearns, 1836), p. 149.
31. Booker T. Washington, *Up from Slavery*, in *Three Negro Classics* (New York: Avon Books, 1965 [1901]), p. 31; Ala., 6:340. See also Ga., 13(3):237; S. C., 2(1):316.
32. Ga., 13(3):245.
33. S. C., 2(1):99.
34. Ga., 12(2):112; S. C., 2(2):55; Fla., 17:174; see also Olmsted, *Back Country*, p. 76.
35. See, for instance, *Plantation Manual*, SHC, p. 1.
36. Ala., 6:73.
37. Ga. Supplement 1, 4(3):103.
38. Texas, 5(3):43.
39. Hughes, *Thirty Years a Slave*, p. 39; Fla., 17:158; White Hill Plantation Books, SHC, p. 13; S. C., 2(2):114.
40. C. Vann Woodward, ed., *Mary Chesnut's Civil War* (New Haven: Yale University Press, 1981), pp. 33–34.
41. Hughes, *Thirty Years a Slave*, p. 22.
42. Ophelia Settle Egypt, J. Masuoka, Charles S. Johnson, eds., *Unwritten History of Slavery: Autobiographical Accounts of Negro Ex-Slaves* (Washington, D.C.: Microcard Editions, 1968 [1945]), p. 41.
43. Ark., 11:21; see also Ulrich Bonnell Phillips, ed., *Plantation and Frontier Documents, 1649–1863*, 2 vols., (Cleveland: Arthur H. Clarke, 1909), 1:27.
44. Frederick Douglass, *My Bondage and My Freedom* (New York: Arno Press, 1968 [1855]), p. 69.
45. Laura M. Towne, *Letters and Diary of Laura M. Towne Written from the Sea Islands of South Carolina 1862–1884*, Rupert Sargent Holland, ed. (New York: Negro Universities Press, 1969 [1912]), pp. 144–145. See also Frances Anne Kemble, *Journal of a Residence on a Georgian Plantation*, p. 55.
46. Ga., 13(3):190.
47. Douglass, *My Bondage and My Freedom*, p. 36.
48. Elizabeth Hyde Botume, *First Days Amongst the Contrabands* (Boston: Lee and Shepard, 1893), p. 132.
49. Davis, *Plantation Life in the Florida Parishes*, p. 191. See also pp. 168, 173.
50. Kemble, *Journal of a Residence on a Georgian Plantation*, pp. 118–119.

51. Cheryll Ann Cody, "Naming, Kinship, and Estate Dispersal: Notes on Slave Family Life on a South Carolina Plantation, 1786 to 1833," *William and Mary Quarterly* (1982), 39(1):207; and Cody, "Slave Demography and Family Formation. A Community Study of the Ball Family Plantations, 1720–1896." (Ph.D. Dissertation, University of Minnesota, 1982), pp. 370, 379.

52. Martia Graham Goodson, "An Introductory Essay and Subject Index to Selected Interviews From the Slave Narrative Collection," (Ph.D. dissertation, Union Graduate School, 1977), p. 33.

53. Cody, "Naming, Kinship, and Estate Dispersal," pp. 207–208, 209.

54. Ala., 6:73.

55. Herbert G. Gutman, *The Black Family in Slavery and Freedom, 1750–1925* (New York: Pantheon Books, 1976), pp. 216–222.

56. J. H. Easterby, ed., *The South Carolina Rice Plantations as Revealed in the Papers of Robert W. Allston* (Chicago: University of Chicago Press, 1945), p. 291.

57. Bassett, ed., *The Southern Plantation Overseer*, pp. 19–20, 32.

58. Ga., 12(2):57.

59. Woodward, *Chesnut's Civil War*, p. 829.

60. Norman Yetman, *Voices from Slavery* (New York: Holt, Rhinehart and Winston, 1970), p. 13.

61. J. Mason Brewer, *American Negro Folklore* (New York: Quadrangle, 1968), p. 233. See also Egypt, ed., *Unwritten History*, p. 134.

62. S. F. Nadel, "Witchcraft in Four African Societies: An Essay in Comparison," in *American Anthropologist* (1952), 34:18; see also John Demos, "Underlying Themes in the Witchcraft of Seventeenth-Century New England," in *Colonial America; Essays in Politics and Social Development*, Stanley N. Katz, ed. (Boston: Little, Brown, 1971), p. 115.

63. For an excellent discussion of these slave beliefs see Lawrence W. Levine, *Black Culture and Black Consciousness, Afro-American Folk Thought from Slavery to Freedom* (Oxford: Oxford University Press, 1977;, pp. 55–80, and Albert J. Raboteau, *Slave Religion, The "Invisible Institution" in the Antebellum South*, pp. 14–15, 85–86.

64. See for instance Ga., 13(4):351; Ind., 6:59; Ga., Supplement 1, 4:49.

65. For information on conjurers see Levine, *Black Culture and Black Consciousness*, pp. 56–57, 67–74, and Raboteau, *Slave Religion*, pp. 80–86, 275–288.

66. Ga., Supplement 1, 4:549.

67. *Ibid.*, 559.

68. Ga., 13(4):351.

69. Ark., 8(2):161.

70. Miss., Supplement 1, 7:569.

71. N. C., 15(2):157.

72. Willie Lee Rose, *Rehearsal for Reconstruction: The Port Royal Experiment* (New York: Oxford University Press, 1864), p. 11.

73. Elizabeth Ware Pearson, ed., *Letters from Port Royal: Written at the Time of the Civil War* (New York: Arno Press, 1969 [1906]), p. 44.

74. *Ibid.*, pp. 250, 303–304.

75. *Ibid.*, p. 187.

76. *Ibid.*, p. 303.

77. *Ibid.*, p. 56.

78. Botume, *First Days Amongst the Contrabands*, p. 125.
79. See for instance, *Ibid.*, pp. 55–56, 58, 80, 212.
80. Pearson, *Letters from Port Royal*, p. 1133.
81. Botume, *First Days Amongst the Contrabands*, pp. 210–211.

5. MEN, WOMEN, AND FAMILIES

1. Willie Lee Rose, *Slavery and Freedom*, William Freehling, ed. (New York: Oxford University Press, 1982), p. 29.
2. See the following discussions of the slave family: John Blassingame, *The Slave Community, Plantation Life in the Antebellum South*, 2d. ed., New York, 1979), pp. 149–191; Eugene Genovese, *Roll, Jordan, Roll, The World the Slaves Made* (New York: Vintage Books, 1974), pp. 450–457, 482–534; Herbert Gutman, *The Black Family in Slavery and Freedom, 1750–1925* (New York: Vintage Books, 1976); Leslie Howard Owens, *This Species of Property, Slave Life and Culture in the Old South* (Oxford: Oxford University Press, 1976), pp. 182–213.
3. See for instance B. A. Botkin, ed. *Lay My Burden Down, A Folk History of Slavery*, (Chicago: University of Chicago Press, 1945), pp. 64, 80; C. Vann Woodward, ed., *Mary Chesnut's Civil War* (New Haven: Yale University Press, 1981), p. 213. Ronald O. Killion and Charles Waller, eds., *Slavery Time When I Was Chillun Down on Master's Plantation* (Savannah, Ga.: Beehive, 1973), pp. 37, 95; Frederick Law Olmsted, *A Journey in the Back Country 1853–1854*, (New York: Putnam's Sons, 1907), p. 391. George Rawick, ed., *The American Slave, A Composite Autobiography*, 19 vols. (Westport, Conn.: Greenwood, 1972); S. C. 2(2):47. All subsequent references to this work will be cited with the foregoing construction.
4. Botkin, ed., *Lay My Burden Down*, p. 145.
5. S. C., 2(2):51–52. See also Botkin, ed., *Lay My Burden Down*, p. 145.
6. Henry Bibb, *Narrative of the Life and Adventures of Henry Bibb*, in *Puttin' On Ole Massa*, Gilbert Osofsky, ed. (New York, Harper and Row, 1959), pp. 72–73 (hereafter cited as Bibb in Osofsky, ed., *Ole Massa*).
7. Solomon Northup, *Twelve Years a Slave, Narrative of Solomon Northup*, in Osofsky, ed. *Ole Massa*, p. 345 (hereafter cited as Northup in Osofsky, ed., *Ole Massa*).
8. Killion, ed., *Slavery Time*, pp. 110–111.
9. Frederic Bancroft, *Slave Trading in the Old South* (New York: Frederick Ungar, 1931), pp. 21, 200.
10. Louis Hughes, *Thirty Years a Slave*, (Milwaukee, Wisc.: South Side, 1897), p. 97.
11. Ga., 12(1):23.
12. Benjamin Drew, *The Refugee: A North-Side View of Slavery*, in *Four Fugitive Slave Narratives* (Reading, Mass.: Addison Welsey, 1969), p. 34. See also Bibb in Osofsky, ed., *Ole Massa*, pp. 42, 164; John Anderson, *The Story of A Fugitive Slave* (London: William Tweedie, 1863), p. 129; Linda Brent, *Incidents in the Life of a Slave Girl*, Lydia Maria Child ed. (New York: Harcourt Brace Jovanovich, 1973 [1861]), pp. 37, 43; James W. C. Pennington, *The Fugitive Blacksmith* (London: Charles Gilpin, 1849), p. 202.
13. Ga., 12(2):12–13; see also Ga., 12(1):25.
14. Josiah Henson, *An Autobiography of the Reverend Josiah Henson*, in *Four*

Fugitive Slave Narratives (Reading, Mass.:Addison Wesley, 1969), pp. 13–14. See also Frederick Law Olmsted, *The Cotton Kingdom*, David Freeman Hawke, ed. (New York: Bobbs-Merrill, 1971), p. 139.

15. Brent, *Incidents in the Life of a Slave Girl*, p. 43.

16. Bibb in Osofsky, ed., *Ole Massa*, pp. 74, 81.

17. Rev. J. W. Loguen, *The Reverend J. W. Loguen As a Slave and As a Freeman* (Syracuse, N.Y.: by the author, 1859), p. 223.

18. William Wells Brown, *Narrative of William Wells Brown, A Fugitive Slave*, in Osofsky, ed., *Ole Massa*, p. 213 (hereafter cited as Brown in Osofsky, ed., *Ole Massa*).

19. James Redpath, *The Roving Editor or Talks with Slaves in Southern States* (New York: Burdick, 1859), pp. 40–41.

20. John Spencer Bassett, *The Southern Plantation Overseer, As Revealed in His Letters*, (Northampton, Mass.: Southworth, 1925), p. 129.

21. Edward A. Pollard, *Black Diamonds Gathered in the Darky Homes of the South*, (Washington, D.C.: Pudney and Russell, 1859), pp. 24–25.

22. Botkin, ed., *Lay My Burden Down*, p. 160.

23. Bayside Plantation Records, vol. 2, January 8, 1864, Southern Historical Collection (SHC), The University of North Carolina at Chapel Hill, Chapel Hill, North Carolina.

24. Schomberg collection, New York City, Slave Documents, March 5, 1850 (uncatalogued) and Document no. 2, November 1778; Brent, *Slave Girl*, p. 36; see also Botkin, ed., *Lay My Burden Down*, p. 119; James L. Smith, *Autobiography of James L. Smith*, (Norwich, Conn.: Press of the Bulletin Co., 1881), p. 4.

25. Ala., 6:103–105.

26. John W. Blassingame, ed., *Slave Testimony. Two Centuries of Letters, Speeches, Interviews, and Autobiographies*, (Baton Rouge: Louisiana State University Press, 1977), p. 13. See also Botkin, ed., *Lay My Burden Down*, p. 125.

27. Frederick Law Olmsted, *A Journey in the Seaboard Slave States* (New York: Dix and Edwards, 1856), p. 36.

28. William Still, *The Underground Railroad, A Record of Facts, Authentic Narratives, Letters, etc.* (Philadelphia: Porter and Coates, 1872), p. 142.

29. Frances Anne Kemble, *Journal of a Residence on a Georgian Plantation*, John A. Scott, ed., (New York: Knopf, 1961 [1863]), pp. 245–246.

30. Gutman, *The Black Family*, pp. 14–18, 149–151, 11–14, 271–273, 53–58, 105–113.

31. Mrs. Nicholas Ware Eppes, *The Negro of the Old South* (Chicago: Joseph G. Branch, 1925), pp. 54–57.

32. Elizabeth Hyde Botume, *First Days Amongst the Contrabands*, (Boston: Lee and Shepard, 1893), p. 155.

33. *Ibid.*, p. 244.

34. Botkin, ed., *Lay My Burden Down*, 125.

35. Edwin Adams Davis, ed., *Plantation Life in the Florida Parishes of Louisiana, 1836–1846, As Reflected in the Diary of Bennet H. Barrow*, (New York: Columbia University Press, 1943), 139.

36. Harriet Martineau, *Society In America*, 3 vols. (London: Saunders and Otley, 1837), 2:333–334.

37. Ophelia S. Egypt, J. Masuoka, Charles S. Johnson, eds., *Unwritten*

History of Slavery: Autobiographical Accounts of Negro Ex-Slaves (Nashville, Tenn.: Fisk University Press, 1945), p. 143.

38. Ala., 6:322.

39. Woodward, ed., *Chesnut's Civil War*, p. 53.

40. Helen T. Catterall, *Judicial Cases Concerning American Slavery and the Negro*, 5 vols. (Washington, D.C.: Carnegie Institute of Washington, 1936), 2:123–124; see also Louis B. Wright and Marion Tinling, eds., *The Secret Diary of William Byrd of Westover, 1709–1712* (Richmond, Virginia: Dietz, 1941), pp. 192, 383; Davis, ed., *Plantation Life in the Florida Parishes of Louisiana*, p. 45; Jack P. Greene, *The Diary of Colonel Landon Carter of Sabine Hall, 1752–1778*, 2 vols. (Charlottesville: Virginia Historical Society, 1965), 1:383; Ala., 6:1; Genovese, *Roll, Jordan, Roll*, pp. 483–484.

41. Catterall, *Judicial Cases Concerning the American Negro*, 3:363.

42. *Ibid.*, 2:513 and 3:363n.

43. Michelle Zimbalist Rosaldo, "Woman, Culture, and Society: A Theoretical Overview," in *Woman, Culture and Society*, Michelle Zimbalist Rosaldo and Louise Lamphere, eds. (Stanford: Stanford University Press, 1974), p. 19; Peggy Sanday, "Female Status in the Public Domain," in *Ibid.*, pp. 199–200.

44. Ophelia S. Egypt, J. Masuoka, Charles S. Johnson, eds. *God Struck Me Dead, Religious Conversion Experiences and Autobiographies of Negro Ex-Slaves.* (Nashville, Tenn.: Fisk University Press, 1945), pp. 156–157.

45. *Ibid.*, pp. 147–149. See also Ga., 13(3):262.

46. Olmsted, *Back Country*, p. 154.

47. Ga., 13(3):79; see also *Ibid.*, 134:14, 141; Northup in Osofsky, ed., *Ole Massa*, p. 347; Letter, Richard J. Arnold to Mr. Swanson, May 22, 1837, in Arnold and Screven Family Papers, Series B, 1811–1869, SHC.

48. S. C., 2(1):231.

49. Anderson, *Life of John Anderson*, p. 129.

50. Rosaldo, "Woman, Culture, and Society: A Theoretical Overview," p. 39. For examples of societies where this has occurred see James T. Siegal, *The Rope of God* (Berkeley: University of California Press, 1969), pp. 53, 55; Martha Champion Randle, "Iroquois Women, Then and Now," in *Symposium on Local Diversity in Iroquois Culture*, William Fenton, ed. (Washington, D.C.: Government Printing Office, 1951), pp. 170–171; John A. Noon, *Law and Government of the Grand River Iroquois* (New York: Viking Fund, 1949), p. 109.

51. Blassingame, *The Slave Community*, p. 179.

52. Genovese, *Roll, Jordan, Roll*, p. 486; see also Robert William Fogel and Stanley L. Engerman, *Time on the Cross, The Economics of American Negro Slavery* (Boston: Little, Brown, 1974), p. 142.

53. Ohio, 16:16.

54. Brent, *Slave Girl*, p. 9.

55. Woodward, ed., *Chesnut's Civil War*, p. 526.

56. Frederick Douglass, *My Bondage and My Freedom* (New York: Mulligan, New York, and Auburn, 1855), p. 27. Douglass himself knew very well that the cook had special advantages when it came to supplementing the family's food. Aunt Katy, the cook at Colonel Lloyd's plantation, always gave her own children extra food while denying the same to Douglass. See *Ibid.*, pp. 54–55, 75.

57. Mo., 11:267.
58. *Ibid.*, p. 53.
59. Redpath, *Roving Editor*, p. 27. The term divorce is used in this text with the understanding that legal marriage, and therefore divorce, among slaves was prohibited.
60. Olmsted, *Seaboard Slave States*, p. 555.
61. Bassett, ed., *Plantation Overseer*, p. 84.
62. Ulrich B. Phillips and James David Glunt, eds., *Florida Plantation Records from the Papers of George Noble Jones* (St. Louis, Mo.: Historical Society, 1927), p. 63.
63. J. Mason Brewer, *American Negro Folklore*, (Chicago: Quadrangle, 1968), p. 229.
64. Gutman, *Black Family*, pp. 157–159; Ulrich B. Phillips, *American Negro Slavery* (Baton Rouge: Louisiana State University Press, 1918), p. 294.
65. See for instance, Bassett, ed., *The Southern Plantation Overseer*, pp. 31, 139, 141; Ulrich B. Phillips, ed., *Plantation and Frontier Documents, 1649–1863*, 2 vols. (Cleveland: Arthur H. Clarke, 1909), 1:1098, 312; Kemble, *Journal of a Residence on a Georgian Plantation*, pp. 95, 127.
66. It is almost ironic that the nineteenth-century slave family exhibited many of the same traits that social scientists now see appearing in the contemporary modern middle-class household. The two-income household has put a strain on traditional male-female relationships. It is argued that as women go out to work they gain a sense of personal autonomy and begin to exert more influence in the household than they did previously. The recent rise in divorce rates has been tied to greater *female* independence. See, for example, Edward Shorter, *The Making of the Modern Family*, (New York: Basic Books, 1977), pp. 278–280.
67. Susan Carol Rogers, "Woman's Place: A Critical Review of Anthropological Theory," in *Comparative Studies in Society and History*, (January 1978), 20:137–162.
68. The slave family conforms to criteria some anthropologist use to describe a matrifocal family. See Raymond T. Smith, "The Nuclear Family in Afro-American Kinship," *Journal of Comparative Family Studies*, (Autumn 1970), 1:62–70; R. T. Smith, "The Matrifocal Family," in *The Character of Kinship*, Jack Goody, ed. (London: Cambridge University Press, 1973), p. 125; R. T. Smith, *The Negro Family in British Guiana, Family Structure and Social Status in the Villages* (London: Routledge and Kegan Paul, 1956), pp. 257–260; Nancie L. Gonzalez, "Toward a Definition of Matrifocality," in *Afro-American Anthropology*, Norman E. Whitten, Jr. and John F. Szwed, eds., (New York: The Free Press, 1970), pp. 233–243; Nancy Tanner, "Matrifocality in Indonesia and Africa and Among Black Americans," in Rosaldo, ed., *Woman, Culture and Society*, 129–156.

6. FROM SLAVERY TO FREEDOM

1. *Narrative of Sojourner Truth, A Bondwoman of Olden Time*, Olive Gilbert, comp. (New York: Arno, 1968 [1878]), pp. 133–134.
2. *Ibid.*, pp. 137–139.
3. James L Roark et. al., *The American Promise: A History of the United States*

(Boston: Bedford Books, 1998), pp. 556, 576; I would like to thank Jennifer Briar for helping me with the research for this new chapter. Thanks also to Christopher Fisher and Yasmin Rahman. This chapter synthesizes some of the very excellent studies written on Reconstruction. It relies heavily on the writings of the following historians: Elsa Barkley Brown, "Negotiating and Transforming the Public Sphere: African American Political Life in the Transition from Slavery to Freedom," *Public Culture* (1994), 7: 107–146; Catherine Clinton, "Reconstructing Freedwomen," in *Divided Houses: Gender and the Civil War,* Catherine Clinton and Nina Silber, eds. (New York: Oxford University Press, 1992), pp. 306–319; Laura Edwards, "Sexual Violence, Gender, Reconstruction, and the Extension of Patriarchy in Granville County, North Carolina," *The North Carolina Historical Review* (July 1991), 68(3): 237–260; Eric Foner, *Reconstruction: America's Unfinished Revolution, 1863–1877* (New York: Harper and Row, 1988); Noralee Frankel, *Break Those Chains at Last: African Americans 1860–1880* (New York: Oxford University Press, 1996); Sharon Ann Holt, "Making Freedom Pay: Freedpeople Working for Themselves, North Carolina, 1865–1900," *The Journal of Southern History* (May 1994), 60(2): 239–262; Jacqueline Jones, *Labor of Love, Labor of Sorrow: Black Women, Work, and the Family from Slavery to the Present* (New York: Vintage Books, 1985); Leon F. Litwack, *Been in the Storm So Long: The Aftermath of Slavery* (New York: Vintage Books, 1980); Julie Saville, *The Work of Reconstruction: From Slave to Wage Laborer in South Carolina, 1860–1870* (Cambridge, Mass.: Cambridge University Press, 1994); Leslie Schwalm, *A Hard Fight for We: Women's Transition from Slavery to Freedom in South Carolina* (Urbana: University of Illinois Press, 1997); Leslie Schwalm, " 'Sweet Dreams of Freedom': Freedwomen's Reconstruction of Life and Labor in Lowcountry, South Carolina," *Journal of Women's History* (Spring 1997), 9(1): 9–38.

4. Quoted in Frankel, *Break Those Chains at Last,* p. 21.

5. See pp. 138–140.

6. Frankel, *Break Those Chains at Last,* p. 21.

7. Schwalm, *A Hard Fight for We,* p. 149; Frankel, *Break Those Chains at Last,* p. 22.

8. Quoted in Frankel, *Break Those Chains at Last,* p. 23.

9. Quoted in B. A. Botkin, ed., *Lay My Burden Down: A Folk History of Slavery* (Chicago: University of Chicago Press, 1945), p. 206.

10. Quoted in Herbert G. Gutman, *The Black Family in Slavery and Freedom, 1750–1925* (New York: Pantheon Books, 1976), p. 386.

11. *Ibid.*

12. *Ibid.,* pp. 386–387.

13. *Ibid.,* p. 386.

14. Jones, *Labor of Love, Labor of Sorrow,* p. 50.

15. Quoted in *ibid.,* p. 50, and Frankel, *Break Those Chains at Last,* p. 32.

16. Frankel, *Break Those Chains at Last,* p. 23.

17. Litwack, *Been in the Storm So Long,* p. 107.

18. Jones, *Labor of Love, Labor of Sorrow,* pp. 47–48.

19. Quoted in Frankel, *Break Those Chains at Last,* p. 23.

20. *Ibid.,* p. 25.

21. Jones, *Labor of Love, Labor of Sorrow,* p. 49.

22. Frankel, *Break Those Chains at Last,* p. 25.

23. *Ibid.*

24. Jones, *Labor of Love, Labor of Sorrow,* p. 49.

25. *Ibid.*

26. *Ibid.*, pp. 50–51.

27. Frankel, *Break Those Chains at Last*, p. 26.

28. See Alice Childress, *"Like One of the Family": Conversations from a Domestic's Life* (Boston: Beacon Press, 1986 [1956]).

29. Litwack, *Been in The Storm So Long*, pp. 106–107.

30. *Ibid.*, p. 117.

31. Eugene Genovese, *Roll, Jordan, Roll: The World the Slaves Made* (New York: Vintage Books, 1972), p. 99.

32. See pp. 46–61.

33. Litwack, *Been in the Storm So Long*, p. 301.

34. See pp. 74–76.

35. Quoted in Litwack, *Been in the Storm So Long*, p. 297, and Frankel, *Break Those Chains at Last*, p. 44.

36. The Freedman's Bureau was established to help the newly freed make the transition to freedom. Like the Union army, its agents were not always sympathetic to freedmen, and often did more harm than good. For example, they often facilitated white apprenticeships of black children against the will of black parents. Agents also compelled freedpeople to sign disadvantageous labor contracts. See Schwalm, *A Hard Fight for We*, pp. 199–204, 252–254.

37. Quoted in Frankel, *Break Those Chains at Last*, p. 99.

38. Litwack, *Been in The Storm So Long*, p. 231.

39. *Ibid.*, p. 229.

40. *Ibid.*, p. 237; Schwalm, *A Hard Fight for We*, pp. 251–254; Tera W. Hunter, *To 'Joy My Freedom: Southern Black Women's Lives and Labors After the Civil War* (Cambridge, Mass.: Harvard University Press, 1997), pp. 35–36.

41. Schwalm, *A Hard Fight for We*, p. 251.

42. *Ibid.*, pp. 253–254.

43. Litwack, *Been in The Storm So Long*, p. 236.

44. *Ibid.*, pp. 236–237; Schwalm, " 'Sweet Dreams of Freedom,' " p. 27.

45. Schwalm, " 'Sweet Dreams of Freedom,' " p. 19.

46. Schwalm, *A Hard Fight for We*, p. 222.

47. Jones, *Labor of Love, Labor of Sorrow*, pp. 56–57; Hunter, *To 'Joy My Freedom*, pp. 74–76.

48. See, for example, Schwalm, *A Hard Fight for We*, pp. 210–211.

49. See p. 143.

50. Litwack, *Been in The Storm So Long*, p. 116.

51. *Ibid.*, p. 176.

52. Schwalm, *A Hard Fight for We*, p. 178.

53. *Ibid.*

54. Jones, *Labor of Love, Labor of Sorrow*, p. 71.

55. Clinton, "Reconstructing Freedwomen," p. 317.

56. *Ibid.*, pp. 315–316.

57. *Ibid.*, p. 316.

58. *Ibid.*, pp. 311–312.

59. Edwards, "Sexual Violence, Gender, Reconstruction, and the Extension of Patriarchy," pp. 244–245.

60. Clinton, "Reconstructing Freedwomen," p. 311.

61. Brown, "Negotiating and Transforming the Public Sphere," p. 112.

62. Clinton, "Reconstructing Freedwomen," pp. 311, 315.

63. K. Sue Jewell, *From Mammy to Miss America and Beyond: Cultural Images and the Shaping of U. S. Social Policy* (London: Routledge, 1993), p. 45.

64. The emphasis on the lynching of black men had severe consequences for black women. See "Divided Against Myself," in *Too Heavy A Load: Black Women in Defense of Themselves, 1894–1994,* Deborah Gray White (New York: W. W. Norton, 1998).

65. Brown, "Negotiating and Transforming the Public Sphere," p. 112 n. 8.

66. Litwack, *Been in The Storm So Long,* p. 240.

67. *Ibid.*

68. See pp. 149–151, 241.

69. Frankel, *Break Those Chains at Last,* pp. 102–103.

70. *Ibid.,* p. 103.

71. See p. 150.

72. *Ibid.*

73. Litwack, *Been in The Storm So Long,* p. 242, and Schwalm, *A Hard Fight for We,* pp. 245–246.

74. Frankel, *Break Those Chains at Last,* p. 103.

75. Schwalm, *A Hard Fight for We,* pp. 244–245.

76. *Ibid.,* pp. 246–247.

77. Jones, *Labor of Love, Labor of Sorrow,* p. 62.

78. *Ibid.;* Foner, *Reconstruction,* p. 87; Schwalm, *A Hard Fight for We,* p. 250; Holt, "Making Freedom Pay," p. 247.

79. Clinton, "Reconstructing Freedwomen," p. 309.

80. Jones, *Labor of Love, Labor of Sorrow,* pp. 53–54.

81. Schwalm, *A Hard Fight for We,* p. 210.

82. Roger L. Ransom and Richard Sutch, *One Kind of Freedom: The Economic Consequences of Emancipation* (Cambridge, Eng.: Cambridge University Press, 1977), pp. 44–46.

83. Holt, "Making Freedom Pay," pp. 236–238.

84. *Ibid.,* pp. 241–244.

85. *Ibid.*

86. *Ibid.,* p. 247. See also Saville, *The Work of Reconstruction,* pp. 126, 130.

87. See Saville, *The Work of Reconstruction,* pp. 105–106.

88. *Ibid.,* p. 248.

89. For example, see: Jones, *Labor of Love, Labor of Sorrow,* pp. 62, 67; Laura F. Edwards, *Gendered Strife and Confusion: The Political Culture of Reconstruction* (Urbana: University of Illinois Press, 1997), pp. 20–21, 151; Foner, *Reconstruction,* p. 87.

90. Litwack, *Been in The Storm So Long,* p. 245.

91. Foner, *Reconstruction,* p. 86.

92. *Ibid.,* p. 85.

93. See, for example, Litwack, *Been in The Storm So Long,* pp. 334–335.

94. *Ibid.,* p. 244.

95. Schwalm, *A Hard Fight for We,* p. 205.

96. Holt, "Making Freedom Pay," pp. 240–241.

97. Foner, *Reconstruction,* p. 88.

98. Schwalm, *A Hard Fight for We,* p. 262.

99. Edwards, "Sexual Violence, Gender, Reconstruction, and the Economics of Patriarchy," pp. 247–248.

100. Schwalm, *A Hard Fight for We,* p. 232; Foner, *Reconstruction,* p. 290;

Brown, "Negotiating and Transforming the Public Sphere," p. 123.

101. Brown, "Negotiating and Transforming the Public Sphere," pp. 118–123.

102. *Ibid.*, 122.

103. Litwack, *Been in The Storm So Long*, p. 246. See also Saville, *The Work of Reconstruction*, p. 145.

104. Donald J. Mulvihill, *Crimes of Violence, A Self-Report to the National Commission on the Causes and Prevention of Violence* (Washington, D. C.: U. S. Government Printing Office, 1969), 2: 209, 212. See also John Dollard, *Caste and Class in a Southern Town*, 3rd ed. (New York: Doubleday, 1957), pp. 147, 152; Gerda Lerner, *Black Women in White America: A Documentary History* (New York: Random House, 1972), pp. 234, 142–193.

105. Susan Brownmiller, *Against Our Will: Men Women, and Rape* (Toronto: Bantam, 1975), pp. 234, 410–412.

106. See Elizabeth Clark-Lewis, *Living In, Living Out: African American Domestics in Washington, D. C., 1910–1940* (Washington D. C.: Smithsonian Press, 1994).

Selected
Bibliography

UNPUBLISHED SOURCES

Schomberg Collection, New York City:
    Slavery Collection (uncatalogued)
University of North Carolina, Southern Historical Collection:
    Edward Clifford Anderson Papers
    Arnold-Screven Family Papers
    Robert Ruffin Barrow Papers
    Frances Hanson Diary
    Thomas Butler King Papers
    Macay and McNeely Family Papers
    Myers Family Papers
    Newstead Plantation Diary
    Norfleet Family Papers
    Plantation Manual (source unknown)
    A. and A. T. Walker Book
    Walter T. Scott Diary
    Louis Campbell Sheppard, "Recollections"
    William Henry Sims Papers
    The Reminiscences of Mrs. Margaret Isabella Weber
    Witherspoon and McDowell Family Papers
    White Hill Plantation Books

PUBLISHED PRIMARY SOURCES

Anderson, John. *The Story of the Life of John Anderson, A Fugitive Slave.* London: William Tweedie, 1863.

Andrews, E. A. *Slavery and the Domestic Slave-Trade in the United States* Boston: Light and Stearns, 1836.

Bassett, John Spencer. *The Southern Plantation Overseer as Revealed in His Letters.* Northhampton, Mass.: Southworth, 1925.

Boggs, Marion Alexander, ed. *The Alexander Letters.* Athens: The University of Georgia Press, 1980.

Bosman, William. *A New and Accurate Description of The Coast of Guinea.* London: Frank Cass, 1967 [1705].

Botkin, B. A., ed. *Lay My Burden Down: A Folk History of Slavery* Chicago: University of Chicago Press, 1945.

Botume, Elizabeth Hyde. *First Days Amongst the Contrabands.* New York: Arno, 1968 [1893]).

Bremer, Fredericka. *Homes of the New World,* 2 vols. New York: Harper and Brothers, 1853.

Brent, Linda. *Incidents in the Life of a Slave Girl.* Edited by Lydia Maria Child. New York: Harcourt Brace Jovanovich, 1973, [1861].

Burke, Emily. *Reminiscences of Georgia.* Oberlin, Ohio: James M. Fitch, 1850.

Cartwright, Samuel. "Slavery in the Light of Ethnology." In *Cotton Is King and Pro-Slavery Arguments.* Edited by E. N. Elliot. Augusta, Ga.: Pritchard, Abbott & Loomis, 1860.

Catterall, Helen T., ed., *Judicial Cases Concerning American Slavery and the Negro,* 5 vols. Washington, D.C.: Carnegie Institute of Washington, 1936.

Cobb, Thomas R. R. *An Inquiry into the Law of Negro Slavery in the United States of America to which is prefixed An Historical Sketch of Slavery.* New York: Negro University Press, 1968 [1858].

Coffin, Joshua, ed. *An Account of the Principal Slave Insurrections.* In *Slave Insurrections, Selected Documents.* New York: American Anti-Slavery Society, 1968 [1822–1860].

Coffin, Levi. *Reminiscences of Levi Coffin.* Cincinnati, Ohio: Robert Clarke, 1898.

Crabtree, Beth G. and James W. Patton, eds. *The Diary of Catherine Ann Devereux Edmondston.* Raleigh: North Carolina Division of Archives and History, 1979.

Craft, William and Ellen. *Running a Thousand Miles for Freedom, or The Escape of William and Ellen Craft From Slavery.* London: William Tweedie, 1860.

Davis, Adwon Adams. *Plantation Life in the Florida Parishes of Louisiana, 1836–1846, as Reflected in the Diary of Bennet H. Barrow.* New York: Columbia University Press, 1943.

DeBow, J. D. B. *Statistical View of the United States, Compendium of the Seventh Census.* Washington, D.C.: Senate Printer, 1854.

DeBow's Review 1850–1860.

A Defense of Southern Slavery Against the Attacks of Henry Clay and Alex'r Campbell. In *A Defense of Southern Slavery and Other Pamphlets.* New York: Negro Universities Press 1969 [n.d.].

Donnan, Elizabeth, ed. *Documents Illustrative of the History of the Slave Trade to America,* 4 vols. Washington: Carnegie Institute of Washington, 1930.

Douglass, Frederick. *My Bondage and My Freedom.* New York: Mulligan, New York and Auburn, 1855.

Drayton, William. *The South Vindicated from the Treason and Fanaticism of Northern Abolitioinists.* Philadelphia, Penn: H. Manley, 1836.

Drew, Benjamin. *The Refugee: A North-Side View of Slavery.* In *Four Fugitive Slave Narratives.* Reading, Mass.: Addison Wesley, 1969 [1856].

Easterby, J. H., ed. *The South Carolina Rice Plantation as Revealed in the Papers of Robert F. W. Allston.* Chicago: University of Chicago Press, 1945.

Eastman, Mary H. *Aunt Phyllis's Cabin; or Southern Life As It Is.* Philadelphia: Lippincott, Grambo, 1852.

Eppes, Mrs. Nicholas Ware. *The Negro of the Old South.* Chicago: Joseph G. Branch, 1925.

Egypt, Ophelia S., J. Masuoka, Charles S. Johnson, eds. *Unwritten History of*

Slavery, Autobiographical Accounts of Negro Ex-Slaves. Nashville, Tenn.: Fisk University Press, 1945.

Fitzhugh, George. *Sociology for the South; or The Failure of Free Society.* Richmond, Va.: A. Morris, 1854.

Fitzhugh, George. *Cannibals All! or Slaves Without Masters.* Cambridge, Mass.: The Belknap Press of Harvard University Press, 1960 [1857].

Gilbert, Olive, comp. *Narrative of Sojourner Truth, A Bondwoman of Olden Time.* New York: Arno, 1968 [1878].

Gilman, Caroline. *Recollections of a Southern Mistress.* New York: Harper and Brothers, 1838.

Greene, Fletcher M., ed. *Ferry Hill Plantation Journal.* In *The James Sprunt Studies in History and Political Science.* Chapel Hill: University of North Carolina Press, 1961.

Greene, Jack P., ed. *The Diary of Colonel Landon Carter of Sabine Hall, 1752–1778,* 2 vols. Charlottesville, Va.: Virginia Historical Society, 1965.

Grimké, Angelina, "An Appeal to the Women of the Nominally Free States." In *Root of Bitterness, Documents of the Social History of American Women.* Edited by Nancy F. Cott. New York: Dutton, 1972.

Grimké, Sarah, "Letters on the Equality of the Sexes and the Condition of Women." In *The Feminist Papers.* Edited by Alice S. Rossi. New York: Bantam, 1978.

Groshart, Alexander B., ed. *The Poems and Literary Prose of Alexander Wilson,* 2 vols. Paiseley, Scotland: Alex Gardner, 1876.

Hamilton, Thomas. *Men and Manners in America,* 2 vols. Edinburgh: William Blackwood, 1833.

Hening, William Waller, ed. *The Statutes At Large Being A Collection of All the Laws of Virginia.* Richmond, Va.: Samuel Pleasants, 1823.

Henson, Josiah. *An Autobiography of the Reverend Josiah Henson.* In *Four Fugitive Slave Narratives.* Reading, Mass.: Addison Wesley, 1969 [1881].

Hughes, Louis. *Thirty Years a Slave.* Milwaukee, Wisc.: South Side Printing Co., 1897.

Industrial Resources of the Southern Western States, 3 vols. Washington: U.S. Government Printing Office, 1854.

Johnson, Charles S., ed. *God Struck Me Dead. Religious Conversion Experiences and Autobiographies of Negro Ex-Slaves.* Nashville, Tenn.: Fisk University Press, 1945.

Kemble, Frances Anne. *Journal of a Residence on a Georgian Plantation.* Edited by John A. Scott. New York: Knopf, 1961.

Kennedy, John Pendleton. *Swallow Born or Sojourn in the Old Dominion.* New York: Harcourt, Brace, 1929 [1832].

Killion, Ronald O. and Charles Waller, eds. *Slavery Time When I was Chillun Down on Master's Plantation* Savannah, Ga.: The Beehive Press, 1973.

Loguen, Rev. J. W. *The Rev. J. W. Loguen as a Slave and as a Free Man.* Syracuse, New York: by the author, 1859.

Martineau, Harriet. *Society in America,* 3 vols. London: Saunders and Otley, 1837.

Mill, John Stuart and Harriet Taylor Mill, "The Subjection of Women." In *Essays of Sex Equality.* Edited by Alice S. Rossi. Chicago: University of Chicago Press, 1970, [1869].

Montagu, Ashley. "Edward Tyson, M.D., F.R.S., 1650–1708." *Memoirs of the*

American Philosophical Society, vol. 20. Philadelphia: The American Philosophical Society, 1943.

Morgan, John H. "An Essay on the Production of Abortion Among Our Negro Population." *Nashville Journal of Medicine and Surgery* (August 1860), 19:117–123.

Muhlenberg, Henry. *The Journals of Henry Melchior Muhlenberg*. Theodore Tappert and John W. Doberstein, eds. and trans. 3 vols. Philadelphia: The Evangelical Lutheran Ministerium of Pennsylvania and Adjacent States and the Muhlenberg Press, 1941.

Myers, Robert Manson. *Children of Pride, A True Story of Georgia and the Civil War*. New Haven: Yale University Press, 1972.

Nairne, Thomas. *A Letter From South Carolina Giving an Account of the Soil, Air Products, Trade, Government, Laws, Religion, People, Military Strength, etc. of that Province*. London: J. Clarke, 1732.

Northup, Solomon. *Twelve Years A Slave, Narrative of Solomon Northup*. In *Puttin' On Ole Massa*. Edited by Gilbert Osofsky. New York: Harper and Row, 1969.

Nott, J. C. and George R. Gliddon. *Types of Mankind*, 7th ed. Philadelphia: Lippincott, Grambo, 1854.

Olmsted, Frederick Law. *A Journey in the Seaboard Slave States* New York: Dix and Edwards, 1856.

——. *A Journey in the Back Country, 1853–1854*. New York: G. P. Putnam's Sons, 1907.

——. *The Cotton Kingdom*. Edited by David Freeman Hawke. New York: Bobbs-Merrill, 1971.

Page, Thomas Nelson. *Social Life in Old Virginia Before the War*. New York: C. Scribner's Sons. 1897.

Pearson, Elizabeth Ware, ed. *Letters from Port Royal: Written at the Time of the Civil War*. New York: Arno, 1969 [1906].

Pendleton, E. M. "On the Susceptibility of the Caucasian and African Races to the Different Classes of Disease." *Southern Medical Reports* (1949 [1856]) 2:336–342.

Pennington, James W. C. *The Fugitive Blacksmith*. London: Charles Gilpin, 1849.

Phillips, Ulrich B. and James David Glunt, eds. *Florida Plantation Records from the Papers of George Noble Jones*. St. Louis, Mo.: Historical Society, 1927.

Pollard, Edward. *Black Diamonds Gathered in the Darky Homes of the South*. Washington, D.C.: Pudney and Russell Publishers, 1859.

Rawick, George. *The American Slave: A Composite Autobiography*, 19 vols. Westport, Conn.: Greenwood, 1972.

——. *The American Slave: A Composite Autobiography. Supplement. Series 2*, 10 vols. Westport, Conn.: Greenwood, 1977.

Rawick, George, Jan Hillegas, and Ken Lawrence. *The American Slave: A Composite Autobiography: Supplement. Series 1*, 12 vols. Westport, Conn.: Greenwood, 1978.

Redpath, James. *The Roving Editor, or Talks With Slaves in Southern States*. New York: Burdick, 1859.

Ripley, Eliza. *Social Life in Old New Orleans, Being Recollections of My Girlhood*. New York: Appleton, 1912.

Russell, William Howard. *My Diary North and South (Canada, Its Defenses, Con*

dition, and Resources), 3 vols. London: Bradbury and Evans, 1863.
Sawyer, George S.. *Southern Institutes or, An Inquiry into the Origin and Early Prevalence of Slavery and the Slave Trade*. Philadelphia: Lippincott, 1858.
Schoepf, Johann David. *Travels in the Confederacy, 1783–1784*, 2 vols. Philadelphia: Campbell, 1911.
The Seventh Census, Report of the Superintendent of the Census. Washington, D.C.: Robert Armstrong, 1853.
Smedes, Susan Dabney. *Memorials of a Southern Planter*. Edited by Fletcher M. Greene. New York: Knopf, 1968.
Smith, James L. *Autobiography of James L. Smith*. New York: Negro Universities Press, 1969 [1881].
Smith, William. *A New Voyage to Guinea*. London: Frank Cass, 1967 [1744]).
Southern Cultivator, 1850–1860.
Southern Historical Manuscripts. Westport, Conn.: Greenwood, 1973.
Still, William. *The Underground Railroad, A Record of Facts, Authentic Narratives, Letters, etc.* Philadelphia: Porter and Coates, 1872.
Stowe, Harriet Beecher. *Uncle Tom's Cabin*. New York: Washington Square Press, Inc., 1962 [1852].
Stroyer, Jacob. *My Life in the South*. Salem, Mass.: New Comb and Gavs, 1898.
Tasistro, Louis F. *Random Shots and Southern Breezes*, 2 vols. New York, Harper and Brothers, 1842.
Towne, Laura M. *Letters and Diary of Laura M. Towne Written from the Sea Islands of South Carolina, 1862–1884*. Edited by Rupert Sargent Holland. New York: Negro Universities Press, 1969 [1912].
Tucker, George. *Progress of the United States in Population and Wealth in Fifty Years*. New York: Augustus M. Kelley, 1964 [1855].
Tucker, H. B. *George Balcome, A Tale of Missouri*, 2 vols. New York: Harper and Brothers, 1836.
Turner, J. A., ed. *The Cotton Planters' Manual*. New York: Orange Judd, 1865.
Tyler, Ronnie C. and Lawrence R. Murphy eds. *The Slave Narrative of Texas*. Austin, Tex.: Encino Press, 1974.
Van Evrie, John H. *Negroes and Negro Slavery*. New York: Van Evrie Horton, 1861.
Washington, Booker T. *Up from Slavery*. In *Three Negro Classics*. New York: Avon, 1965 [1901].
Wright, Louis B. and Marion Tinling, eds. *The Secret Diary of William Byrd of Westover, 1709–1712*. Richmond, Va.: The Dietz Press, 1941.
Yetman, Norman. *Voices from Slavery*. New York: Holt Rhinehart and Winston, 1970.

SECONDARY SOURCES

Aidoo, Agnes Akousua. "Ashante Queen Mothers in Government and Politics in the Nineteenth Century." In *The Black Woman Cross-Culturally*. Edited by Filomina Chioma Steady. Cambridge, Mass.: Schenkman, 1981.
Bancroft, Frederic. *Slave Trading in the Old South*. New York: Frederick Ungar, 1931.
Bauer, Raymond and Alice Bauer. "Day-to-Day Resistance to Slavery." *Journal of Negro History* (October 1942), 27:388–419.
Beauvoir, Simone de. *The Second Sex*. New York: Vintage, 1974 [1952].

Berlin, Ira. *Slaves Without Masters, the Free Negro in the Antebellum South.* New York: Random House, 1974.

Blassingame, John W. *The Slave Community, Plantation Life in the Antebellum South.* New York: Oxford University Press, 1972.

Blassingame, John W., ed. *Slave Testimony. Two Centuries of Letters, Speeches, Interviews, and Autobiographies.* Baton Rouge: Louisiana State University Press, 1977.

Bloch, Ruth H. "American Feminine Ideals in Transition: The Rise of the Moral Mother, 1785–1815." *Feminist Studies* (June 1978), 4:101–126.

Brewer, J. Mason. *American Negro Folklore.* Chicago: Quadrangle, 1968.

Brownmiller, Susan. *Against Our Will. Men, Women and Rape* Toronto: Bantam, 1975.

Bruchey, Stuart, ed. *Cotton and the Growth of the American Economy: 1790–1860.* New York: Harcourt, Brace, and World, 1967.

Calderhead, William. "How Extensive Was the Border State's Slave Trade: A New Look." *Civil War History* (March 1972), 18:42–55.

Chafe, William, H.. *Women and Equality, Changing Patterns in American Culture.* Oxford: Oxford University Press, 1977.

Clinton, Catherine. *The Plantation Mistress. Woman's World in the Old South.* New York: Pantheon, 1982.

Cody, Cheryll Ann. "Slave Demography and Family Formation. A Community Study of the Ball Family Plantations, 1720–1896." Ph.D. disscertation, University of Minnesota, 1982.

——. "Naming, Kinship, and Estate Dispersal: Notes on Slave Family Life on a South Carolina Plantation, 1786–1833." *William and Mary Quarterly* (1982), 39:192–211.

Conrad, Alfred and John R. Meyer. "The Economics of Slavery in the Ante-Bellum South." *The Journal of Political Economy* (April 1958), 66:95–130.

Crabon, Michael. "Jamaican Slavery." In *Race and Slavery in the Western Hemisphere: Quantitative Studies.* Edited by Stanley Engerman and Eugene Genovese. Princeton: Princeton University Press, 1975.

Craven, Wesley Frank. *White Red and Black, The Seventeenth-Century Virginian.* Charlottesville: The University Press of Virginia, 1971.

Davis, Angela. "Reflections on the Black Woman's Role in the Community of Slaves." *Black Scholar* (December 1971), 3:3–15.

Degler, Carl N. *Neither Black Nor White, Slavery and Race Relations in Brazil and the United States.* New York: Macmillan, 1971.

Demos, John. "Underlying Themes in the Witchcraft of Seventeenth-Century New England." In *Colonial America; Essays in Political and Social Development.* Edited by Stanley N. Katz. Boston: Little, Brown, 1971.

Dollard, John. *Caste and Class in a Southern Town,* 3d ed. New York: Doubleday, 1957 [1937].

Dow, George Francis. *Slave Ships and Slaving.* Salem: Mass.: Marine Research Society, 1927.

DuBois, W. E. B. *The Gift of Black Folk: The Negroes in the Making of America.* Boston: Stratford, 1924.

Dunbar, Paul Lawrence. *Lyrics of Lowly Life; Complete Poems.* London: Chapman and Hall, 1897.

Dunn, Richard. "The Tale of Two Plantations: Slave Life at Mesopotamia in

Jamaica and Mount Airy in Virginia, 1799–1828." *William and Mary Quarterly* (January 1977), 34:32–65.

Dupire, Marquerite. "The Position of Women in a Pastoral Society (The Fulani Wo Daa Be, Nomads of the Niger)." In *Women of Tropical Africa*. Edited by Denise Paulme. Berkeley: University of California Press, 1963.

Elkins, Stanley M. *Slavery, A Problem in American Institutional and Intellectual Life*, 2d ed. Chicago: University of Chicago Press, 1968 [1959].

Farley, Reynolds. *Growth of the Black Population, A Study of Demographic Trends.* Chicago: Markham, 1970.

Farley, Reynolds. "The Demographic Rates and Social Institutions of the Nineteenth-Century Negro Population: A Stable Population Analysis." *Demography* (1965), 2:386–398.

Fogel, Robert William and Stanley Engerman. *Time on the Cross, The Economics of American Negro Slavery.* Boston: Little, Brown, 1974.

Frazier, E. Franklin. *The Negro Family in the United States.* Chicago: University of Chicago Press, 1939.

Frederikson, George M. and Christopher Lasch. "Resistance to Slavery." In *The Debate Over Slavery, Stanley Elkins and His Critics.* Edited by Ann J. Lane. Urbana: University of Illinois Press, 1971.

Gains, Francis Pendleton. *The Southern Plantation. A Study of The Development and the Accuracy of a Tradition.* Gloucester, Mass.: Peter Smith, 1962.

Genovese, Eugene D. *The Political Economy of Slavery, Studies in the Economy and Society of the Slave South.* New York: Random House, 1961.

———. *Roll, Jordan, Roll, The World the Slaves Made.* New York: Vintage Books, 1974.

Gessain, Monique. "Coniagui Women." In *Women of Tropical Africa.* Edited by Denise Paulme. Berkeley: University of California Press, 1963.

Gonzalez, Nancie L. "Toward a Definition of Matrifocality." In *Afro-American Anthropology.* Edited by Norman E. Whitten, Jr., and John F. Szwed. New York: Free Press, 1970.

Goodson, Martia Graham. "An Introductory Essay and Subject Index to Selected Interviews From the Slave Narrative Collection." Ph.D. dissertation, Union Graduate School, 1977.

Gordon, Linda. *Woman's Body, Woman's Right, A Social History of Birth Control in America.* New York: Penguin, 1974.

Greene, Lorenzo J. "The New England Negro as Seen in Advertisements for Runaway Slaves." *Journal of Negro History* (April 1944), 29:125–146.

Gutman, Herbert G. *Slavery and the Numbers Game, A Critique of Time on the Cross.* Urbana: University of Illinois Press, 1975.

———. *The Black Family in Slavery and Freedom, 1750–1925.* New York: Pantheon, 1976.

Hagler, D. Harland. "The Ideal Woman in the Antebellum South: Lady or Farmwife." *Journal of Southern History* (August 1980), 46:405–418.

Hernton, Calvin C. *Sex and Racism in America.* New York: Grove, 1966.

Herskovits, Melville. *The Myth of the Negro Past.* Boston: Beacon, 1978 [1941].

Johnson, Michael P. "Smothered Slave Infants: Where Slave Mothers at Fault?" *The Journal of Southern History* (November 1981), 47:493–520.

Johnson, Guion B. *A Social History of the Sea Islands.* Chapel Hill: University of North Carolina Press, 1930.

Jones, Jacqueline Jones. " 'My Mother Was Much of a Woman': Black Women,

Work, and the Family Under Slavery." *Feminist Studies* (Summer 1982), 8:235–267.

Jordan, Winthrop. *White Over Black, American Attitudes Towards the Negro, 1550–1812.* Baltimore, Ma.: Penguin, 1968.

Kennedy, Theodore. *You Gotta Deal With It. Black Family Relations in a Southern Community.* New York: Oxford University Press, 1980.

Kipple, Kenneth F. and Virginia Himmelsteib King. *Another Dimension to the Black Diaspora. Diet, Disease, and Racism.* Cambridge: Cambridge University Press, 1981.

Kraditor, Aileen S., ed. *Up From the Pedestal.* Chicago: Quadrangle, 1968.

Kulikoff, Allan. "A 'Prolifick' People: Black Population Growth in the Chesapeake Colonies, 1700–1790." *Southern Studies* (Winter 1977), 16:391–428.

Kulikoff, Allan. "The Beginnings of the Afro-American Family in Maryland." In *The American Family in Social-Historical Perspective,* 2nd. ed. Edited by Michael Gordon. New York: St. Marton's, 1978.

Ladner, Joyce. *Tommorrow's Tommorrow. The Black Woman.* New York: Doubleday, 1971.

Leith-Ross, Sylvia. *African Women: A Study of the Ibo of Nigeria* London: Routledge and Kegan Paul, 1939.

Lerner, Gerda. *Black Women in White America: A Documentary History.* New York: Vintage, 1972.

——. *The Majority Finds Its Past, Placing Women in History.* New York: Oxford University Press, 1979.

Levine, Lawrence W. *Black Culture and Black Consciousness, Afro-American Folk Thought from Slavery to Freedom.* Oxford: Oxford University Press, 1977.

Littlefield, Daniel C. *Rice and Slaves, Ethnicity and the Slave Trade in Colonial South Carolina.* Baton Rouge: Louisiana State University Press, 1981.

McDougall, Marion Gleason. *Fugitive Slaves [1619–1865].* New York: Bergman, 1967 [1891].

Menard, Russell R. "The Maryland Slave Population, 1658 to 1730: A Demographic Profile of Blacks in Four Countries." *William and Mary Quarterly* (January 1975), 32:29–54.

Mikell, Jenkins. *Rumbling of the Chariot Wheels.* Columbia: University of South Carolina Press, 1923.

Mintz, Sidney and Richard Price. *An Anthropological Approach to the Afro-American Past: A Caribbean Perspective.* Philadelphia, Penn.: ISHI, 1976.

Mitchell, Carolyn. "Health and the Medical Profession in the South." *Journal of Southern History* (1944), 10:424–447.

Morgan, Edmund S. *American Slavery, American Freedom, The Ordeal of Colonial Virginia.* New York: Norton, 1975.

Moynihan, Daniel Patrick. *The Negro Family: The Case for National Action.* Washington, D.C.: United States Department of Labor, 1965.

Mullin, Gerald W. *Flight and Rebellion, Slave Resistance in Eighteenth-Century Virginia.* London: Oxford University Press, 1972.

Mulvihill, Donald J. *Crimes of Violence, A Staff Report to the National Commission on the Causes and Prevention of Violence,* 3 vols. Washington, D.C.: U.S. Government Printing Office, 1969.

Nadel, S. F. "Witchcraft in Four African Societies: An Essay in Comparison." *American Anthropologist* (1952), 34:18–29.

Nichols, Charles H. *Many Thousand Gone, The Ex-Slaves' Account of Their Bondage and Their Freedom*. Bloomington: Indiana University Press, 1963.
Noon, John A. *Law and Government of the Grand River Iroquois*. New York: Viking Fund, 1949.
Ortner, Sherry B. "Is Female to Male as Nature Is to Culture?" In *Woman, Culture, and Society*. Edited by Michelle Zimbalist Rosaldo and Louise Lamphere. Stanford, California: Stanford University Press, 1974.
Owens, Leslie Howard. *This Species of Property, Slave Life and Culture in the Old South*. Oxford: Oxford University Press, 1976.
Paterson, Orlando. *Sociology of Slavery*. London: MacGibbon and Kee, 1967.
Paulme, Denise, ed. *Women of Tropical Africa*. Berkeley: University of California Press, 1963.
Peterson, Merrill D., ed. *The Portable Thomas Jefferson*. New York: Viking, 1975.
Phillips, Ulrich B. *Plantation and Frontier: Documents, 1649–1863*, 2 vols. Cleveland, Ohio: Arthur H. Clarke, 1909.
———. *American Negro Slavery, A Survey of the Supply, Employment and Control of Negro Labor as Determined by the Plantation Regime*. Baton Rouge: Louisiana State University Press, 1966 [1918].
Pleck, Elizabeth H. "A Mother's Wages: Income Earning Among Married Italian and Black Women 1896–1911. In *The American Family in Social-Historical Perspective*. 2nd ed. Edited by Michael Gordon. New York: St. Martin's, 1978.
Postell, William Desite. *The Health of Slaves on Southern Plantations*. Baton Rouge: Louisiana State University Press, 1951.
Raboteau, Albert J. *Slave Religion, The "Invisible Institution" in the Antebellum South*. New York: Oxford University Press, 1978.
Randle, Martha Champion. "Iroquois Women, Then and Now." In *Symposium on Local Diversity in Iroquois Culture*. Edited by William Fenton. Washington, D.C.: Government Printing Office, 1951.
Rogers, Susan Carol. "Woman's Place: A Critical Review of Anthropological Theory." *Comparative Studies in Society and History* (January 1978), 20:123–162.
Rosaldo, Michelle Zimbalist. "Woman, Culture, and Society: A Theoretical Overview." In *Woman, Culture and Society*. Edited by Michelle Zimbalist Rosaldo and Louise Lamphere. Stanford, Calif. Stanford University Press, 1974.
Rose, Willie Lee. *Rehearsal for Reconstruction: The Port Royal Experiment*. New York: Oxford University Press, 1864.
Sanday, Peggy. "Female Status in the Public Domain." In *Woman, Culture and Society*. Edited by Michelle Zimbalist Rosaldo and Louise Lamphere. Stanford, Calif. Stanford University Press, 1974.
Savitt, Todd L. *Medicine and Slavery. The Diseases and Health Care of Blacks in Antebellum Virginia*. Urbana: University of Illinois Press, 1978.
Schafer, Judith Kelleher. "New Orleans Slavery in 1850 as Seen in Advertisements." *Journal of Southern History* (February 1981), 46:33–56.
Scholten, Catherine M. "On the Importance of the Obstetric Art: Changing Customs of Childbirth in America, 1760–1825." *William and Mary Quarterly* (1977), 34:426–445.
Scott, Anne Firor. *The Southern Lady. From Pedestal to Politics, 1830–1930*. Chi-

cago: The University of Chicago Press, 1970.

Sellers, James. *Slavery in Alabama.* University, Alabama: University of Alabama Press, 1950.

Sheridan, Richard. "Mortality and the Medical Treatment of Slaves in the British West Indies." In *Slavery in the Western Hemisphere: Quantitative Studies.* Edited by Stanley Engerman and Eugene Genovese. Stanford: Stanford University Press, 1975.

Shorter, Edward. *The Making of the Modern Family.* New York: Basic Books, 1977.

Siegal, James T. *The Rope of God.* Berkeley: University of California Press, 1969.

Smith, Raymond. *The Negro Family in British Guiana, Family Structure and Social Status in the Villages.* London: Routledge and Kegan Paul, 1956.

Smith, Raymond T. "The Nuclear Family in Afro-American Kinship." *Journal of Comparative Family Studies* (Autumn 1970), 1:57–70.

Smith, Raymond. "The Matrifocal Family." In *The Character of Kinship.* Edited by Jack Goody. London: Cambridge University Press, 1973.

Smith, Daniel Scott. "Family Limitation, Sexual Control and Domestic Feminism in Victorian America." In *Clio's Consciousness Raised, New Perspectives on the History of Women.* Edited by Mary S. Hartman and Lois Banner. New York: Harper and Row, 1974.

Stack, Carol *All Our Kin. Strategies for Survival in a Black Community.* New York: Harper and Row, 1974.

Stampp, Kenneth. *The Peculiar Institution. Slavery in the Ante-Bellum South.* New York: Random House, 1957.

Strasser, Susan. *Never Done. A History of American Housework.* New York: Pantheon, 1982.

Sudarkasa, Niara. "Female Employment and Family Organization in West Africa." In *The Black Woman Cross-Culturally.* Edited by Filomina Chioma Steady. Cambridge. Mass.: Schenkman, 1981.

Sudarkasa, Niara. "Interpreting the African Heritage in Afro-American Family Organization." In *Black Families.* Edited by Harriete Pipes McAdoo. Beverly Hills, Calif.: Sage, 1981.

Sutch, Richard. "The Breeding of Slaves for Sale and Westward Expansion of Slavery 1830–1860." In *Race and Slavery in the Western Hemisphere; Quantitative Studies.* Edited by Stanley Engerman and Eugene Genovese. Princeton: Princeton University Press, 1975.

Swados, Felice. "Negro Health on the Antebellum Plantation." *Bulletin of the History of Medicine* (1941), 10:460–472.

Sydnor, Charles Sackett. *Slavery in Mississippi.* Gloucester, Mass.: Peter Smith, 1965.

Tanner, Nancy. "Matrifocality in Indonesia and Africa and Among Black Americans." In *Woman, Culture, and Society.* Edited by Michelle Zimbalist Rosaldo and Louise Lamphere. Stanford, Calif.: Stanford University Press, 1974.

Taylor, Joe Gray. *Negro Slavery in Louisiana.* Baton Rouge, Louisiana: Louisiana Historical Association, 1963.

Trussel, James and Richard Steckel. "The Age of Slaves at Menarche and Their First Birth." *Journal of Interdisciplinary History* (Winter 1978), 8:477–505.

Van Gennep, Arnold. *The Rites of Passage.* Chicago: University of Chicago Press, 1960.
Wallace, Michelle. *Black Macho and the Myth of the Superwoman.* New York: Dial, 1979.
Wood, Ann Douglas. " 'The Fashionable Diseases': Women's Complaints and Their Treatment in Nineteenth-Century America." *The Journal of Interdisciplinary History* (Summer 1973), 4:25–52.
Wood, Peter H. *Black Majority. Negroes in Colonial South Carolina from 1670 through the Stono Rebellion.* New York: Norton, 1974.
Woodward, C. Vann, ed. *Mary Chesnut's Civil War.* New Haven: Yale University Press, 1981.
Zelnick, Melvin. "Fertility of the American Negro in 1830–1850." *Population Studies* (1966), 20:77–83.

Index